M000034971

TRANSFORMISSION

Making Disciples Through Short-Term Missions

TRANSFORMISSION

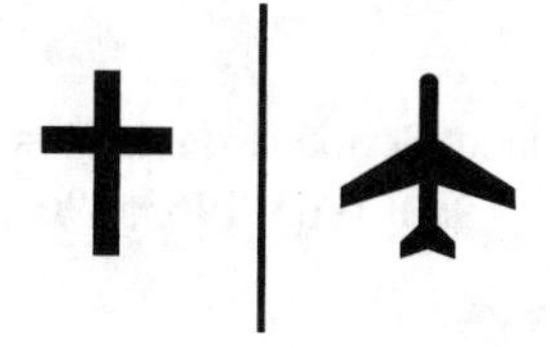

MICHAEL S. WILDER + SHANE W. PARKER

NASHVILLE, TENNESSEE

TransforMission:
Making Disciples Through Short-Term Missions

ISBN: 978-0-8054-4774-3

Published by B&H Publishing Group
Nashville, Tennessee

Dewey Decimal Classification: 266
Subject Heading: MISSIONS \ EVANGELISTIC WORK \
CHRISTIAN LIFE

Abbreviations used for journals, periodicals, major reference works, and series conform to *The SBL Handbook of Style*, ed. Patrick H. Alexander et al. (Peabody, MA: Hendrickson, 1999).

Printed in the United States of America

1 2 3 4 5 6 7 8 9 10 11 12 • 17 16 15 14 13 12 11 10
R

CONTENTS

Dedication

To my best friend and wife, Ginger:

Thank you for your support and your endless encouragement;
thank you for exemplifying the Proverbs 31 woman in our home.

To my daughters, Daly Amelia,
Ashton Leigh, and McKenzie Grace:

You are amazing, and I am pleased to see
who you are becoming in Christ;
may your heart always be tender toward the nations.

To my parents and siblings:

You have challenged me at every turn;
you have believed in me without hesitation.
Thank you!

To the glory of God:

May the gospel go forth to the nations.

—Michael

Dedication

To my partner in life, ministry,
and indescribable love, Lydia:

You are truly a woman of godly courage, strength, virtue, and sacrifice;
I will always deeply adore you.

To my children, Wiley and Evie:

You will never grasp the full extent to which I love you,
but the love is dynamic and unending.
May God grow you to know Jesus
and pour out your lives to make Him known.

To my parents:

You have given up energies, time, resources—your lives—
in order to love, nurture, and support me;
I love you and am so grateful for your lives.

To the glory and honor of Jesus, who is worthy:

"For you were slain, and by your blood you ransomed people
for God from every tribe and language
and people and nation."
(Rev 5:9b ESV)

—*Shane*

INTRODUCTION

CALLING THEM TO GREATNESS: SHORT-TERM MISSION FOR LIFE TRANSFORMATION

Have you ever spent time with a person who was so passionate about something that you were captivated by his words? At that moment it seemed as if what was driving him was contagious, so tangible that it might ignite you if you stood too close to that life. William Carey must have possessed that type of infectious personality. One writer estimates the legacy of "the father of modern missions" in these terms: "What Martin Luther was to the Protestant Reformation, Carey was to the Christian missionary movement."[1]

When we talk about Carey, we often think about his urging the leaders of the Northampton Baptist Association to consider "whether the command given to the apostles to teach all nations was not binding on all succeeding ministers to the end of the world."[2] It seems almost certain that this statement was delivered with great fervor; unfortunately, it was met with an equal or greater degree of cynicism. John Ryland, for example, replied, "Young man, sit down. . . . When God pleases to convert the heathen, He will do it without consulting you or me."[3] Even though several at this meeting discouraged Carey from pursuing missions, God had placed deep in the heart of this young lay pastor and cobbler the desire to make disciples of all nations. Perhaps that moment with the Northampton leaders was Carey's crucible, a jolting catalyst that galvanized his determination

---

[1] J. Anderson, "The Great Century and Beyond," in *Missiology,* ed. J. M. Terry, E. Smith, and J. Anderson (Nashville: B&H, 1998), 200.

[2] S. P. Carey, *William Carey, D.D., Fellow of Linnaean Society* (New York: George H. Doran, 1923), 50.

[3] Ibid.

to fulfill the Great Commission among a group of people in a land and culture he did not know.

Carey was unwilling to be dissuaded on an issue so critical to the heart of God, so he began to write what has become known as the manifesto on modern missions, *An Enquiry into the Obligations of Christians to Use Means for the Conversion of the Heathens*, which was published in 1792. In this writing he refutes the notion that the Great Commission has already been fulfilled and implores the Church to be involved in international mission. The writing of the *Enquiry* eventually led to the formation of the Baptist Missionary Society, and Carey and his family became the first missionaries to obtain support through this group. Though William Carey often wrote and spoke eloquently about the Christian's obligation to the unreached people of the world, perhaps his most powerful message was preached on May 30, 1792, at Nottingham, just prior to the beginning of his missionary career. From the pulpit, he declared with great force, "Attempt great things, expect great things." This message still strikes at the heart of believers who see God's command to make disciples of all nations as their battle cry. Carey determined to attempt that which seemed possible only if God proved Himself strong. Prove Himself strong, God did. Carey invested the remainder of his life among the people of India, producing over forty translations of the Bible, establishing a dozen mission stations, successfully combating the evil social practices of infanticide and widow burning among the Hindus, and watching as his three sons became missionaries.[4]

"Attempt great things, expect great things."
—WILLIAM CAREY

As we attempt great things for the sake of the gospel, God accomplishes great things in our midst. Certainly God is not bound by our energies or service, but God has chosen to use our participation in fulfilling the Great Commission as a means to evangelize the world. The apostle Paul is clear when he writes, "How then will they call on Him in whom they have not believed? How will they believe in Him whom they have not heard? And how will they hear without a preacher?" (Rom 10:14).

God has chosen us to serve as disciple-makers in this world. It is our responsibility to communicate unashamedly, through word and action,

[4] S. Moreau, G. Corwin, and G. McGee, *Introducing World Missions: A Biblical, Historical, and Practical Survey* (Grand Rapids: Baker, 2004), 202.

the gospel of our Lord Jesus Christ to a world of hungering and thirsting unbelievers.

The phenomenal truth is this: As we actively participate in spreading the story of Christ's redemptive work, we are also somehow transformed in the process. Just as William Carey's attitudes, values, and life purpose were changed when he engaged a nation with the gospel, so it will be for us as we begin to fulfill the Great Commission of Jesus.

May we be reminded that we are not singular individuals standing in the gap for a lost and dying world. Instead, we are a part of the Church that God continues to use in fulfillment of the tasks of discipleship and mission. He has called out people like the apostles, the early church fathers, Aurelius Augustine, Thomas Aquinas, John Wycliffe, Martin Luther, John Calvin, John Wesley, George Whitefield, William Carey, Jonathan Edwards, Lottie Moon, Adoniram Judson, George Mueller, David Livingstone, J. Hudson Taylor, C. T. Studd, John Paton, Charles Spurgeon, D. L. Moody, Amy Carmichael, Gladys Aylward, Jim Elliot, and scores of others throughout history to be the "means" of which Carey spoke. He is still calling out people like these to participate in mission and service in the kingdom—those who have a heart to pursue and prioritize the things of God. Such individuals are willing to attempt great things for God's glory and expect great things from the God who is faithful to this end.

Among the activities being attempted are short-term mission ventures. The number of those participating in such experiences is astounding. Missiologist Robert Priest suggests that due to the "decentralized" nature of the short-term movement, his own estimate of between one and four million annual North American participants may be too low.[5] Of the total number going, from North America alone two million are adolescents between the ages of 13 and 17. Also, 30 percent of all North American teenagers have engaged in religious missions or service projects, with 13 percent of these having been a part of two to four such experiences.[6]

> Thirty percent of all North American teenagers have engaged in religious missions or service projects.

The reality behind these statistics is that God is using this generation to reach the nations. He is also using active participation in fulfilling the

[5] R. Priest, "Are Short-Term Missions Good Stewardship?," *Christianity Today* 49 (July 2005). Cited 9 April 2007. Online: http://www.ctlibrary.com/ct/2005/julyweb-only/22.0.html.

[6] C. Smith, *Soul Searching: The Religious and Spiritual Lives of American Teenagers* (New York: Oxford Univ. Press, 2005), 53–54.

Great Commission as a means of life transformation. God is not only interested in the recipients of mission activity; He is also interested in the participants. God's Word is clear that along with reconciling us to Himself, He has made a commitment to restore us to a more accurate image of His Son. This restoration process has captured many writers' attention.

This restoration process has captured our attention as well. We are both veteran youth pastors and researchers in the field of youth ministry and missiology. From our biblical understanding, our research, and our experience, we are convinced that God is doing something remarkable in the lives of students and their adult leaders as they actively participate in short-term missions. Our conviction is that short-term mission is one way God is taking the gospel to the nations and, concurrently, transforming the individual participants.

We were recently visiting in the home of David, a close friend and young pastor. While there, we watched video footage of his two-year term as a missionary to Zambia. We saw images of Zambian nationals listening intently during Bible study, playing sports with the local missionaries, and laughing together. David looked at the video with the excitement and attention of someone seeing it for the first time and mentioned his openness to returning one day, should the Lord allow it. He is someone who has been revolutionized for, and altered by, mission experience.

Looking at David, it is clear that the contagious passion so evident in William Carey has infected another mind, heart, and spirit for God's glory among the nations. But when did this passion ignite, and what was the catalyst and fuel for the fire that it has become? In response to these questions, David points to a process of short-term deployment that began in high school, continued through college, and culminated with his two-year stint in Zambia. When speaking of this transforming process, David identifies these short-term opportunities as a key agent in "making [his] passion for missions whole," "giving it structure," and "completing it." In particular, he recognizes the value of the difficulty and effort these experiences have entailed; they have stripped away any romantic notion of mission service, leaving him with an authentic understanding of the challenges and joys of being involved in the fulfillment of the Great Commission.

David's story is representative of what God is doing on an individual basis—one person at a time. As was true with Carey, so it is with David and others. The transformation of values, thoughts, desires, and lives takes place through attempting difficult and rewarding mission tasks, while expecting God to bring honor to His name through such efforts.

In the balance of this volume, we want to raise some questions with you as a leader. Whether you are a student minister, missiologist, church leader, adult volunteer, college or seminary student, or mission-sending agency personnel, you share a concern for student and adult involvement in mission. We would like to assess strategies for promoting this involvement by exploring several questions: What mechanisms is God employing to achieve this advance in mission? What is taking place in the lives of believers who are obediently participating in the fulfillment of the Great Commission? What are the theological and theoretical foundations for the life transformation that is occurring? What is the most effective means of conducting short-term mission experiences?

We also want personally to challenge you as you proceed through this volume. Some of the questions we hope will be raised for you include: Am I obediently fulfilling the Great Commission? Am I taking the gospel to both my neighbor and the nations? Am I using short-term missions as a strategic component in my ministry setting? If so, am I doing it well? Do I have a clear understanding of how God transforms people?

We hope this book will better equip you to create effective mission environments wherein students and adults alike will experience life transformation, resulting in a greater commitment to biblical Christianity. We also want this book to inspire you to mobilize generations who will faithfully fulfill the Great Commission. May you be found as one who "attempts great things" and "expects great things."

PART I

SHORT-TERM MISSION IN PERSPECTIVE: EXPLORING THE BIGGER PICTURE

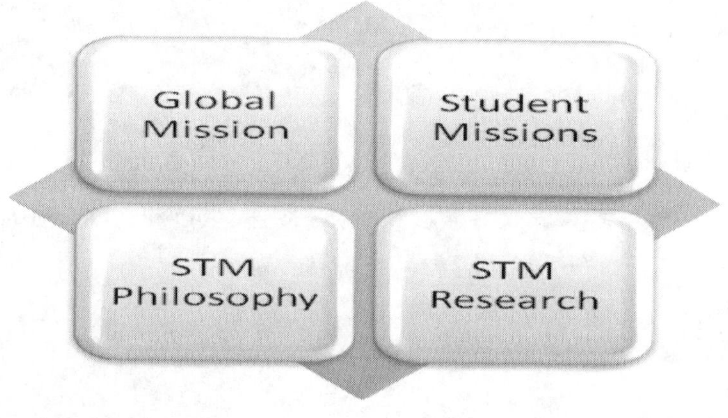

I just saw a picture from high school. It was an old photo of five of us hanging out during a lunch break. It was a snapshot of 17-year-old classmates, paused for a minute in a life moving at breakneck pace. At that moment none of us could know that it was a picture of two future wives and mothers, an eventual funeral home director, a White House staff member (yes, that White House), and a married minister with two children.

The picture did not depict those futures, but it did tell us a great deal about that moment in our lives and world. We were all good athletes, in excellent shape. We had a lot of time to connect. We had poor fashion sense (trends in hairstyles have definitely changed). We were once close to one another. Time, neglect of health, frenzied lives, and distance have changed all of that. An image like that could not tell us about our respective futures, but it did capture what was once our present.

In Part I we will take a look at our present and our past. Such an assessment can tell us a great deal about the global mission today, its biblical basis, and what it means to mobilize students for this task now and in the future. It should also help us take a more informed look at the idea of short-term mobilization, especially as it involves your church and your students.

Our hope is that those young people who are a part of your ministry will have pictures they look at years from now that tell them about who they were, what they were doing, and who they wanted to be. We hope these chapters will help you think through how to ensure that when each individual looks back at such images, he sees a globally aware and engaged student determined to become the mission-focused adult he one day embodies.

CHAPTER 1

HOLDING THE VIEW-MASTER: THE WHERE, WHAT, AND WHO OF GLOBAL MISSION

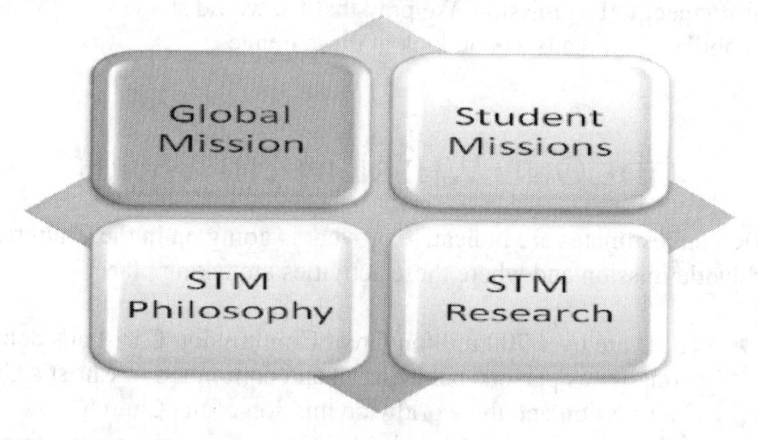

CLICKING THROUGH THE SLIDES

Capturing this snapshot of mission around the world involves asking a few basic questions. Really, several pictures are related but different—kind of like a View-Master. If you are too young to remember the chunky red viewing toy with the slot-machine-like arm on the side to make it work, let us give you a brief tutorial. You take a plastic disc (a few usually came with the viewer), and insert it into the top of the View-Master. Along the entire outside edge of these discs were small film windows. As you pull down the plastic arm while looking through the lenses, you click through the slides and see each picture up close. Each slide related to the others on the disc. (Our favorites were the superhero discs; Spider-Man never looked so cool in a frozen pose.) Though related, the pictures were different, because together they often told a story—a story bigger than one frame could contain.

In similar fashion, trying to get a respectable grasp on the state of global mission is a much more expansive task than a chapter will allow. In truth, its complexity and gravity prevents it from being fully outlined or distilled in a series of volumes. Our more reasonable hope here is to click through the View-Master with you, looking at just a few slides. The pictures we view will constitute an exploration of, not an exhaustive answer to, these questions: *Where* are lives being changed through mission? *What* types of ministry are taking place? *Who* are these missionaries? Even at this elemental level, God may begin using these statistics, stories, and details of dynamic movements to shape where and how you and your students connect to His mission. We pray that He would shape your "vision" for mobilizing students as you look at these images.

SLIDE ONE: WHERE IN THE WORLD

Recent estimates are indicative of what is going on in the Church and worldwide mission and where these activities are taking place:

- There are over 700 million Great Commission Christians defined primarily as persons believing in and committed to Christ's Great Commission and the worldwide mission of the Church.
- Estimates show that Christian believers make up almost a third of the world population, or just over 2,000,000,000 persons.
- The annual increase is 58.4 million newly evangelized for the first time (160,000 a day).
- The world population is expanding by 79.4 million per year (287,530 per day).
- Those unevangelized comprised *[sic]* 74.6% of the world population in 1800, but by 2007 they . . . [were] 28% of the global population.
- If the actual numbers of the unevangelized are evaluated, the picture is somewhat different. There were 674,350,000 in 1800, whereas the projection of those unevangelized in 2025 will be

> 2,156,012,000. These people will comprise *[sic]* 27.3% of the estimated world population.[1]

The Church has grown exponentially over the past two centuries, but the need to walk in faithfulness to the Great Commission has never been more crucial. Believers who are called to this global faithfulness are not confined to one discrete world region. Figure 1.1 indicates where the members of the Church, worldwide, call home.

Asia	353,822,000
Africa	417,001,000
Europe	532,715,000
Latin America	525,162,000
North America	223,621,000
Oceania	22,668,000

Figure 1.1: The Global Church Population by World Area

As these estimates indicate, the mass of the Church has largely moved south. This shift has prompted some missiologists to conclude that initiatives and trend-setting moves will be generated principally from the "Southern Church" in the years to come.[2] It will take future snapshots to determine the breadth of this effect.

Among People Groups

In the meantime, trends in both the Southern and Northern Hemispheres show that missionaries maintain ways to identify populations that they might engage with the gospel. Over time this classification process has taken different shapes. In recent decades missionaries have established ministries based on the identification of people groups, distinct "cultural

[1] T. Johnson, "Status of Global Mission 2007: An Annual Update," Lausanne World Pulse, n.p. [cited 19 November 2008]. Online: http://www.lausanneworldpulse.com/research.php/627/02-2007?pg=all.

[2] S. Escobar, *The New Global Mission* (Downers Grove, IL: InterVarsity, 2003), 15–16.

and/or sociological groupings" of which the global populace is composed.[3] The 1982 Lausanne Committee on World Evangelization provided a definition of a "people group": "For evangelization purposes, a people group is the largest group within which the Gospel can spread as a church planting movement without encountering barriers of understanding or acceptance."[4]

UNREACHED PEOPLE PROFILE HUI OF CHINA

Population

12,695,000 Hui in China

Identity

The Hui are an official minority of China.

Language

The Hui speak standard Mandarin; although, in some locations, Persian and Arabic words have been added to their vocabulary.

History

By the middle of the seventh century, Arab and Persian traders and merchants traveled to China in search of riches. In addition, in the thirteenth century the Mongols turned people into mobile armies during their Central Asian conquests and sent them to China.

Religion

Almost all Hui are Sunni Muslims. They worship in thousands of mosques throughout China.

Christianity

Although there are a small number of scattered Hui believers in China, the Hui are probably the largest people group in the world without a single known Christian fellowship group.

The Joshua Project
www.joshuaproject.net

---

[3] S. Wilson, "Peoples, People Groups," in *Evangelical Dictionary of World Missions,* ed. A. S. Moreau (Grand Rapids: Baker, 2000), 744.

[4] The Joshua Project, "What Is a People Group?," Lausanne Committee on World Evangelization, n.p. [cited 10 November 2008]. Online: http://www.joshuaproject.net/what-is-a-people-group.php.

This description is helpful because of its emphasis on the twin priorities of seeing the *gospel* and the *Church* established among these "nations."

Among the Unreached Peoples

The stark reality is that not all of these groups have equal access to the good news. The Joshua Project, which focuses on the study of people groups and mission, defines an *unreached people group* as a "people group among which there is no indigenous community of believing Christians with adequate numbers and resources to evangelize this people group."[5] The situation for the least-reached looks like this:

- There are approximately 16,453 ethno-linguistic groups in the world.
- Of these groups, 6,853 are still unreached.
- The total number of individuals in these groups is 2.67 billion, which makes up 40.2% of the world's population.
- The single largest unreached group is the Japanese, who are 120,000,000 in number.
- There are 3,324 Muslim people groups, who are 1,300,000,000 in number.
- There are 2,714 Hindu people groups, who are 900,000,000 in number.
- There are 573 Buddhist people groups, who are 375,000,000 in number.
- Of the 7,216 groups in the 10/40 Window, there are 5,399 which are unreached.
- These 5,399 groups make up 74.8% of the unreached groups.
- They include 2.32 billion people.[6]

The challenges of governments limiting access, cultural understanding/research, language acquisition, and Bible translation into the various groups' languages all make reaching these people both complex and overwhelming. In the area of Scripture translation alone, there are 4,400 languages that have no portion of Scripture available to them. While there are

[5] Ibid.

[6] Ibid.

current translation efforts for 1,600 of these, for the other 2,800 languages no one is working on Bible translations.[7]

Slide Two: What in the World

Bible translation is just one of the many forms that the work of a twenty-first-century missionary might take. Andrew Walls has identified "Five Marks of Mission," which are not intended to be exhaustive but do encompass major areas of this cross-cultural ministry:

1. To proclaim the Good News of the Kingdom.
2. To teach, baptize, and nurture new believers.
3. To respond to human need by loving service.
4. To seek to transform unjust structures of society.
5. To strive to safeguard the integrity of creation and sustain and renew the life of the earth.[8]

These expansive veins of mission contain so many ministry types that one agency president indicated that at one time his organization had listed 100 different categories for missionary assignment.[9] The diverse roles that today's agencies and churches are looking to incorporate into their strategy include missionary platforms that are sometimes explicitly tied to churches and ministries as well as some that are more indirectly linked.

Gritty issues like poverty, modern slavery, human trafficking, genocide, the AIDS epidemic, hostile governments, and refugee crises are all facing the Church. These realities remind us that we are called to make mission Christ centered and gospel oriented. This requires engaging the whole person, in the totality of his circumstances, with the eternal hope of our great God and His "transforming gospel."[10] Many agencies, churches, and individual believers are clearly envisioning and endorsing multiple ways to do just that.

---

[7] Ibid.

[8] A. Walls and C. Ross, eds., *Mission in the 21st Century: Exploring the Five Marks of Mission* (Maryknoll, NY: Orbis, 2008), xiv.

[9] J. Rankin, *To the Ends of the Earth* (Nashville: B&H, 2006), 209.

[10] D. Carson, "Conclusion: Ongoing Imperative for World Mission," in *The Great Commission,* ed. M. Klauber and S. Manetsch (Nashville: B&H, 2008), 183.

Slide Three: Who in the World

Since there are so many different manners of involvement, there must also be a diverse group of people who are answering the call to serve. Our picture would be incomplete if we did not take a brief look at these people who are investing in cross-cultural relationships, places, and ministries.

The Missionary Force

Of the total foreign missionary force, 249,000 are men and 209,000 are women.[11] These include not only missionaries from North America and Europe but also scores of those serving through Third World mission organizations. There are estimated to be hundreds of such sending vehicles across Asia, Africa, and Latin America.[12]

The ages of these missionaries vary, with many beginning their service as young adults.[13] These new recruits are, generally, recent graduates from colleges, universities, graduate schools, or seminaries that have been equipped for ministry and are seeking to use this preparation in cross-cultural settings. There is also a trend among some agencies and churches toward identifying opportunities that enable older adults to use their career skills overseas. The Finishers Project, for example, makes mobilizing the boomer generation an objective.[14]

Connecting Motive and Mission

There are also scores of different motives pushing students, recent graduates, and older adults to plug into mission. Some of these motivations are related to certain brands of mission philosophy. For example, some may have a deep drive to free child slaves in India that causes them to join International Justice Mission, while others may long to see churches planted among tribal peoples in Papua New Guinea, which leads them to connect with ministries like New Tribe Mission or To Every Tribe Ministries. Ministries like these, as well as many others, facilitate opportunities for individuals looking to act on specific ministry passions.

---

[11] Johnson, "Status of Global Mission 2007."

[12] J. Reapsome, "The Next Generation of Innovators," in *Innovation in Mission,* ed. J. Reapsome and J. Hirst (Atlanta: Authentic, 2007), 183.

[13] S. Shadrach, *The Fuel and the Flame* (Atlanta: Authentic, 2003), 212–13.

[14] See "Vision" in Finishers Project, n.p. [cited 18 November 2008]. Online: http://www.finishers.org/.

There is, however, an essential drive toward biblical service that should undergird the motives of even these worthy causes. The principal motive for mission should be that *God's glory be seen, that He be worshipped, and that these things take place among every people group on the earth.* Preaching to a missionary society in colonial America more than 200 years ago, Jonathan Edwards argued that "the glory of God, a regard to his honor and praise in the spread of the gospel, ought to be the governing motive in all missionary exertions and the animating principle in the breast of missionaries."[15] Sifting all that is done through this evaluative filter can clarify what we are intending as our outcome in mission.

LENGTH OF TERM

This desire to further God's glory was a driving force behind William Carey's decision to leave everything and go. Carey went to India with no expectation of returning home frequently, partly because at that time the ability to travel back and forth with ease did not exist. Modern travel has changed that forever. Even many career missionaries who go overseas for a "lifetime" come back on home assignment at regular intervals and in some cases speak to family and friends almost daily, using video communication programs that are now readily available.

This means that definitions of, and options for, timeframes deployed to the field have changed. *Long-term*, or career, missionary service usually applies to any period of two or more years in length. Any term that is between three months and two years is generally labeled *mid-term*, although some organizations and missiologists categorize these as short-term.[16] *Short-term* trips can be characterized as any trip that is three months or less. These designations are only basic guidelines because deployment terms and expectations are established by each agency or church.[17]

Some organizations and churches use these different levels as progressive steps to what they hope will be longer seasons of service. As conceived, the tiered approach will get someone involved in mission at the entry level and, progressively, facilitate movement through the next steps. Advocates of this approach believe that such exposure helps the new missionary to see firsthand what life is like on the mission field and enables

---

[15] J. Edwards, "To the Glory of God," in *Classic Texts in Mission and World Christianity,* ed. N. Thomas (Maryknoll, NY: Orbis, 1995), 60.

[16] R. Blue, *Evangelism* and *Missions* (Nashville: Thomas Nelson, 2001), 149–54.

[17] R. Peterson, "Innovation in Short-Term Mission," in *Innovation in Short-Term Mission,* ed. J. Reapsome and J. Hirst (Atlanta: Authentic, 2006), 51.

the sending agency or church to determine if the missionary demonstrates the ability to be successful during longer periods of deployment. Some organizations, however, mobilize exclusively for short-term mission. Many of these agencies coordinate opportunities for students and adults from local churches. The intention, many times, is to grant participants baseline exposure to mission while encouraging greater global awareness and involvement as a result.

Looking at Their Pictures

Looking at these slides of the present can help us be realistic about who we are, what we are to be, and where we want to go. The people inhabiting this global environment will change before we can even finish this sentence; they will grow in number in some places and decline in others. The places and peoples will be different tomorrow than they are today due to progress, revolution, and sometimes devastation. If we are going to get students involved in this mission now, we need to anticipate these changes, by first gaining a sense of their foundation in mission, and then implementing designs that will challenge them to missional attitudes, thoughts, and informed actions.

Discussion Questions

1. Describe the state of the Church today in terms of its reach.
2. Detail the spread of the gospel throughout the earth.
3. What are some of the various types of ministry opportunities that exist on the mission field?
4. What should the Christian's motive be for participating in missions?
5. When reading the statistics in the chapter, were you surprised in any way? If so, by what? Were you moved to reconsider your present and future involvement in missions?

Chapter 2

What Students Are Doing: The Yesterday and Today of Student Missions

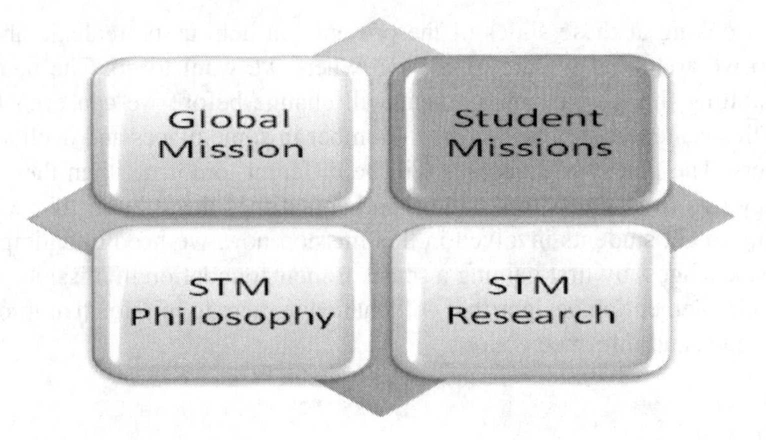

Standing in a Long Line of Missionaries

You have got to see the film *EE-Taow!*[1] It recounts the story of a missionary couple who traveled to Papua, New Guinea, and rooted their ministry in teaching the Bible, chronologically, among the Mouk tribal people. Once they had studied the language and culture sufficiently, they began to tell the story of biblical creation, fall, and redemption; however, even before he began teaching the Bible, missionary Mark Zook told the Mouk about the historical trek of the gospel, as it had "gone around the world and was now coming to them."[2] This has been a long historical journey that involves the life-giving truth of Christ being carried by those who would stop at nothing to see it advance a little farther into a new tribe or people or nation.

---

[1] *EE-Taow!*, DVD (Sanford, CA: New Tribes Mission, 1999).

[2] Ibid.

This is also a timeless story with which today's students can immediately connect. They are not simply making a difference in their generation; they are also standing in a long line with those God has been raising up to establish His Church and exalt His name all over the globe for roughly two millennia.

Historically, a determined heart for mission advance has been a hallmark of the lives of those who believe in Jesus. While the whole of this rich mission history is beyond the scope of our exploration, a brief look at biblical mission, and the place of youth and college students in past and present movements, will be important to understanding the role of contemporary short-term mission in fulfilling the Great Commission and developing students.

The Starting Point of Mission

Many times our discussions of what the Bible teaches about the idea of mission start with a handful of New Testament texts, but Walter Kaiser argues that this is an inadequate approach to capturing the biblical picture:

> The Bible actually begins with the theme of missions in the Book of Genesis and maintains that driving passion throughout the entire Old Testament and on into the New Testament. If an Old Testament "Great Commission" must be identified, then it will be Genesis 12:3—"all the peoples of the earth will be blessed through you [Abraham]." This is the earliest statement of the fact that it will be God's purpose and plan to see that the message of his grace and blessing comes to every person on planet earth. The message did not begin there. The basis for it, in fact, went all the way back to Genesis 3:15.[3]

In Gen 3:15 (ESV), God issues a key postfall promise to the serpent: "I will put enmity between you and the woman, and between your offspring and her offspring; he shall bruise your head, and you shall bruise his heel."Andreas Köstenberger and Peter O'Brien note that "Christian scholars have understood this as the *protoevangelium*, the first glimmer of the

[3] W. Kaiser, *Mission in the Old Testament* (Grand Rapids: Baker, 2000), 7.

gospel."[4] Desmond Alexander further clarifies that this promise of "good news" in "the seed of woman" is to be seen as "referring to a single individual and not numerous descendants."[5] The move toward the fulfillment of this promise, then, becomes the key narrative element in the remainder of both the book of Genesis and the whole Old Testament.[6] The manner in which this fulfillment unfolds is clarified and refined in each of the further promises of the Abrahamic (Gen 12:1–3) and Davidic (2 Sam 7) covenants.

By the time we reach the end of the first 11 chapters of the book of Genesis, there are 70 established "nations." Against this backdrop the promise to Abram is given in Gen 12:1–3 (ESV):

> Now the LORD said to Abram, "Go from your country and your kindred and your father's house to the land that I will show you. And I will make of you a great nation, and I will bless you and make your name great, so that you will be a blessing. I will bless those who bless you, and him who dishonors you I will curse, and in you all the families of the earth shall be blessed."

This pledge is not isolated in its emphasis on Abraham's offspring being a blessing to all nations through the Man of Promise, "the seed" of Gen 3:15.[7] A similar message of Gentile inclusion and engagement with the reality of God is captured in both Exod 19:5–6 and Psalm 67.[8] Each of these passages offers an explicit injunction to Israel and her constituent members to understand and rejoice in God's inclusion of the Gentiles.

Christopher Wright is keen to point out that the mission emphasis in the Old Testament is largely on *God* bringing blessing and restoration to the nations rather than on a far-reaching missionary deployment from among Israel's ranks. However, there are notable exceptions to this: the eschatological sending of messengers in Isaiah 66; Jonah's task; Elijah's ministry to the widow of Zarephath (1 Kgs 17:8–24); and Elisha's trip to

4 A. Köstenberger and P. T. O'Brien, *Salvation to the Ends of the Earth: A Biblical Theology of Mission* (Downers Grove, IL: InterVarsity, 2001), 27.

5 D. Alexander, "Further Observations on the Term 'Seed' in Genesis," *Tyndale Bulletin.* 48 (1997): 363.

6 J. Sailhammer, *Genesis,* Expositor's Bible Commentary (Grand Rapids: Zondervan, 1990), 55–56.

7 J. Stott, "The Living God Is a Missionary God," in *Perspectives on the World Christian Movement,* ed. R. Winter and S. Hawthorne; 3d ed. (Pasadena, CA: William Carey, 1999), 4.

8 W. Kaiser, "Israel's Missionary Call," in Winter and Hawthorne, *Perspectives*, 11.

Damascus (2 Kgs 8:7–15).[9] These are certainly unique examples, but they do demonstrate an incipient practice of God sending messengers to the nations as part of His activity among them.[10] This "sending of messengers" image is more fully developed and expressed in the outline of mission in the New Testament.

The Continuing Task of Mission

Since the theme of mission finds its extension, rather than its origin, in the New Testament, Bryant Hicks argues that "the early followers of Jesus Christ did not perceive missions as a new concept or function for God's people. They perceived the task of bringing the nations to faith in Yahweh as the responsibility of Israel from its beginnings."[11] As George Peters notes, "The Great Commission does not make Christianity a missionary religion; it is such because of the character and purpose of God."[12]

In the New Testament this God-centered mission is restated and clarified. The core of this clarification is most commonly labeled the "Great Commission," which is customarily confined to the content of Jesus' teaching given to His disciples immediately preceding His ascension (Matt 28:16–20); however, New Testament scholar Robert Plummer applies this concept and title to all passages that address "Christians' obligation to share the gospel with non-believers."[13] In order for the Great Commission to be rightly understood and expressed, he argues, it must be realized in broader terms than simply "explicit imperatives."[14]

Plummer offers an understanding of the theme of the Great Commission that includes several elements: (1) the command to make disciples (Matt 28:19); (2) "the role of God's Spirit in empowering and directing the gospel's spread" (Acts 5:32); and (3) Paul's epistles, for example, which focus on "the gospel as God's dynamic word that inevitably accomplishes his purpose" (Col 1:6).[15] The movement of the gospel into and among the

[9] C. Wright, *The Mission of God* (Downers Grove, IL: InterVarsity, 2006), 503.

[10] Ibid., 502–3.

[11] B. Hicks, "Old Testament Foundations for Missions," in *Missiology,* ed. J. M. Terry, E. Smith, and J. Anderson (Nashville: B&H, 1998), 51.

[12] G. Peters, *A Biblical Theology of Missions* (Chicago: Moody, 1972), 176.

[13] R. Plummer, "The Great Commission in the New Testament," *Southern Baptist Journal of Theology* 9 (2005): 4.

[14] Ibid., 9.

[15] Ibid.

nations of the earth is comprised of all three of these active Great Commission elements.

MISSION AS DISCIPLE-MAKING

In Matt 28:16–20, the "making" of disciples is the nucleus of the apostles' mission. New Testament scholar John Harvey observes that for "Matthew, the focus of the disciples' mission is less one of public proclamation than one of intensive instruction. This perspective, of course, is in accord with Matthew's portrait of Jesus as a teacher who repeatedly instructs his disciples at length and in depth."[16] Disciple-making here is seen as *instruction* that is thoroughgoing and rooted in "all things" that Jesus has commanded His disciples; however, it also prizes the importance of the apostolate following the *model* of Jesus in its teaching.

This replicative discipleship process is further developed by Lucien Legrand: "'Making disciples' conjures up the image of a master initiating his disciples through an organized process in the rabbinical style, progressively communicating a teaching and a lifestyle corresponding to this 'tradition.' This kind of activity suggests more the instructor's podium than the 'feet of those who announce good news.'"[17] Instructing the followers of Jesus means communicating both a teaching and a lifestyle. While gospel living may be more caught than taught, as the cliché goes, these two aspects of communication should nevertheless be more interdependent: lifestyle teaches the student, and biblical teaching that "lives" is both understood by and integrated into the learner's life.

MISSION AS SPIRIT-DIRECTED ADVANCE

Throughout the early chapters of the Acts of the Apostles, Luke's emphasis is on the Holy Spirit and His working *within* the believing witnesses to disseminate the truth (e.g., 2:4,37–41; 4:8,13; 6:5,10; 7:54,57). While each of these instances displays the work of the believer as he is empowered by the Spirit, Acts 5:32 contains a nuanced understanding of what is actually taking place. Peter declares, "And we are witnesses to these things; and so is the Holy Spirit, whom God has given to those who obey Him." Unlike those texts that point to the work of the Spirit in and through the witnesses, the statement here seems to indicate that the Spirit also bears witness to the truth of the gospel in direct parallel to the proc-

[16] J. Harvey, "Mission in Matthew," in *Mission in the New Testament,* ed. W. Larkin and J. Williams (Maryknoll, NY: Orbis, 1998), 131–32.

[17] L. Legrand, *Unity and Plurality* (Maryknoll, NY: Orbis, 1990), 78.

lamation of the apostolic witnesses.[18] Bill Larkin comments on this dual emphasis in Acts:

> Luke does not neglect the "salvation accomplished" portion of the gospel: the Messiah must suffer and rise from the dead. However, the main focus is on "salvation applied"—the church in mission taking the gospel to the ends of the earth. Luke constantly reminds us that this is the mission of the Triune God. Not only does he send and guide his missionaries (apostles, witnesses to the resurrection, evangelists, believers), but he is directly calling people to himself as his word grows and the number of his people increases.[19]

This activity by God, both parallel to and in concert with His "sent ones," serves as the real power behind the disciple-making effort. His Spirit bears witness to His absolute magnificence, as the extension of His gospel accomplishes His purposes, ultimately among every people group.[20]

Mission as the Extension of God's Word

In his letter to the Colossian believers, Paul observes about this gospel "which has come to you, . . . [that] in the whole world it is bearing fruit and growing—as it also does among you, since the day you heard it and understood the grace of God in truth" (Col 1:6 ESV). Here the gospel is active in "bearing fruit and growing." As Plummer puts it:

> Paul's understanding of the gospel as God's dynamic word that inevitably moves forward and accomplishes the divine purpose provides a theological basis for the church's mission. . . . [For] Paul, when the gospel is genuinely present in a congregation, he is confident that the dynamic nature of that word will guarantee its ongoing triumphant progress.[21]

As this global mission finds fulfillment through going, teaching, and baptizing, the Spirit accomplishes disciple-making and the successful

---

[18] W. Larkin, "Mission in Acts," in *Mission in the New Testament,* ed. W. Larkin and J. Williams (Maryknoll, NY: Orbis, 1998), 177.

[19] Ibid., 185.

[20] J. Hamilton, *God's Indwelling Presence* (Nashville: B&H, 2006), 85.

[21] Plummer, "The Great Commission in the New Testament," 9.

establishment of the Church by this "word." Such are the active process and method that are fulfilling the Great Commission.

THE ROLE OF STUDENTS IN MISSION: YESTERDAY

Now we come to the role of students in this Great Commission story. In 1970, missions historian Pierce Beaver argued that the changing world necessitated informed strategies that were new and culturally engaging; however, in pushing for innovation, he added this cautionary note: "It will help as we pray, study, plan and experiment if we know the past history of mission strategy."[22] Beaver's outline of this "past history" of organized mission strategies and movements includes the eighth-century efforts of Boniface; the deplorable Crusades against Muslims; the subsequent work of Francis of Assisi and Ramon Lull to evangelize Muslim peoples; the sixteenth- to eighteenth-century worldwide advance of Christianity through Portuguese, Spanish, and French colonialism; the seventeenth-century Jesuit approaches to mission; and the New England Puritan outreach efforts to Native Americans.[23]

The completion of this dynamic task, through different types of mission efforts and sacrifice, is entrusted to the whole Church.[24] While every individual student or adult is not directed to invest his life in career mission service, the holistic involvement of the Church in the Spirit-enabled making of disciples is vital. The Church's primary task between the resurrection and return of Christ is mission, as the Eleven are seen as "representative of later generations of believers."[25] The contributions of these "later generations of believers" to mission expansion have included individual students, youth and young adult groups, and entire student missionary movements. These are just a few of those groups and individuals who have shaped student initiatives, the whole of mission, and indeed the world.

THE MORAVIANS

Student missionaries have mainly been connected to broader youth and college movements. One of these was spearheaded by Count Nic-

[22] P. Beaver, "The History of Mission Strategy," in Winter and Hawthorne, *Perspectives,* 252.

[23] Ibid., 241–45.

[24] Harvey, "Mission in Matthew," in Larkin and Williams, *Mission,* 135–36.

[25] Köstenberger and O'Brien, *Salvation to the Ends of the Earth,* 108–9.

olaus Ludwig von Zinzendorf (1700–60), who is widely recognized as "the father of the eighteenth century Moravian missionary movement."[26] Philip Spener, the noted Pietist, was Zinzendorf's godfather, so it comes as no surprise that Nicolaus was heavily influenced by the movement. August Hermann Francke, the other notable name in Pietism, also knew Zinzendorf: Nicolaus would eventually study at the university founded by Francke, located in Halle, Germany. Here Zinzendorf joined five classmates to form the Order of the Grain of Mustard Seed, which focused on prayer and action centered around four distinctive goals:

1. Bearing witness to the power of Jesus Christ.
2. Drawing other Christians together in fellowship.
3. Helping those who were suffering for their faith in Christ.
4. Carrying the gospel of Christ overseas.[27]

Concurring with the prevailing notion that modern mission movements find their genesis, at least in part, in the Moravian activities beginning in 1732, David Howard concludes that it was a group of praying students who provided the initial spark for this foundational mission push.

As a result of such fervent prayer, by 1734 the first Moravian missionaries went to share the gospel among those recognized as "the most despised and neglected people."[28] This group of missionaries, with their intense focus on mission as the responsibility of the local church rather than specialized personnel or organizations, stands as the first unified example of its kind among Protestants.[29]

THE WESLEYS

Another link in this chain of student mission involvement is John Wesley (1703–91), along with his brother Charles (1707–88). As church historian Justo Gonzalez observes:

> Although the Moravian church never had a large membership, and soon was unable to continue sending and supporting such a high number of missionaries, its example contributed to the great missionary awakening of the

---

[26] J. Reapsome, "Zinzendorf, Nicolaus Ludwig von," *Evangelical Dictionary of World Missions*, 1044–45.

[27] D. Howard, "Student Power in World Missions," in Winter and Hawthrone, *Perspectives,* 278.

[28] Beaver, "The History of Mission Strategy," 246.

[29] C. Grant, "Europe's Moravians," in Winter and Hawthrone, *Perspectives*, 276.

> nineteenth century. But perhaps the greatest significance of the movement was its impact on John Wesley and, through him, on the entire Methodist tradition.[30]

The Pietism that fueled the Moravians found its way into the life of Susanna Wesley and was passed along to each of her children, including John. John's brother Charles, while a student at Oxford, formed what became known as the "Holy Club," a group of students who studied "the classics and the New Testament."[31] Howard notes that they were so called because of the "derision" of their peers. The group also wore the label of "Methodists" because of their intentionally systematic "method" toward all things.[32]

John joined the group after returning to Oxford as a teaching fellow, and there he found himself involved in genuine ministry with the marginalized people of society. This experience would shape the understanding and passion of both John and Charles, so that they would eventually set sail for Georgia to minister there among the English colonists and Native Americans without the gospel. Only later, partly through the faithful witness of Moravian missionaries, would John trust Christ and find true "spiritual awakening" in Him.[33]

THE SIMEONITES

The impact of Charles Simeon (1759–1836) on student mission thought and action is seen through his ministry at Cambridge as a Fellow of King's College.[34] The influence he had on students, the most ardent of whom wore the label "Simeonite," showed itself in the formation of the Jesus Lane Sunday School for children (1827), an auxiliary of the British and Foreign Bible Society (1811); the Cambridge Union for Private Prayer (1848); the Cambridge University Church Missionary Union (1858); and the Cambridge Inter-Collegiate Christian Union (1877).[35] Each of these organizations was born out of, and sustained by, the initiative of Simeon's students.

---

[30] J. Gonzalez, *The Reformation to the Present Day,* vol. 2, *The Story of Christianity* (New York: Harper Collins, 1985), 209.

[31] Howard, "Student Power in World Missions," in Winter and Hawthorne, *Perspectives,* 278.

[32] Ibid.

[33] R. Olson, *The Story of Christian Theology* (Downers Grove, IL: InterVarsity, 1999), 484.

[34] D. Howard, *Student Power in World Missions* (Downers Grove, IL: InterVarsity, 1979), 68–69.

[35] Ibid.

The Cambridge Seven

The impact of this Cambridge-born swell of youth making bold moves for the living out of mission continued to build. Perhaps the most notable students to ride this wave were seven promising young men who would eventually be known as "The Cambridge Seven." This band of revolutionaries made a decision that defied all logic, according to many around them, when they committed themselves as career missionaries to Hudson Taylor's newly formed China Inland Mission. Among these seven, the outstanding cricketer C. T. Studd (1860–1931) remains the most prominent name. As Ruth Tucker notes, "To many people, including members of Studd's own family, the decision of the seven university students was a rash move and a tremendous waste of intellect and ability."[36] Studd would go on to devote the rest of his life to mission in India and Africa, even after his stint in China was concluded. The "wasteful" sacrifice of a life for the sake of the gospel, which Studd and the others seemed to embody, was not confined to the students of Cambridge or to the continent of Europe. Like many movements of God, similar changes were taking place in other areas of the world.

The Student Volunteer Movement

In North America, the Haystack Prayer Meeting of 1806, as it would come to be called, gave birth to both the Society of Brethren at Andover Theological Seminary and the American Board of Commissioners for Foreign Missions.[37] These catalytic societies represented the beginnings of North American foreign missions, influencing the ministries of Robert Wilder and the Princeton Foreign Missionary Society, along with the college ministry of the American YMCA, each of which proved to be a stream feeding the river that eventually became the Student Volunteer Movement for Foreign Missions (SVM).

With some 251 students meeting in the summer of 1886 for a Bible conference in Mt. Hermon, Massachusetts, speakers A. T. Pierson and D. L. Moody saw 100 students sign commitments to missionary service.[38] This proved to be the launch of something far greater, as the SVM was formally organized in 1888, appointing J. R. Mott as its first chairman. In

---

[36] R. Tucker, *From Jerusalem to Irian Jaya,* 2d ed. (Grand Rapids: Zondervan, 2004), 315.

[37] Howard, "Student Power in World Missions," in Winter and Hawthrone, *Perspectives,* 216.

[38] P. Pierson, "The Student Volunteer Movement for Foreign Missions (SVM)," in *Evangelical Dictionary of World Missions,* 914.

considering this unique movement of God through His student army, Mott made a profound observation:

> It is a most inspiring fact that the young people of this generation do not apologize for world-wide missions. It would seem that that Christian who in these days would apologize for missions is either ignorant or thoughtless, because a man who apologizes for missions apologizes for Christianity, because that is essentially a missionary enterprise. He apologizes for the Bible, because missions constitutes its central theme. He apologizes for the prayer of his Lord and for the Apostles' Creed. He apologizes for the fatherhood of God, and in doing so also for the brotherhood of man. If he is a Christian, he apologizes for every whit of spiritual life that is in himself; and, worst of all, he apologizes for Jesus Christ, who is the Propitiation not for our sins only but for the sins of the world. I repeat, he is either ignorant or thoughtless. Not only do the students and other young people of our day, however, not apologize for this world-wide enterprise, but they believe in it as has no preceding generation of young people. They are believing in it with a depth of conviction, and manifesting their belief with a practical sympathy and purpose and action, such as has never been witnessed in any preceding age in the history of the Church.[39]

While the historical veracity of Mott's claims could be debated, the overwhelming movement of God among students in those days was such that Mott believed it to be unparalleled among previous generations of youth. Paul Pierson's recounting of the sheer volume of student volunteers mobilized seems to support the spirit of Mott's comment:

> Almost 600 volunteers from 159 institutions attended the quadrennial convention in 1891. The following year Wilder traveled to Britain, and the movement was launched in a number of European countries. It grew rapidly until after World War I. The 1920 convention was attended by 6,890 people from 949 schools, and that year 2,783 new volunteers enrolled. By 1940 at least 20,500 missionar-

[39] J. Mott, "The Responsibility of the Young People for the Evangelization of the World," in Winter and Hawthorne, *Perspectives*, 317–18.

> ies had sailed from North America and Europe to various mission fields. The movement more than tripled the number of missionaries from North America.[40]

The vital spirit that drove these students is captured in Samuel Zwemer's 1911 call to students to take up the mantle of going to the unreached Muslim peoples:

> Face to face with these millions in darkness and degradation, knowing the condition of their lives on the unimpeachable testimony of those who have visited these countries, this great unfinished task, this unattempted task, calls today for those who are willing to endure and suffer in accomplishing it.[41]

The student volunteers were willing. At its zenith, the movement's unparalleled success was extensive:

> In fact, one out of every thirty-seven U.S. students during that era signed SVM's missions declaration, and if you applied that same ratio to the number of college students that we have in the United States today, we would see almost 400,000 young people signing up to be missionaries.[42]

Unfortunately, this brand of missional courage, and the solidarity that accompanied it, diminished after the First World War, as theological laxity and ambiguity disabled what had once been a pillar of the movement. By the 1950s, the organization had joined efforts with others, eventually forming the University Christian Movement. By 1969, the once dynamic SVM had been officially dissolved, due in part to a lack of clear leadership and unifying vision.[43]

The Big Shift

Shortly after the end of the SVM, a seismic shift took place in mission thinking, which resulted in the emergence of a variety of short-term offerings at the end of the twentieth century.[44] This shift from "professional

[40] Pierson, "The Student Volunteer Movement for Foreign Missions (SVM)," 914.
[41] S. Zwemer, "The Glory of the Impossible," in Winter and Hawthorne, *Perspectives*, 315.
[42] S. Shadrach, *The Fuel and the Flame* (Atlanta: Authentic, 2003), 20.
[43] Pierson, "The Student Volunteer Movement for Foreign Missions (SVM)," 914.
[44] J. Rankin, *To the Ends of the Earth* (Nashville: B&H, 2006), 48.

missionaries only" to the "inclusion of short-termers" was recognized as possessing not only practical value, but also biblical validity.[45] This theological position is evident in "The Manila Manifesto" of the Lausanne Committee for World Evangelization:

> Our manifesto at Manila is that the whole church is called to take the whole gospel to the whole world, proclaiming Christ until he comes, with all necessary urgency, unity and sacrifice (Luke 2:1–7; Mark 13:26–27; 13:32–37; Acts 1:8; Matt 24:24; 28:20)."[46]

The involvement of short-term participants in the aforementioned elements of Great Commission advance is a component of this "holistic" mission thrust of the Church. Similar, though not equal, short-term, team-oriented experiences are some of the building blocks of the larger advancement of God's redemptive message, just as they were in the Old Testament (e.g., 1 Sam 7:15–17; Nehemiah 2–10; Jonah 1–4) and the establishment of the Church in the apostolic era (e.g., Acts 10:23; 13:2–4; 15:39–41).

This historical progression, from the perspective of the local church, involved a shift from a distant connection of home-based supporters, through mission presentations, and conferences, to tangible firsthand involvement:

> As the new millennium drew closer, the effects of globalization began to change the significance of these vicarious mission experiences. Short-term missions increased the number of Christians who had firsthand experiences to share at annual conferences. Mission pastors were added to the staffs of churches, colleges launched summer mission trips, and mission societies were drawn into the action, albeit reluctantly, by engaging in formal short-term mission programs. The emergence of groups that specialized in mobilizing people, particularly the young, became household names among dedicated Christians. Youth with a Mission (YWAM) and Operation Mobilization (OM), specialists in mobilizing young people, have two of the best-known acronyms in the world of missions.[47]

[45] M. Pocock, G. Van Rheenen, and D. McConnell, *The Changing Face of World Missions* (Grand Rapids: Baker, 2005), 247–48.

[46] Lausanne Committee for World Evangelization, *The Manila Manifesto* (Pasadena, CA: Castle, 1989), 35.

[47] Pocock, Van Rheenen, and McConnell, *The Changing Face of World Missions,* 247–48.

Groups like these built whole structures to support this army of young people interested in exploring and engaging in mission.

The Role of Students in Mission: Today

Both life-stage and social-dynamic issues make it necessary to look at college students of the past in comparison to youth and college students of today. While those mentioned above were predominantly college students, they were also early to late adolescents, by our contemporary standards, with students in colonial colleges and universities ranging from early adolescence to their early thirties.[48] So age itself actually supports the inclusion of these students as we look at precedents for today's middle- and high-school age youth.

The social dynamics of those the same age, at these two distinct points in history, are clearly worlds apart. While this may seem like a reason to look elsewhere for historical comparisons for today's teenagers, the opposite might be true. Significant social shifts in the placement and contributions of youth in the past century have fueled the idea that a "dependence and education now, responsibility and independence later" approach to teenage development undermines strong growth.[49]

Fueling this seismic shift in the social displacement of youth were the ideas of genetic psychologist G. Stanley Hall (1844–1924), who coined the term *adolescence*. Hall theorized that in Western society Jean-Jacques Rousseau's (1712–88) naturalist focus on children as developing organisms, and teenagers as situated in an intermediate state between childhood and adulthood, was correct.[50] However, Hall added the notion that this stage was not only biological but also social in its construction.[51] Therefore, as a society understands the need to educate in order to ensure optimal social development, added years of education and dependency naturally follow.

As Hall's theory shaped thinking and eventually practice, the progression from a preindustrial, to industrial, to postmodern adolescence left in its wake an adolescent experience that had shifted from contributing

[48] I. Mohsenin, "Age Structure of College Students," *History of Education Quarterly* 23 (1983): 491.

[49] D. White, "The Social Construction of Adolescence," in *Awakening Youth Discipleship* (Eugene, OR: Cascade, 2008), 4.

[50] H. Ozmon and S. Craver, *Philosophical Foundations of Education,* 7th ed. (Upper Saddle River, NJ: Merrill Prentice Hall), 131–32.

[51] J. Savage, *Teenage* (New York: Penguin, 2007), 66–67.

directly to society—through labor, thought, and participation—to a subculture focused largely on education and individual consumerism.[52] David White argues that these "developments relegate most youth to institutions in which they have less than full power for longer than any age cohort in the history of the world, leaving them considerably less free to make their distinctive mark on history, and are quickly shaping them as passive consumers rather than active agents and shapers of history."[53] A growing number of believing students today do not seem willing to continue this trend toward consumerism and self-absorption. They are crying for a return to social structures and challenges that enable them to contribute to revolutions of thought and action, rather than continue watching from the sideline.

THEY ARE NOT WAITING ON CHANGE

One of musician John Mayer's hit songs is titled "Waiting on the World to Change." The lyrics express his and his friends' desire to see things that are wrong with the world made right; however, they feel powerless to initiate steps toward any remedy. So, they have decided simply to wait for these changes to come.[54] Mayer and all of his friends might be "waiting on the world to change," but an increasing number of today's students are not. Instead, they are investing their lives in making it happen.

This generation of youth and college students is being enlivened to respond to the call of God in similar ways to those in generations past. Jonathan Rice notes that the "enthusiasm" and boldness of these developing "missionaries" are similar to those of centuries past, and the same applies when it comes to their motivations.[55] For example, the surge of those students interested in humanitarian relief and assistance work is not a pioneering trend, when compared with the lives of key players in the development of modern missions.

Timothy George argues that the coupling of gospel proclamation and substantial humanitarian service was a common expression of the mission efforts born out of the evangelical awakenings of the eighteenth and nineteenth centuries. Giants like Whitefield, Wesley, Wilberforce, and Carey

[52] Ibid.

[53] White, "The Social Construction of Adolescence," 4.

[54] J. Mayer, "Waiting on the World to Change," *Continuum,* compact disc, Sony, © 2006.

[55] J. Rice, "The New Missions Generation," *Christianity Today*. Online: http://www.christianitytoday.com/ct/2006/september/19.100.html (accessed on July 18, 2008).

were each involved in holistic ministry.[56] Whitefield cared for orphans, Wesley advocated for the safety of coal miners, Wilberforce fought for the freedom of slaves, and Carey served as a "school-planter" and social activist confronting the practice of widow-burning.[57]

They Are Not Taking Their Coffins

While these characteristics are similar, a key difference is that today's students generally go for shorter terms of service rather than for the remainder of their lives. While many missionaries over the past three centuries "took their coffins with them," Rice observes that "missions-minded students in 1806—and even 1946—believed that the call to overseas service was for life. Now they're not so sure. With the increasing convenience of international air travel, today's students are more spontaneous about overseas missions. For many, missions is an event, not a vocation that requires the sacrifice of years."[58] In the past, short-term exposure had been seen as one available option among several, whereas now, for many, it has become a driving paradigm of thinking about mission involvement.

The explosive increase in short-term deployment over the last four decades is remarkable:

> For the year 1965 student researcher Thomas Chandler noted "only" 540 individuals from North America involved in short-term mission. In 1989 another estimate put the number at 120,000. Three years later it had more than doubled to 250,000. Today, we estimate at least 1,000,000 short-termers sent out from a globally-sent perspective every year. And considering just the 40,000 U.S. sending entities alone, it is highly probable that our estimate of one million short-termers is actually far too conservative.[59]

The inability to pinpoint exact figures is due in part to the fact that roughly 35,000 churches, 3,700 North American mission agencies, and 1,000 North American schools make up the 40,000 "sending entities" mentioned

---

[56] T. George, "Evangelical Revival and the Missionary Awakening," in *The Great Commission* (Nashville: B&H, 2008), 59.

[57] Ibid.

[58] Rice, "The New Missions Generation."

[59] R. Peterson, G. Aeschliman, and W. Sneed, *Maximum Impact Short-Term Mission* (Minneapolis: STEM, 2003), 255.

above.[60] And given that even these figures are estimations, precise numbers become virtually impossible to come by.

Missiologist Robert Priest believes the number might be closer to 1.5 million short-termers.[61] Since this advance directly affects what is done in mission, Priest "calls on missiologists to place this movement at the center of research, missiological reflection, and classroom instruction."[62] He also makes a key insight about the importance of this research for church leaders, and especially for those of us who serve with the students: "What we have is a grassroots movement in which, for example, youth pastors as a normal and expected part of their job take their youth groups to Mexico, West Virginia, Guatemala or Haiti on mission trips. Many congregations now routinely organize mission trips for all ages scheduled to fit around school and work schedules."[63] If short-term experiences are a responsibility of student ministers, provocative events to change students' lives, and a vehicle for them to engage in the fulfillment of the Great Commission, then we must decide how to approach these opportunities with such commitments in mind.

DISCUSSION QUESTIONS

1. From the information presented in this chapter, provide a biblical defense for missions.
2. Detail the historical progression of the student mission movement.
3. Describe the current role of students in missions today.
4. What are you doing to develop an army of global-minded Christian students?

[60] Ibid., 252.
[61] R. Priest et al., "Researching the Short-Term Mission Movement," *Missiology* 34 (2006): 432.
[62] Ibid., 431.
[63] Ibid., 433.

CHAPTER 3

WHAT PEOPLE ARE SAYING: THE TWO SIDES OF SHORT-TERM MISSION

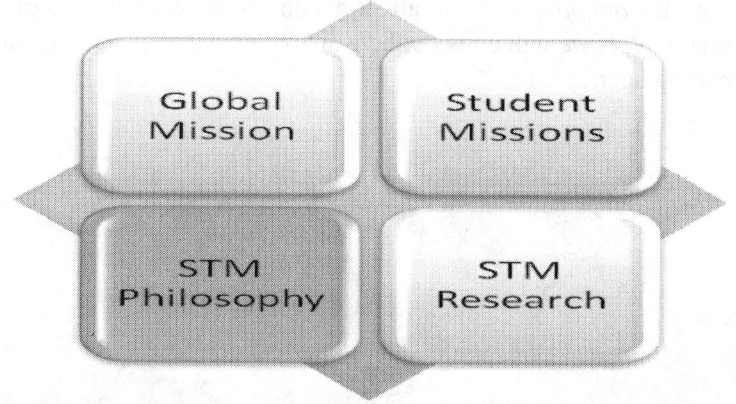

RESULTS AND OPINIONS MAY VARY

Of the estimated millions of annual short-term mission (STM) participants from North America alone, hundreds of thousands are middle- and high-school students. These students spend collective millions each year to take part in these trips. With massive numbers of students being mobilized, and churches and individuals forking out this kind of money to make it happen, we would assume that there is fundamental agreement on the inherent benefits of such trips. However, instead of a unified voice on the matter, there is a continual splintering among missiologists, sending agencies, churches, and those who serve in student ministry. In order to simplify and frame our particular philosophy of STM, we want to draw out some of the issues and themes that prove challenging when considering mobilizing students for short-term missions.

THE LONG AND SHORT OF IT

In a conversation about STM, it is essential to clarify what makes an experience "short-term." In most student ministry models, a short-term trip will fall along the lower end of the spectrum, with the majority of these opportunities lasting one to two weeks. We will focus attention primarily on trips of this length, while considering the long-range goals of such experiences. All of the players involved in the promotion, planning, execution, and follow-through of these experiences have the task of intentionally thinking about how to maximize the effect these few days have on the other 50 weeks of the year. How each of these individuals, or groups, envisions his *ongoing role* will affect his ability to facilitate this process. The role players we will consider here are the church, the participant, and the sending agency.

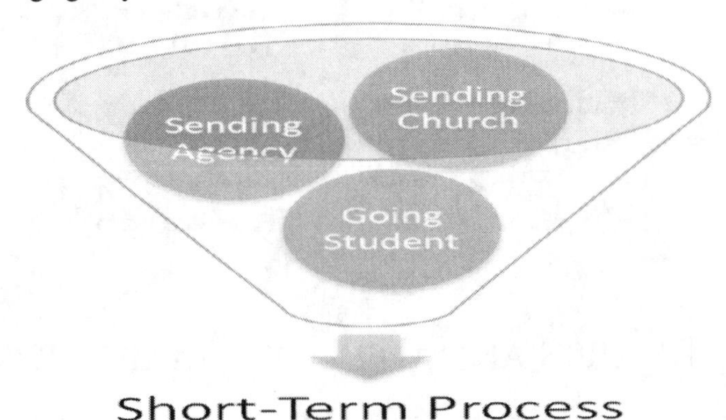

Figure 3.1: Key Players in the Short-Term Process

ESTABLISHED BY THE SENDING CHURCH

When looking at the "vehicle" of STM, people frequently ask questions about which one of these key players is driving these trips. Specific questions include: Who is directing the trip? Who is in the position of authority over mobilization? Who decides where to go and how to get it done? Depending on whom you ask, the answer to all these questions could be the church, short-term participants, the sending agency, or even the national hosts.

Since the disciple-making charge has been given to the church, that is where the ultimate vision for STM strategy and development, as it is experienced in the lives of the participants, should begin. This is not to say that participant input or the tremendous resource of agencies should not be major factors in vision development; however, they have different roles to play.

In looking at how we engage students in lifelong mission activity and attitudes, Steve Shadrach uses the image of a tree. He affirms the primacy of the church, arguing that this "is where the workers are nourished, fed, and prayed for. These are the rank-and-file believers who intercede, give, and send. Just as the roots of a tree provide the stability and resources for the trunk and branches, world-Christian churches do the same for student groups and mission agencies."[1] This interrelated view of the function of the sending church, the going student, and the organizations that assist in seeing strategy formulated enables the whole of the mobilizing process to be cast in a church-driven mold. This is an important distinction because our mandate is for the church, not just for its individual members.[2]

Developed through the Student Participant

Without these individual members answering the call to be missionaries, however, there will be no fulfilled mission. Church and parachurch ministries can develop and implement cross-cultural strategies, but such efforts are wasted if there is no one to carry out these operations. As Shadrach reminds us, "Virtually every major missions movement in history has been instigated and fueled by college-aged young people. Then, and now, they are the primary suppliers of crucial personnel for the over-ripened harvest."[3] These frontline ambassadors are resourced by, and members of, the local church. As they are discipled within the church body, students are equipped to be the type of global-minded believers that flourish in a life of ministry.

In order for this to happen effectively, these students have to be challenged to broader responsibilities and models of service that influence the globe, not just their limited sphere of daily experience.[4] College students

[1] S. Shadrach, *The Fuel and the Flame* (Atlanta: Authentic, 2003), 246.

[2] See M. Dever, "The Doctrine of the Church," in *A Theology for the Church,* ed. D. Akin (Nashville: B&H, 2007), 814.

[3] Shadrach, *The Fuel and the Flame*, 246.

[4] T. Rainer and S. Rainer, *Essential Church* (Nashville: B&H, 2008), 87, argue that the "church is missing a grand opportunity to influence the world for Jesus Christ. Many of our students do have some level of desire for the church to help guide their life . . . . The bottom line: guidance, biblical truth, and responsibility are the missing ingredients." Here, the researchers note that responsibility in ministry and service are key elements to retaining youth and college students in church ministries.

and youth are all too often "underchallenged" in our ministries when they are starving for edgy, dynamic ways to contribute to something bigger and more significant.[5]

CONNECTED THROUGH THE SENDING AGENCY

Once we have talked about the church as the foundational preparer and the participant as the one sent, what is left for the sending agency to do? The agency can help the church direct its vision toward continuous, ongoing field ministry. This is no small matter. Shadrach elaborates on the value of this task:

> We don't need more mission agencies—we've got hundreds of excellent ones ready and able to penetrate every unreached people group. But they are waiting for student ministries and local churches to wake up and provide them with the needed workers and the resources to turn them loose. The roots of the trunk can't reach up into the sky to heights unknown; only the branches are designed to do that.[6]

The vast majority of the complaints about short-term teams stem from a lack of cultural and long-term ministry awareness. Based on a "facilitating" approach to an agency's function, whether the "missionary" is to be sent for two weeks or two decades, the seamless commitment to long-term field initiatives can be maintained.

Some would argue that if the church is the driving organism in short- and long-term mission, then this precludes any need for agencies. The church should simply send their students and long-term missionaries and cut out the middleman. Jim Plueddemann offers an insightful response to this way of thinking:

> Mission boards provide not only logistic and spiritual support but also structures for field-based visionary planning and for accountability. For individual churches to send missionaries around the world would be like local towns sending their own soldiers into war and having the soldiers report back to the mayor of their home town rather than to the officer in the field. Such a plan not only

[5] A. Reid, *Raising the Bar* (Grand Rapids: Kregel, 2004), 20.
[6] Shadrach, *The Fuel and the Flame*, 246.

> would be more expensive, it would create chaos in the battle. Sending churches and mission boards are mutually dependent on each other.[7]

Interdependency, or at least ongoing cooperation, between all of those involved in the mobilizing process is a means to cohesion. If our main ministry is to middle- and high-school students, then the ministries and people that influence them must all be enlisted. In the case of college students, there may be an opportunity for their institution, or campus organization, to develop partnerships with sending agencies and churches in order to direct energies and interest.

Conspicuously Absent: The Recipients

For those of you who are perceptive, we have not overlooked the people to whom we send our students—national recipient-hosts. We will discuss their role later in our discussion. Our conversation will primarily deal with what happens in the ongoing process of STM deployment and student discipleship within the local church. Although the host-receivers both are influenced by and exert influence upon the students, our primary attention will focus primarily on the responsibilities of stateside personnel in this process of mission. Part of this responsibility involves, of course, a cooperative, colearning affiliation with our hosts. This posture guards against, among other things, perceptions of a superior "missionary-as-hero" attitude.[8] We will pursue these and other cross-cultural relational connection issues in chapters 10–13.

It Depends on Whom You Ask: The Two Sides of STM

Gathering the information we need to discuss how these players might make STM a functional part of their strategy requires looking at some of the potential drawbacks of poorly conceived and executed STM, while

[7] J. Plueddemann, "SIM's Agenda for a Gracious Revolution," *International Bulletin of Missionary Research* 23 (1999): 158.

[8] K. Birth, "What Is Your Mission Here?" *Missiology* 34 (2006): 497. Birth argues that "social categories and relationships into which short-term missionaries fit during their trips do not necessarily reflect the social categories that are used to discuss, deride, or promote short-term missions." Therefore, the cultural perceptions of the hosts, the relationship established on field, and even the debriefing that leaders offer must possess an awareness of these cultural nuances.

also entertaining the potential benefits, the upside, when the rationale and approach of such opportunities are solid. Stan Guthrie recognizes some of these likely pitfalls and benefits of short-term mobilization:

> Short-term work, whether two weeks or two years, can indeed be effective and pleasing to God. Yes, it can cost a lot of money, disrupt nationals and missionaries, encourage short-term thinking, and inoculate some against career missions involvement. But done well, it can open participants' eyes to the sometimes gritty realities of the world, make them aware of their own ethno-centrism and the gifts and courage of non-Western believers, and spark a lifelong commitment to missions. In the best cases, some real kingdom work gets done, too.[9]

Using his observations as a guide, we will explore both the downside and the upside of STM in order to gain a better understanding of some of the key issues involved.

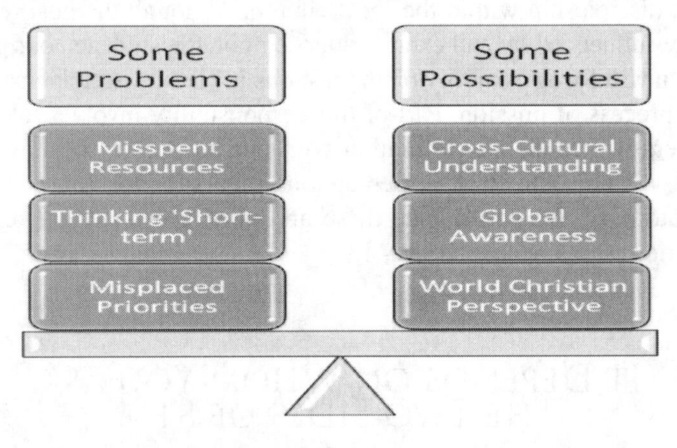

Figure 3.2: Example Issues on the Two Sides of STM

THE DOWNSIDE: SOME PROBLEMS WITH STM

Instead of witnessing positive results from STM, many have largely experienced the downside of short-term practice. Some of you may take issue with allocating so many financial and logistical resources for short-

[9] S. Guthrie, *Missions in the Third Millennium* (Carlisle, UK: Paternoster, 2000), 89.

termers or the disruption they can cause to the efforts of nationals and missionaries. Others may point out that, many times, short-term projects do not seem to produce long-term strategy or personnel as promised. These problems are well worth acknowledging before trying to assess STM in light of potential benefits.

Misspending the Resources

We all jumped into a van and headed down busy streets of a crowded Southeast Asian city. I had just spoken at a student event, and our group, along with the church leaders, thought it had gone really well, but I was having a hard time. We had been traveling around the country for several weeks, participating in similar ministry events. Over the weeks I had begun to see the ability of the national leaders to do what we were doing far more effectively than we could. If anything, some of them just needed a little training. So I began to wonder if it would not have been better to send resources to secure their training rather than spend the thousands of dollars on our travel, lodging, and meals.

When we look at the extensive financial resources poured into STM each year, in comparison with the ongoing needs of long-term field personnel, it does seem that our monies could be spent more wisely. Angie Fann, a proponent of STM, readily admits as much:

> The last time I led a mission trip, we raised, between the twelve of us, more than $20,000. Did you know that, depending on the country, it takes only somewhere between twenty and thirty thousand to support one missionary for an entire year? And we were only there for a week![10]

Funds for mission may be better used in the hands of those on the ground, long-term in these areas, rather than put toward an effort that lasts just a few days or weeks, in many cases. However, there is also a matter of long-term investment in these ministries. While long-term, relational mission is optimal, many sending bodies lack an ongoing strategy to develop those who would take up the work next—the missionaries of tomorrow.

Also, there is the issue of spending money that could go to support ministries and the economies in host countries. Jo Ann Van Engen sees several problems with many short-term experiences. Not only are they expensive, she argues, but the STM teams "almost always do work that could

[10] A. Fann, *How to Get Ready for Short-Term Missions* (Nashville: Thomas Nelson, 2006), 59.

be done (and usually done better) by the people of the country they visit."[11] She identifies a definite need for believers to share in other's struggles across the globe, but "short-term missions as they stand are not the answer. Third-world people do not need more rich Christians coming to paint their church and make them feel inadequate. They *do* need more humble people who are open and willing to share in their lives and struggles."[12] The key phrase here is "as they stand." Van Engen goes on to say that taking our responsibilities in mission seriously can actually begin with visiting another country, short-term.

Van Engen's suggestion is not the end of STM but a *refocusing for long-term development and investment*. This refocusing involves seeing STM not as a "service to perform" but "a responsibility to learn."[13] She believes that effective STM must be cast as part of the ongoing practice of the participant through pre-field elements (cultural and language preparation); on-field practices (learning while there, spending time with nationals); and post-field habits (while at home, getting involved through research and advocacy for global ministry).[14] Van Engen concludes by reiterating that while STM are expensive, they are "worth every penny" if they represent the beginning of a long-term commitment to global mission attitudes and living.[15]

Disrupting Nationals and Missionaries

When there is ongoing field work in a region, it is often disruptive for a group to come in for just a few weeks. Add to this the certainty that for some of those on the field, these group visits occur year-round, or at least seasonally, and one has a potential recipe for disaster. A group of teenagers and adults that have little or no training may do more harm than good without even realizing it. This has been the perspective not only of many long-term missionaries but also of scores of nationals that have witnessed what they deem "insensitive" and "domineering" short-term teams.[16]

Without dismissing this difficulty, the problem is not primarily with the short-term team but largely with the process of connecting the team and the field missionaries and preparing both of them for the trip. If a field

---

[11] J. A. Van Engen, "The Cost of Short-Term Missions," *The Other Side* 36 (2000): 21.

[12] Ibid., 22.

[13] Ibid.

[14] Ibid., 23.

[15] Ibid.

[16] E. Zehner, "Short-Term Missions: Toward a More Field-Oriented Model," *Missiology* 34 (2006): 510–11.

is not equipped to handle short-term teams, that is not evil; it is simply the current reality. The missionaries and their agencies need to understand this and resist pressure to host teams they cannot support or would greatly disrupt what they are doing. If the long-term team can support one member as a link to short-term teams, this provides one way to facilitate groups or individual involvement. The sheer volume of those interested in going makes this solution a necessity in some areas.

Ron Blue, former president of CAM International (formerly, the Central American Mission) and chair of the World Missions and Intercultural Studies Department at Dallas Theological Seminary, remarks that since the number of those interested is so massive, "career missionaries could easily drop the work to which they feel God has led them in their place of service and dedicate all their time to provide liaison for short-term teams. In some cases this is literally what has happened."[17] He argues that in order to prevent this undermining of long-term field work, and for STM itself to be effective, short-term efforts must be "channeled" and developed by those leading and planning. In this regard, Mack Stiles's observation is important: "Good short terms stand on three legs: partnerships with a sending church, partnerships with hosts and partnerships with missionaries."[18] Understanding such connections from all sides can go a long way toward ironing out operational, logistical, and sometimes interpersonal kinks between short-term and long-term mission efforts.

For those who go as participants, Blue advocates a process of careful "selection," "adequate training," formal church "deployment," "debriefing" upon return from the field, and "advancement" of the short-term strategy through leader development.[19] He indicates that this process, along with the motivation to engage intelligently the field with the gospel, will enable discipleship and possible long-term mission involvement to take place.

Starting Short-Term, Staying Short-Term

Many of us enjoy having our passports stamped, and what is even better is to have a whole collection of stamps. We want to be able to say that we have been all over the world. Sometimes variety is seen not only as the spice of life but as *the way* to do STM. For many student ministries and

[17] R. Blue, *Evangelism* and *Missions* (Nashville: Thomas Nelson, 2001), 174.

[18] M. Stiles and L. Stiles, *Mack and Leeann's Guide to Short-Term Missions* (Downers Grove, IL: InterVarsity, 2000), 139.

[19] Ibid., 175–77.

their churches, the idea is to deploy to as many different destinations as possible while making sure not to repeat destinations too often, if ever.

The trouble with this kind of short-term exposure and involvement is that it can lead to students and adults limiting their perspective to that short length of service. This is in part because they do not get the opportunity to see growth take place in the lives of nationals. It is easy to think subtly of those people they met as existing only for that particular week to appear in the pictures, videos, and memories of the short-termers. If one is not careful, nationals can become little more than living "souvenirs" from a cross-cultural vacation.

Combating this mind-set, in the course of developing a greater global mind-set in participants, is challenging. Repetitive deployment to the same people group and area, however, can indeed combat this tendency. As Daniel Rickett argues, "Short visits are a part of a multi-year series of engagements. Short-term visits should never stand alone."[20] David Cashin adds:

> Adoption of people groups, like the adoption of children, is a long-term task that is often much more difficult than is initially appreciated. Christian educational institutions are well placed to combine short- and long-term goals as this is part of a program to train workers for long-term service. There is great potential to see their mobilizers coming back again and again to the churches involved to keep their vision for the specific people group alive. The short-term teams have a goal of long-term relationship.[21]

An outlook that is focused on developing relational ties to a people is one way to ensure that STM with students or adults is viewed in relation to enduring field initiatives. This provides participants with both developing relationships with nationals and a small measure of valid cultural understanding.[22] Such attainments are necessary to give participants a truer picture of mission and a greater sense of responsibility to the efforts of the career personnel and strategies.

[20] D. Rickett, "Short Term Missions for Long Term Partnership," *Evangelical Missions Quarterly* 44 (2008): 44–45.

[21] D. Cashin, "Facilitating a New Student Volunteer Movement," *Evangelical Missions Quarterly* (January 2010).

[22] Stiles and Stiles, *Mack and Leeann's Guide to Short-Term Missions*, 49.

Misplacing the Priorities

Some would say that discussing benefits to the students simply demonstrates that STM of this stripe should not even feature the word *mission* in the label. If this were truly mission, the argument runs, the focus would be on the evangelization and discipleship of the nationals, period. The participant's life might indeed change, but that is not to be a first order of concern.

The difficulty with such reasoning is that we are called, chiefly, to *disciple-making among all people groups*. The way we have often read this is in rigid categories. We make disciples by going and serving those in the target culture, while those going are to remain in a sterile, vacuous state and dare not even think about their own development. Such an understanding conflicts with our call to be on mission as witnesses and heralds for the King, while *also* maintaining and growing in our faithful relationship to Him through such service.[23] Our sanctification and our sacrifice are linked. In fact, we would argue that authentic discipleship must incorporate consistent service.[24]

All this is not to say that the fields and people we serve are to be "used" for our students' growth.[25] Short-term mission philosophies that perceive the people and places as little more than cardboard cutouts and exotic backdrops for photos and video footage should be discarded. On the other hand, those trips that presuppose an understanding of STM as *primarily* beneficial to the long-term development of mission-oriented disciples seem to have a fitting place in the ministries of both the church and the sending agency.

The Upside: Some Possibilities with STM

James Engel and William Dyrness argue that if these churches and agencies want to see individual students and adults developed into mission-directed believers, "Nothing speaks more clearly than firsthand exposure and hands-on involvement."[26] Firsthand exposure to the realities,

[23] A. Köstenberger, *The Missions of Jesus and the Disciples According to the Fourth Gospel* (Grand Rapids: Eerdmans, 1998), 269–70.

[24] E. Stetzer and D. Putman, *Breaking the Missional Code* (Nashville: B&H, 2006), 134.

[25] M. Adney, "Shalom Tourist," *Missiology* 34 (2006): 461.

[26] J. Engel and W. Dyrness, *Changing the Mind of Missions* (Downers Grove, IL: InterVarsity, 2000), 125.

people, and impact of a life lived on mission can enable the participant to get his hands dirty in genuine mission environments. In this way, contact through short-term mission is one gateway to seeing our world and our commission more clearly.

THE POSSIBILITY OF CULTURAL UNDERSTANDING: THE PEOPLE OVER THERE

Before I left for Southeast Asia, I heard from several people that, as a speaker, I should not expect the people there to respond a great deal to the messages. The main reason given was that "the people in that culture" were cold, indifferent, and simply not receptive to what was taught. Sure enough, after a couple of weeks of speaking, my calls for response had been met with almost zero immediate action.

What I learned during those weeks, however, was that my public calls for individual commitment were misfiring not because listeners were cold to the message, as I had been told, but because they wanted to come and talk with me later, usually along with their parents or other family members. They understood that in their cultural milieu, contrary to mine, following Christ would affect their entire family, and that was a matter of honor. So they were not going to commit to anything without this larger family conversation. Rugged individualism was not a virtue for them.

Being in a new culture for several weeks and living life with the people there can crack the shell of calloused ethnocentrism and allow the participant to become a colearner with nationals. Duane Elmer looks at cultural learning as, "the ability to glean relevant information about, from, and with other people."[27] Elmer says that *learning about* others helps us "get a basic orientation to the people and their culture" so that we can "check and better adjust our expectations against reality."[28] This kind of "distant" cultural learning reveals our need to go even further in our education once we actually enter another culture. Unless we strive to continue learning in contact with living, breathing people from the new area, our learning *about* can actually serve to give us an incomplete, and therefore misinformed, set of perceptions.[29]

We build on learning *about* others by learning *from* them. Elmer notes that learning from those in another culture allows us to honor them by asking for their insights. We also show them that we truly want to gain an

[27] D. Elmer, *Cross-Cultural Servanthood* (Downers Grove, IL: InterVarsity, 2006), 93.

[28] Ibid., 94–95.

[29] Ibid., 94.

honest appraisal from them about their situation and develop an authentic dialogue.[30] This enables our cross-cultural ministry to be "successful" because we are beginning to place the active priority on people, not tasks.[31] This is a "lifelong attitude" to be adopted.[32]

While "learning about" and "learning from" are progressive steps in developing cultural understanding, Elmer argues that the "rarest form of learning" is *learning with.*[33] He describes this as learning that "happens in relationship, in mutuality, in partnership where neither side is above or beneath."[34] In his words:

> Each is, at the same time, teacher and learner, without either person knowing or caring that those roles are being played out. A strong, resilient trust bonds their relationship. This solidarity fosters the deepest sharing, the joy of authenticity and the wonder of mutually discovering the path of God.[35]

If this type of relational investment is optimal in gaining a balanced and accurate cultural image, it seems that consistent *learning about* and *from,* which includes opportunities to temper and galvanize these attitudes by *learning with,* is a useful pattern. Rightly conceived and strategically applied, STM can be a medium for this type of learning, as it presents a "ground floor" opportunity for students to begin interacting with the people within their culture.

The Possibility of Global Realization: You Cannot Turn the Channel.

Actor Ben Affleck recently visited eastern Congo. He has visited several times in an attempt to understand why an estimated 250,000 refugees are displaced and an estimated five million Congolese people have died in four long years of war. He also wanted other people to understand and act:

> The primary reason I am here is to urge people to give money to the NGOs and charities doing hard work in east-

[30] Ibid., 98–99.

[31] Zehner, "Short-Term Missions: Toward a More Field-Oriented Model," 512–13.

[32] Elmer, *Cross-Cultural Servanthood,* 103.

[33] Ibid.

[34] Ibid.

[35] Ibid.

> ern Congo on meager funds. . . . And if people out there have an existing relationship with a charity, to urge that charity to get involved in eastern Congo. To let people know, Don't just read the horror stories in the newspapers and turn off.[36]

As with a bad dream, or one of those relief commercials for poverty-ravaged children, we tend to try to forget what we just saw. If we are watching television, we usually just turn the channel. We can do this because we are holding the remote. We are, it appears, in control.

I recently spent a couple weeks in Rwanda, and there were times that I wished I had the remote. I wished I could turn off the images that were there of the memorials telling the story of the 1994 genocide. That event was an unthinkable slaughter that led to more than 800,000 deaths in three months. At the memorials I saw rows of skulls with fragments missing. Cracks indicated where the killer's machete made contact with the victim's head. Many of those skulls were small, indicating that the victims had been young children.

As I stood there, just a few feet away from stacks of human remains, I wanted to turn it off, but there was no way to do that. Just as there was no way for those young children, or their parents, to "turn off" their own horrific murder. They experienced with their final moments an extreme demonstration of the capacity for sin that human beings possess. This was a moment when I grew in my conviction that the establishment of the Church among every people for the sake of His name and through making disciples is worth my life. It is worth it because God frees His people from the enslavement of sin—even the sin of murdering men, women, and children.

Of course, it is one thing to be affected in the moment, but we would all agree that the key is to see lasting change in us and our students. Gary Haugen says that we need to see these issues and develop "compassion permanence," which allows us to remember and influence situations like the one in Rwanda, even when we are not there.[37] That is our reasoning for exploring STM philosophy and practice, so that we can identify and develop practices that might enhance and optimize this kind of lasting change. We want to see what practices and concepts might help STM lead to sustainable transformation.

---

36 "Ben Affleck Tours Refugee Camps in Eastern Congo," *The State,* November 21, 2008.

37 G. Haugen, *Good News About Injustice* (Downers Grove, IL: InterVarsity, 1999), 38–39.

The Possibility of Global Disposition: Thinking, Living, and Going Long-Term

It is fairly common for a prospective career missionary to "try out" a short-term trip with an agency, so that each side can see if there might be a long-term fit.[38] This "short-term before long-term" idea has also been applied by some to develop a global awareness, mind-set, and lifestyle.[39] Those who propose STM as a vehicle to shape thinking, lifestyle, and openness to longer terms of service offer both experiential and ideological reasoning.

In his former role as candidate secretary of The Evangelical Alliance Mission (TEAM), Michael Pocock noted several key factors that increased the likelihood of STM participants becoming engaged in career missionary service.[40] First, TEAM required an orientation prior to selection and summer "appointment." A second factor, closely connected to the first, is the rigid preselection process and requirements.[41] Third, TEAM advocated and required on-field service that was challenging and involved high levels of interaction with those from the host culture rather than offering "paint-up and fix-up" ministry that inhibits interaction with nationals. Finally, TEAM required a "post-field debriefing" of the short-term missionaries, in order to recognize both the highlights and negative elements of the experience. This approach to the short-term experience is based on the observation that "many applicants for career service have gotten their feet wet by short-term service."[42]

These suggested "feet-wetting" practices uphold the idea that initial exposure and engagement are means to producing a greater appreciation for and involvement in the global effort.[43] Richard Slimbach observes that if an approach to STM is going to benefit long-term efforts, it must optimize the "development . . . [of] . . . earnest young people . . . [into] . . . valuable resources . . . [through] . . . organizing for learning."[44] In each of these ap-

[38] S. Moreau, G. Corwin, and G. McGee, *Introducing World Missions: A Biblical, Historical, and Practical Survey* (Grand Rapids: Baker, 2004), 191–93.

[39] P. Borthwick, *How to Be a World Class Christian* (Waynesboro, GA: Authentic, 2000), 131.

[40] M. Pocock, "Gaining Long-Term Mileage from Short-Term Programs," *Evangelical Missions Quarterly* 23 (1987): 155–60.

[41] Ibid., 158.

[42] M. Pocock, "The Evangelical Alliance Mission," *Evangelical Missions Quarterly* 22 (1986): 122–25.

[43] A. Atkins, "Work Teams? No, 'Taste and See' Teams," *Evangelical Missions Quarterly* 27 (1991): 387.

[44] R. Slimbach, "First, Do No Harm," *Evangelical Missions Quarterly* 36 (2000): 439.

proaches to STM, the idea is that God can mold lifelong world Christians through intelligent method and practice.

The Difference Maker: STM "Done Well"

So what makes the difference between opportunities that are more trouble than they are worth and those that hold too great a value to pass up? The difference maker, as Guthrie puts it, is that those that add value to the ongoing field effort are "done well."[45] Snags emerge when STM experiences are poorly conceived and badly executed. By contrast, those that are done well foster real cultural understanding, cross-cultural advocacy, awareness, and lifelong involvement. The determining issue is what it means to be faithful to the STM vehicle—to do it well.

Discussion Questions

1. Would you agree or disagree with the authors' conclusion about which of the "key players" is to be the driving force in developing a missions strategy? Why?
2. What are the problems with STM?
3. What are the possibilities with STM?
4. What is your opinion about the value of STM?

[45] Guthrie, *Missions in the Third Millennium*, 89.

CHAPTER 4

WHAT RESEARCHERS ARE FINDING: ROSE-COLORED GLASSES, BLINDERS, OR BIFOCALS?

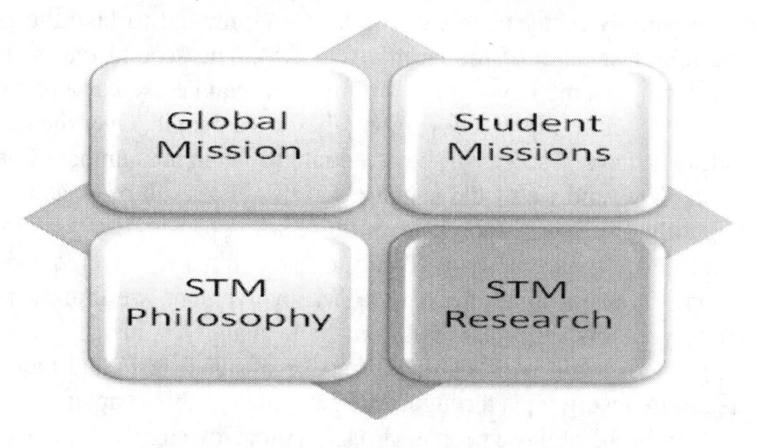

CHOOSING THE RIGHT LENSES

Yes, you did read it right; we did not mistype this chapter title. And, no, we did not choose to add a chapter on ophthalmologic research. In this chapter we want to help you see the potential transforming effects of short-term mission.

We are convinced that God could have made Himself known to an unregenerate world without using people, but that was not His plan. He determined in eternity past that He would use believers just like us to tell the world of His merciful plan.

Though we cannot know the mind of God on all things, we can know His thoughts to the degree that they are revealed in Scripture. And there is no question what Jesus spoke to His disciples prior to His ascension. Imagine our Lord delivering the Great Commission with all boldness and with absolute confidence in His followers. When Jesus spoke those words,

He made clear what He expected. Those same expectations—to order one's life so as to engage fully the Great Commission—are placed on us as well.

So, if God could have communicated the message of redemption without us, why were we included? The most poignant of all possible responses for our discussion is the transforming effect of being involved in taking the message of the gospel to a lost world. Believers who participate in making disciples of all nations are transformed. God knew this, and this in part is why He gave the Great Commission to the Church.

We think there are two primary reasons churches are choosing short-term missions as a means of fulfilling the Great Commission. The first is they are simply being obedient to Christ's command to take the gospel to the remotest parts of the earth (Acts 1:8). The second reason is that churches understand how short-term missions can be used as a part of the deliberate discipleship process among their own people. Over the last four decades, we have observed an exponential growth in the number of participants in STM, and we would suggest that this is a result of what churches are actually observing in the lives of those who go.

Before we share with you what our research has discovered about the potentially transforming effects of STM involvement, we think it best to relate to you how short-term missions have changed some lives we know well. We will begin with a story from one of our friends and then intersperse more testimonies throughout the balance of this chapter.

Kathy is one of those people who has a great love for the Lord and a desire to make Him known among the nations. She is a seminary student who works at a children's home where she ministers daily to children who come from dysfunctional families. She also substitute teaches at a middle school in her community in order to build relationships with the students for the purpose of sharing God's love with them. Kathy will tell you that her heart for unbelievers drives all that she does. We want to share with you an E-mail that she sent us a few months ago as she was preparing to go to Zambia on a mission trip. It reflects the global-minded Christian thinking that we desire to see develop within our youth ministries and graduating students.

When Kathy returned home from her trip, she had an even greater commitment to take the gospel to hurting people across the street and across the ocean. In just a few weeks she is headed back to Zambia for four more months, despite the fact that she contracted malaria on her previous trip. God has wrought in her heart, in part due to her STM experiences, a commitment to go to the line—every day and everywhere.

I can remember vividly being a young girl going on family vacations to Cape Cod. It still is one of those nostalgic places for me. The ocean was (and continues to be) my favorite place. The smells, sounds, and taste of the ocean air are where I'm home.

One of my favorite parts of vacationing down the Cape was when my uncle would take me out on his sailboat. As a young child I would say to my uncle, "I want to go there," pointing to the horizon. I wanted to go where the ocean and sky suddenly became one, where the white, puffy clouds danced with gentle waves. I wanted to go to the end of the earth. No matter how far we traveled, we never made it to the line. As much as I would beg for us to go all the way to the line, my uncle would lovingly tell me, "When you're older."

Well, I'm older now, and as I write this I'm preparing to go to the line [Zambia]. There's not a doubt in my mind that those days in my uncle's sailboat were used by God to give me a heart for missions . . . in Southern Indiana, the US, and the world.

Each day God allows me to go to the line countless times. In the beginning God separated the heavens from the earth. Every day when we step out of our front door, we go to the line, we go to the place where the gospel meets the world, and we have the opportunity to share His Son with others. I wonder what opportunity He will give me today to show someone that they can meet Jesus and go to the line? —Kathy

The anecdotal stories in this chapter, in conjunction with our combined 35 years of ministry experience, have driven us to investigate what is actually taking place during short-term mission experiences. During our investigation we have become ever more convinced that the larger discussion is shifting from "Should we do short-term missions?" to "Why and how should we do short-term missions?"

In the previous chapters we have argued the *why* of short-term missions. We have discussed the rapid spread of the gospel to unreached people groups, examined how God has historically used the short-term missions approach in mission advance, and unashamedly, yet realistically, attempted to defend the participant paradigm. In this chapter we will further discuss the *why* of short-term missions as it pertains to the life transformation that is often experienced by the participant.

Terry Linhart states it well:

> Some would say their research focus on those that go is misguided. The purpose of mission and service is to give one's self away for the sake of others and the Gospel. Yet, for many ministry leaders, there is an additional purpose—because of their involvement on a short-term trip, participants will learn, grow, and want to further share in God's mission in the world. Because of this curricular hope for growth in people's lives and the significant amount of financial resources spent for such experiences, an examination of the nature of the learning process seems worthwhile.[1]

Indeed we do believe that this investigation is worthwhile.

David Johnstone, an administrator at George Fox University, wrote an article about how to close the learning loop in STM trips among college students. While he avoids weighing in on the controversy about STM, he advocates the value of these experiences:

> I will suggest that, while the impact may be varied for those at the receiving end of a short-term mission/service [or even study] trip, the impact is potentially enormous for the student who is traveling and volunteering. This fact alone is worth the journey. The educational significance of these experiences is vast. The challenges to their worldview, their heightened cultural sensitivity, and increased self-awareness brought about by these trips cannot be easily replicated by other experiences.[2]

We appreciate these comments as well as Johnstone's discussion on how to cement the changes in the participants' lives, which we will refer to in the last section of the book. Many would argue that STM is a perfect pedagogical approach to initiate spiritual, cognitive, affective, and behavioral transformation. Again, the question is not, *Should* we do short-term missions? but, *How* should we do them?

---

[1] T. D. Linhart, "They Were So Alive!: The Spectacle Self and Youth Group Short-Term Mission Trips," *Missiology* 34 (2006): 452.

[2] D. Johnstone, "Closing the Loop: Debriefing and the Short-Term College Mission Team," *Missiology* 34 (2006): 523–29.

Grappling with the Important Stuff

In applying various models, youth ministry leaders for decades have wrestled with the question, How can I best design my youth ministry in order to produce maturing disciples? Certainly the goal of developing mature disciples who more accurately reflect the image of God is undisputed in discussions on youth ministry, but how each church arrives at this objective varies.

Historically, a number of basic strategies and methodologies have been employed to fulfill this biblical purpose of discipleship. Some have used mentoring; some, small groups; some, in-depth Bible studies; and some, youth camps and leadership development retreats. These strategies are still a vital part of the youth minister's tool bag, yet in recent years there has been an emphasis on short-term mission involvement as a way to cultivate spiritual growth in students and adult leaders.

Some have rightly advocated a balanced approach to youth ministry that includes opportunities for students to mature spiritually through active participation in Bible study, discipleship, worship, and missions.[3] We agree with the assessment that youth ministers must include missions participation as a part of their strategy.

Several years ago, Richard Ross, a youth professor at Southwestern Baptist Theological Seminary, was leading a teaching session in which he made the bold assertion that every Christian student needs to commit at least one semester of his college years in missions service.[4] This challenge receives its primary impetus from the Great Commission, but it is also based on the recognition that when people are engaged in missions, they grow spiritually and develop ministry and leadership skills.

How Important Is It for Students to Put Their Faith into Action?

Numerous studies have been conducted that point toward the idea that service-type project involvement increases one's commitment to the church, matures one's faith, and aids in the development of a global perspective. For example, Search Institute conducted a national study of 560 congregations in six denominations. Adults were asked to recall their church experiences in

[3] R. Ross, *Youth Ministry Handbook* (Nashville: Convention Press, 1989), 52.

[4] R. Ross, class lecture (delivered at Youth Ministry Institute of New Orleans Baptist Theological Seminary, 2000). In conjunction with this challenge, Ross suggested that churches should encourage parents to establish a missions savings fund for their child by giving a monetary gift at the child's dedication or baptism.

childhood and adolescence. The findings indicate that those who rated higher in faith maturity were more likely to have been involved in service projects as a child or an adolescent. The findings also indicate that involvement in service opportunities was a better predictor for faith maturity than one's experiences in Sunday school, Bible studies, or worship services.[5]

In the same study, adolescents were asked to assess how important their church was to them. Students who had spent 40 hours or more involved in service through their local church were twice as likely to affirm the importance of church in their lives as compared with those who had not. Similarly, the results indicate that those who were heavily involved in service were more than twice as likely to believe that they would be actively engaged in church at ages 21 and 40 than those who had served zero hours. In other words, this study suggests that the more an adolescent participates in service opportunities through the local church, the greater his loyalty and commitment to that church. Moreover, a greater possibility exists that the adolescent will remain actively involved in church throughout his adult years and live life with a more mature Christian faith.[6]

It is truly important for students to put their faith into action; as they do, they are often transformed. Jim Burns writes about the impact that short-term missions have on the fervency of a participant: "The key to igniting volunteers to become world Christians is found in one word: experience. Once people have been given a taste of what missions is all about, there will be no holding them back."[7] He argues that the experience is what brings about the possibility of attitudinal and behavioral change. Michael Anthony also comments on the effects of short-term missions:

> I have experienced the life-changing effect that a short-term mission trip can have on a person. I have seen God

[5] P. L. Benson and C. H. Eklin, *Effective Christian Education: A National Study of Protestant Congregations* (Minneapolis: Search Institute, 1990), 26–29.

[6] Ibid. Adolescents were asked whether they strongly agreed with the statement, "The church I attend matters a great deal to me." Only 20 percent of the students who had given no time in service through their local church agreed with the statement, while 43 percent of those who had invested at least 40 hours or more in their lifetime in service through their local church strongly agreed. Only 28 percent of those who had spent 5 hours or less serving said that church membership is important, while 45 percent of those who had spent more than 40 hours serving responded that church membership is vitally important. The question was asked with regard to whether a person thought that he or she would be involved in church at age 21 and at age 40. The percentage more than doubled at both 21 years old and at 40 years old for those who served 0 hours compared with those who served more than 40 hours (14 to 40 percent; 17 to 39 percent, respectively).

[7] J. Burns, "Igniting Volunteers to Become World Christians" in *The Short-Term Missions Boom: A Guide to International and Domestic Involvement,* ed. M. J. Anthony (Grand Rapids: Baker, 1994), 31.

> touch the lives of my students through these experiences as well. Many will never be the same as a result of what they have seen and experienced. You cannot hold a dying child in your arms, look into its eyes and not be shaken by the experience.[8]

Ridge Burns, noting the effects of short-term mission experiences on his ministry and life writes, "All I know is that when I evaluate my more than fifteen years in youth ministry, the one type of experience that has had the most impact on kids in my youth groups has been mission trips. And these same mission trips have had an unbelievable impact on my life."[9]

The testimonies recorded above are the result of individual Christians who made a decision to commit themselves in service to others, share their personal faith, and fulfill the Great Commission. We would suggest that the change in attitudes and behaviors may well have resulted from the Holy Spirit working in the midst of an experience. Our contention is that short-term missions *can* act as the necessary catalytic experience in the Christian formation process.

Rose-Colored Glasses

Sunglasses are amazing—they block out harmful ultraviolet light, reduce glare, and generally make the ride into work more pleasant. Back in the day, the Eskimos used whalebone goggles with slits to reduce the glare off the ice during hunting season, the Chinese invented a tea lens with brown tint, and the English developed green lenses in 1561 to aid failing eyes.[10] Today you can walk into virtually any retail store and find sunglasses in all sizes and shapes with just as much variety in the color of the lenses. Some lenses are gray and seem to dull out the landscape, while some are brown and bring a warm feeling, and others are rose colored and make the whole countryside come to life—the grass is greener, the flowers are more brilliant, and even the sunset is more intense.

Instead of putting on rose-colored glasses while examining the potential transformative effects of STM, we have chosen to use a pair of bifocals.

[8] M. J. Anthony, ed., *The Short-Term Missions Boom: A Guide to International and Domestic Involvement,* introduction by Michael Anthony (Grand Rapids: Baker, 1994), 9.

[9] R. Burns and N. Bacchetti, *The Complete Student Missions Handbook* (Grand Rapids: Zondervan, 1990), 16.

[10] See http://www.lighthouse.org/aboutus/prevention/sunglasses/ (accessed September 10, 2008).

Our intent is to scrutinize closely the results of prior studies, while also peering off into the "what could it be like if done well" distance.

Putting on the Bifocals

This may be a good place for full disclosure—neither one of us wear bifocals, YET. We have, however, picked up someone else's bifocals and peered above and below the line. We invite you to do the same: put on a set of imaginary bifocals with us, and let us look below the line to see what research has been saying about the transformative effects of STM.

More than 100 studies have been conducted on the value of short-term missions to date. Roughly 60 percent of those have been qualitative studies, while 40 percent have been quantitative in nature.[11] In addition to these studies, countless numbers of articles have been published in both academic and popular periodicals. So it is an understatement to say that the material on STM is voluminous. The overwhelming majority of the research has focused on the effects STM has on the participants, with much less attention paid to the recipients of the ministry work.

Pilgrims and Museum Goers

If you were to read through any number of these studies, you would find that many descriptors are used for STM and its participants. We share with you two that seem apropos for our discussion. Robert Priest's description of STM as pilgrimages is fairly representative of what most youth pastors would espouse:

> Like pilgrimages, these trips are rituals of intensification, where one temporarily leaves the ordinary, workday life "at home" and experiences an extraordinary, voluntary, sacred experience "away from home" in a limited space where sacred goals are pursued, physical and spiritual tests are faced, normal structures are dissolved, communitas is experienced, and personal transformation occurs. This transformation ideally produces new selves to be reintegrated back into everyday life "at home," new selves which in turn help to spiritually rejuvenate the churches they come from, and inspire new mission vision at home.

[11] K. A. Ver Beek, class lecture on short-term missions, http://www.calvin.edu/academic/sociology/staff/01%20Kurt%20Ver%20Beek%201.mp3; K. A. Ver Beek "Lessons from the Sapling: Review of Research on Short-Term Missions, Study Abroad, and Service Learning," http://www.calvin.edu/academic/sociology/staff/kurt.htm (accessed October 8, 2008).

> But unlike other forms of pilgrimage, these STM trips explicitly intend to serve and help others in distant places. That is, they aim not only for self-transformation, but for change in the places to which they go.[12]

The description of STM as pilgrimage is helpful as it emphasizes the intentionality and the intensity of the experience, accompanied by the stated goal of life transformation.

Linhart, on the other hand, uses a metaphor that reminds one of the movie *A Night at the Museum.* You cannot fall asleep during movies like this. Larry Daley, a night watchman at the natural history museum, experiences the unfathomable—the entire museum comes to life at night, including Attila the Hun, an army of gladiators, a T. rex, an army of Union soldiers, and of course cowboys and Indians. Daley is fighting a losing battle to keep everyone in check, until former President Teddy Roosevelt comes to the rescue. The movie's greatness stems not from the chaos that ensues but from the manner in which the figures of history come to life. Suddenly, the moviegoer becomes a participant in history, learning from every encounter.

Linhart suggests that STM creates a similar experience: Cross-cultural contacts during a short-term trip resembles an interactive museum, as visiting students occasionally play with children or high school students, perform religious dramas or programs, while waving or smiling across the chasm of language barrier. Activities like participation in worship services side by side at church with people they could not talk to, or just looking around at how people lived their daily lives, are all part of the interactive experiences.[13]

Now we want to be careful when using the metaphor of an interactive museum; we do not mean to endorse a "come and see, come and touch for your own personal edification mentality." For, as Linhart himself correctly notes, a participant, due to his lack of linguistic and cultural knowledge, will often misread and misunderstand his observations. We do, however, find value in the idea that STM can be used as an experiential means of exposing students and adults to the desperate spiritual and physical needs of people from every tribe, tongue, and nation. This exposure can be a catalyst in developing a heart for the nations and personal obedience to the *missio Dei.*

---

[12] R. Priest et al., "Researching the Short-Term Mission Movement," *Missiology* 34 (2006): 433–34.

[13] Linhart, "They Were So Alive!," 451–62.

Short-term missions has the potential to transform an individual from being merely a mission goer to a full participant in God's redemptive history.

Types of Transformation

With images of real-life pilgrims descending on an interactive museum in your mind, let us think about the types of transformation that are reportedly occurring among participants as a result of their involvement in STM. From the many studies and articles devoted to the subject, we are able to detect several categories of participant change.[14] The first type of transformation involves the participant's increased *understanding of and commitment to biblical Christianity*, whereby he acknowledges his responsibility to fulfill the Great Commission, express compassion by serving others selflessly, practice spiritual disciplines regularly, adjust his life to the biblical truths of Scripture in obedience to Christ, and live life in biblical community.

Another type of transformation that often receives mention is a greater *openness to volunteer and vocational ministry service.* Many of the studies indicate that participants return from their STM experience with an openness to vocational ministry in general and missions specifically. However, as we will address shortly, some who argue against the value of STM question why we are not then seeing the number of long-term missionaries increasing. At least in terms of volunteerism, though, studies clearly show that participants are more open to future STM trips and to ministering in their own churches and communities.

Studies also indicate that there is often a modification in one's *global perspective.* Cultural sensitivity is usually increased and ethnocentrism decreased as a result of the intercultural experience. The design and locale of some STM trips expose participants to the extreme poverty and diminished health of nationals. In some cases the participants observe inequality in social structures based on economic strata, gender, or community standing. Reportedly, these encounters enlarge the participant's perspective of the world.

Interestingly, several studies address a fourth category of transformation, which is that of the *participant's self-awareness.* The participant, when confronted with the sometimes harsh realities of a cross-cultural experience or even the requirement to serve outside his comfort zone,

[14] These categories are not exhaustive but rather suggestive of the general findings. We think it is helpful for the reader to be provided a means to categorize the findings for the purpose of retention and evaluation.

emerges with a better understanding of who he is and where he needs to mature. The final type of transformation we will share with you is that of the participant exercising and developing his *leadership skills.* Short-term mission trips are seen by many as perfect opportunities to challenge participants and place them in situations that demand the practice of competencies such as interpersonal relations, communication, conflict resolution, and teaching skills.

In the section below we will briefly look at some of the studies touching on the types of transformation enumerated above; note that this examination is not intended to be exhaustive but simply to give a sense of the types of studies and results that have been reported. But first, we have a word for those who refuse to put on either rose-colored glasses or bifocals, preferring instead to wear blinders when the transformative effects of STM are examined: it is time to take the blinders off. We are not advocating that you go from one extreme of seeing no value in STM to seeing it as the ultimate answer. But we are asking that you at least listen to what the research says—both the rosy type and the more balanced approach that we will discuss.

Understanding of and Commitment to Biblical Christianity

Numerous studies have highlighted the effects of STM on the Christian formation of the participant. For example, one of the earliest studies was conducted by Peterson and Peterson in 1991 and involved 366 alumni participants of STEM Ministries (Short Term Evangelical Missions) two-week mission trips to the Caribbean. The study tested the hypothesis that such trips produce "significant changes in the perceptions and behavior of the participants, changes which are likely to increase the participants' contribution to world evangelization."[15] Participants reported dramatic increases in the amount of time spent in prayer for missions, money given to support missions, and commitment to activities related to missions, as well as a willingness to return to the mission field.[16] In 1996, STEM funded a follow-up study and surveyed 432 respondents. The results of the McDonough and Peterson (1999) study indicated that as a consequence of their STM experience, participants increased the amount of missions-focused

[15] R. P. Peterson and T. D. Peterson, *Is Short-Term Missions Really Worth the Time and Money?: Advancing God's Kingdom Through Short-Term Mission* (Minneapolis: STEM, 1991), 3.

[16] D. P. McDonough and R. P. Peterson, *Can Short-Term Mission Really Create Long-Term Missionaries?* (Minneapolis: STEM, 1999), 3.

prayer on a weekly basis and their missions-related giving, as well as reported an increased likelihood of returning to the field.[17]

Beckwith (1991) conducted a case study by immersing herself in a two-week mission trip to the island of St. Vincent along with 40 teenagers from a single church congregation. As a part of the study, she interviewed the 40 students prior to the experience, during the STM, and several months later. The goal was to understand better what components of the STM aided the emotional and social maturation process of the participants.

In answer to the question, "What good will this experience do in your life?" asked during the trip interview, the top three responses related to personal growth, attitudinal changes toward material wealth and blessings, and spiritual growth. In the posttrip interview Beckwith posed the question, "How are you different because of this experience?" The top three responses were personal growth, spiritual growth, and better idea of life in other parts of the world. It is worth noting here that the follow-up responses showed a sharp decline in relation to each of the areas mentioned above, meaning that the STM experience had some, but not as much, influence as the participants originally perceived it would.[18]

Purvis (1993) studied short-term mission involvement in Kentucky Baptist churches. The study's sample included 79 participants, 15 to 80 years old, who had been involved in short-term missions to Kenya and Brazil. A presurvey and two postsurveys were administered (one at two weeks and one at six months). One question in the survey pertained specifically to how the short-term mission experience affected the participant's spiritual growth. The pretest indicated that 74.1 percent expected to grow spiritually as a result of the mission experience. The first posttest showed that 91.7 percent thought they grew as a result of their experience. However, at the six-month mark 62.6 percent of the participants still felt that the mission experience had influenced their spiritual growth.[19]

Jones (1998) surveyed 852 junior and senior high-school students who participated in weeklong projects in needy areas of U.S. cities. The study used a pretest and a posttest administration of the Faith Maturity Scale (FMS) and the Multidimensional Self Concept Scale (MSCS). She selected three projects that primarily involved construction and two projects that involved a combination of construction and community ministry. The FMS

[17] Ibid., 9–20.

[18] I. Beckwith, "Youth Summer Missions Trips: A Case Study" (PhD diss., Trinity Evangelical School, 1991).

[19] T. G. Purvis, "Partnership in Cross-Cultural Mission: The Impact of Kentucky Baptist Short-Term Volunteer Missions" (DMiss diss., Asbury Theological Seminary, 1993).

During the summer of 2004, I had the opportunity to go on a short-term mission trip to Southeast Asia. We traveled to a "closed country," where the government does not allow Christianity to be spread. Little detail was known except that we would be prayer walking through villages. On arrival we were told that we would be led around by government officials to villages which could only be found by government maps. While we walked around these villages, we were told that we could not leave the sight of the government officials. We walked and prayed silently. We felt helpless seeing people who had never heard the name of Jesus Christ and yet not being able to tell them of His love. Before we headed home, the missionary split us up and had us write down what we felt about each village as we were prayer walking. Everyone on the team felt that one particular village would be the most open to the gospel. The missionary would use our conclusion to develop the strategy of spreading the gospel in this area. This trip allowed me to see God working through prayer. I learned that even when we cannot see the fruit, we should be faithful to pray and that God by His wonderful grace works our prayers into His perfect plan.

—Pete

and the MSCS posttest scores were significantly higher for all youth when compared with the pretest scores, indicating a positive impact on the Christian formation of the participants.[20]

Wilson (1999) used a study group of 27 teenagers who participated in a nine-day mission trip to Mexico. He applied a pretest and posttest (45 days after the trip) using the FMS and found no significant changes in the scale as a whole. But he did find that the self-perception of time spent reading the Bible and giving time and money to help others, and concern about global poverty, all increased.[21]

Hopkins (2000) surveyed 64 university students who had participated in a one-week mission trip to the Northwest United States using the Global

[20] K. E. Jones, "A Study of the Differences Between Faith Maturity Scale and Multidimensional Self Concept Scale Scores for Youth Participating in Two Denominational Ministry Projects" (PhD diss., Southwestern Theological Baptist Seminary, 1998). Note that the FMS and MSCS scores for females were higher than the scores of the males. Also worth noting, the scores for the community-oriented projects were significantly lower than the scores for the construction projects.

[21] D. E. Wilson, "The Influence of Short-Term Mission Experience on Faith Maturity" (DMin diss., Asbury Theological Seminary, 1999).

God has gradually changed my heartbeat for the nations. As a result of my participation in short-term missions, I am evermore convinced that I have a personal responsibility to share the gospel throughout the globe. The most meaningful trip for me was a few years ago to Southeast Asia just after the 2004 tsunami. I was part of a team that not only was able to meet the physical needs of the people by cleaning neighborhoods, reclaiming wells, teaching them new skills to earn a living, but also meeting their spiritual needs. When I think that 99 percent of the regional population was Muslim, I am reminded of psalmist's words: "They have neither knowledge nor understanding; they walk about in darkness" (Ps 82.5). One of the lasting impressions I have from the trip is the image of the people being frightened by the sea—they would not even go to the beaches. They were living their lives in absolute fear because they did not know the Sovereign Creator—the One who created the seas. It is a must that we go to the ends of the earth, not only for our own sanctification but also for our participation in the mission of God—the glory of the gospel. —Kim

Social Responsibility Scale (GSRI), an inventory that assesses social responsibility. He applied a pretest, posttest, and a follow-up test four weeks later with both the STM participants and a control group of 36 nonparticipants. He found that the participants demonstrated a stronger sense of social responsibility according to the posttest and that this difference persisted one month later.[22]

Wilder (2004) administered a posttrip survey to 517 students and 187 adults (including youth ministry leaders) who participated in a one-week STM experience within the United States. The study examined the perceptions of youth ministry leaders, adult volunteers, and students by using an instrument consisting of a combination of both closed form and qualitative essay questions. Also, in-depth interviews were conducted with 20 of the youth ministry leaders. Analysis of the data revealed that youth ministry leaders and adult volunteers perceived that STM involvement is a useful aid in the Christian formation and maturation process in

[22] S. M. Hopkins, "Effects of Short-Term Service Ministry Trips on the Development of Social Responsibility in College Students" (PsyD diss., George Fox University, 2000).

the lives of their students. The data clearly indicated that the leaders felt their students, as a result of STM participation, would emerge with greater commitments to evangelism, service, and spiritual growth. The student participants rated these same three areas as the ones enjoying lasting effects of their short-term mission experience. The students also responded using a four-point Likert scale (strongly agree to strongly disagree) in the following manner: 83.9 percent strongly agree that they will intentionally grow more in their relationship with Jesus Christ; 81.4 percent strongly agree that they will worship God with a greater passion; and 74.7 percent strongly agree that they will build stronger friendships with other students and adults in their church as a result of their STM experience. These students perceived an overall positive spiritual effect from their involvement.[23]

My first short-term mission trip was in 2003. I went to Reykjavik, Iceland. AMAZING!!! Aside from the beginning of my relationship with Jesus, I'd never experienced such a life-changing event. The greatness of God was revealed to me! Since then I've been back to Iceland and to Brussels, Belgium. —Chris

Fitzgerald (2005) studied young adults who had participated in STM while attending college. The 113 participants he interviewed perceived that both personal and spiritual growth occurred as a direct result of their experience—specifically, it deepened their relationship with God, pushed them to depend on Him more, and enhanced their commitment to service.[24] Beers's (1999) study of 171 students from Taylor University—72 who participated in a one-month missions program study abroad were compared with 99 who remained on campus during the same time—had similar results. The quantitative element of his study showed no significant changes on the scales utilized; however, the participants also were subjected to the qualitative survey, which indicated that the STM helped them further develop their relationship with God and their willingness to serve others.[25]

[23] M. S. Wilder, "Short-Term Missions as a Strategic Component in Youth Ministry Programming" (PhD diss., The Southern Baptist Theological Seminary, 2004).

[24] T. E. Fitzgerald, "The Student Missionary Experience and Its Impact on Young Adults" (PhD diss., Andrews University, 2005).

[25] S. T. Beers, "Faith Development of Christian College Students Engaged in a One Month Study Abroad Mission Trip" (PhD diss., Ball State University, 1999).

Ver Beek (2006) surveyed 127 participants who were involved in a short-term mission trip to Honduras. The participants had completed their mission trip one to three years prior to filling out the survey. He also used a phone interview with 10 randomly selected survey respondents. The study had three objectives: (1) assessing the long-term impact of the STM experience on a participant; (2) assessing the long-term impact STM teams had on communities they visited; and (3) assessing how the sending and receiving agencies viewed the benefits and difficulties of working with short-term teams. Regarding the long-term impact on the participants, Ver Beek found that 53 percent reported increasing time spent in prayer; 52 percent stated their time spent volunteering increased, 43 percent reported increased involvement in church; and 62 percent identified an increased advocacy for the poor.[26]

I remember being convinced by some friends to participate in my first international mission trip in the summer of 2006. On that trip God truly impacted my life. As we went from village to village in Haiti, I became aware of how powerful the gospel truly is, such a simplistic and potent message that I had made complicated over the years. I realized that if I could walk through a village and share the gospel with people I had never met and didn't even speak their language well, truly I could do the same at home. You could say that my short-term mission experience refocused my desire to fulfill the Great Commission in my own back yard. —Ned

Openness to Volunteer and Vocational Ministry Service

STM has often been touted as a means to promote long-term mission service among participants. Many have argued that it is one of the best ways to produce long-term missionaries. Agreeably, studies have indicated that STM experiences often influence participants to be more open to a vocational ministry call, as well as to volunteer service in one's church and community.

In Peterson and Peterson's study (1991), 76.5 percent of the STM par-

[26] K. A. Ver Beek, "The Impact of Short-Term Missions: A Case Study of House Construction in Honduras after Hurricane Mitch," *Missiology* 34 (2006): 477–95.

ticipants who responded stated they are likely to serve, very likely to serve, or already are serving in the field or have confirmed plans to do so.[27] Similarly, Purvis's (1993) study reported that 92.5 percent of the respondents deemed themselves "available for future short-term ministry."[28]

White (1996) surveyed 77 respondents who had participated in STM occurring from 1990 to 1995. He concluded that short-term experiences increase the participant's openness to serving in missions.[29] Moreover, Manitsas (2000) indicated that as a result of STM experience, participants were more likely to return to the short-term field, a likelihood that persisted six months following the experience.[30]

After several months of preparation and watching the Lord provide for our needs of going, my wife and I left for Paris. The trip was amazing as we spent two weeks prayer walking, handing out bottled waters, talking to people, and worshipping with other believers. The Lord used this opportunity to grow me and open my eyes to serving on the mission field. We came home after this trip knowing that the Lord was calling us to the mission field. We have started the application process with a mission agency and will be leaving for the field in the summer of 2009. The Lord has continued to strengthen my faith since that time, and we are so excited about serving on the mission field. My family is praying that we will glorify our Lord and Savior.

—Chris

McDonough and Peterson (1999) found that STM experience often increases the likelihood of participants becoming career missionaries. One of the notable findings from this study was that 18.7 percent indicated they are likely to return, and 21.3 percent may possibly return, full-time to the mission field; in other words, 40 percent displayed movement toward an openness to serve as career missionaries. The study also revealed that those who return for a trip of at least one month or more were much more

[27] Peterson and Peterson, *Is Short-Term Missions Really Worth the Time and Money?*, 18.

[28] Purvis, "Partnership in Cross-Cultural Mission," 86.

[29] R. White, "Evaluating the Effects on Participants of Summer Mission Teams Sent Out by Southeastern College" (DMin diss., Trinity Evangelical Divinity School, 1996).

[30] D. L. Manitsas, "Short Term Mission Trips: A Vehicle for Developing Personal and Spiritual Well-Being" (PsyD diss., George Fox University, 2000).

likely to become career missionaries than those who went on subsequent trips for less than a month. Also applicable is the participants' willingness to return on STM trips in the future: 72.4 percent expected to return for less than one month; 25.3 percent will return and at least double their time commitment (14.9 percent will return from one to 12 months; 10.4 percent will return from one to four years).[31]

Wilder's study (2004) reported that 77.9 percent of student participants agreed (32.1 percent strongly agreed and 45.8 percent agreed somewhat) that their experience had caused them to be more open to serving at least one semester in missions as a college-aged student. Even more substantial, 92.4 percent (54.9 percent strongly agreed and 37.5 percent agreed somewhat) said they would be more open to God calling them into vocational ministry. Among the adult participants, the results were similar: 60.4 percent agreed (19.2 percent strongly agreed and 41.2 percent agreed somewhat) that their experience had caused them to be more open to serving at least three to six months in mission service in the future and 77.7 percent (38.0 percent strongly agreed and 39.7 percent agreed somewhat) said they would be

> Before I ever went on my first short-term mission trip, I was running from God's call on my life. I was saved, but to me *missions* was a four-letter word. I was so afraid God might call me to live in a hut in the middle of Africa. After reading an article in *Decision* magazine by Billy Graham about missions and evangelism, I was at least willing to go on a short-term trip. My first short-term mission trip was a construction trip to Baldwin, Louisiana. We were rebuilding a home of a blind man who was so sick of his ramshackle house that he took a Skilsaw and literally cut his house in half. He was frustrated that his house was not accommodating to his blindness. When we finished the remodeling, he came in and felt around with his cane and just wept. I wept—my heart was being broken for the call that God had on my life in the realm of missions. Since then, I have been on four of the seven continents doing mission trips, I pursued a masters in missiology from Southern Seminary, and my wife and I served as missionaries in Haiti running an orphanage. We are currently pursuing a career missions position, and I would be honored if God would call us to live in a hut in the middle of Africa. —Dennis

[31] McDonough and Peterson, *Can Short-Term Mission Really Create Long-Term Missionaries?*

more open to God calling them into vocational ministry. Moreover, 64.8 percent strongly agreed and 32.1 percent agreed somewhat that they would be more involved serving in the ministry of their local church.[32]

Alsup (2005) surveyed two groups of students using a pretest and posttest methodology. One group participated in a domestic work-camp setting, while the second group participated in an international work-camp setting. The research indicated a relationship between the students' participation in the STM and an increase in their desire to "become involved in either volunteerism or a career in community service or missions."[33] Similarly, Fitzgerald's (2005) study also found that participation in STM enhanced the participants' commitment to service.[34]

My short-term trip set in concrete all the pieces of the puzzle God had so delicately placed to call me to His long-term service in missions. The call can seem at times a ubiquitous subject. To understand it you must be amidst it; to understand it clearly you must be amidst the God from which it comes. In my own life God has used a great many things to piece together my passion for the Brazilian people. Short-term missions brought research to life in homes, slums, and most of all, in lives. Throughout my short time with YWAM in Belo Horizonte, Brazil, God cultivated an undeniable passion, a passion so deep that my heart has been transplanted into another culture. I am forever connected to that world, forever shaped by its people. I left little pieces of my heart with every girl and every staff member of Casa Recanto! There is no way I could have developed such passion for a people without God! I also know that nothing could have happened in my time overseas had God not shown up! He runs through every action as we reach out! Being a missionary has incredible blessings, but it also has incredible challenges. For every place the Lord has us walk, we will leave a little more of our hearts, and that is how it should be! God just continues to make our hearts grow and expand for the people He has called us to! —Beth *(soon headed to Brazil as a career missionary)*

[32] Wilder, "Short-Term Missions as a Strategic Component in Youth Ministry Programming."

[33] P. Alsup, "An Analysis of the Influence of M-Fuge Participation on Volunteerism and Career Leadership in Service" (EdD diss., The Southern Baptist Theological Seminary, 2005), 172. See also 106–24 for detailed statistical data.

[34] Fitzgerald, "The Student Missionary Experience and Its Impact on Young Adults."

Dean (2001) conducted a study of retention factors among 60 Wesleyan career missionaries and found 18 factors. One of these was STM experience prior to deploying for long-term service.[35]

> My youth pastor provided us with several mission opportunities each summer, and he challenged me to go on a church planting mission to Traverse City, Michigan, for two weeks and on another trip to Louisiana for two weeks. I had to make a choice that summer: play baseball or spend four weeks doing door-to-door survey work and evangelism. The Lord would not let me go on this one, and I finally told my coach that I would not be playing ball that summer. Needless to say, it was some of the best times of my life. The Lord starting dealing with me in the area of giving my life to ministry. There was one thing I never wanted to be growing up, a pastor—the ministry just had no appeal to me, but God had a different plan, and he used these short-term projects greatly in my life. Because of the impact of short-term missions in my own life, I want every person to experience short-term missions because I believe it is a crucial element in the discipleship process. —Tad

GLOBAL PERSPECTIVE

Some studies have also addressed the issue of how STM experiences may expand the global perspective of the participant. For example, Wisbey (1990) surveyed college students and found that their STM experience had caused an increase in their awareness of the vast needs of people around the world.[36] Beers (1999) found that the college students who had participated in a one-month mission trip study abroad became more accepting of people with different religious beliefs. Northcutt (2000) administered a pretest and posttest to 15 college students who previously had not been on a mission trip to the Third World. He asked questions concerning their attitude, knowledge, and behavior toward poverty. He found that the at-

[35] M. W. Dean, "A Study of Retention Factors Among Career Missionaries of Wesleyan World Missions" (PhD diss., Trinity Evangelical Divinity School, 2001).

[36] R. R. Wisbey, "Collegiate Missions in the Context of Short-Term Mission Experiences" (DMin diss., Wesley Theological Seminary, 1990).

In May 2006, God opened the door for me to go on a short-term trip to a remote village in the Andes Mountains of Peru. The village, if to be described by worldly terms, was extremely destitute in that the people who live there do not have running water or electricity. This was the first time I had ever been faced with the realities of life in a Third-World country and truly felt burdened by the needs of my fellowman. And yet, after spending many days getting to know the believers there, I came to a great understanding that has deeply informed my worldview and worked to tear away the layers of American Christianity which is ingrained with capitalistic, self-sufficiency apart from the power of God through the Holy Spirit. As we sang hymns with these believers around a fire one night, in the cold and in languages I did not understand, I could see the joy of Christ in my brother's and sister's faces, and I knew that beyond any worldly wealth I may have, they were rich in Christ and God was mightily working in their midst. —Julia

titude and behavior of the students toward Third-World poverty changed significantly as a result of their exposure during a STM trip.

Lingle (2003) interviewed STM participants from eight churches in central Georgia. One of the findings pertinent to global perspective is that the respondents indicated they gained a more complex view of missionary work as a result of their mission experience—now seeing that it requires a better understanding about the nationals and their beliefs.[37]

Blezien (2004) used a mixed method approach to his study. The quantitative portion of the research involved the use of a pretest and a posttest with 159 college students, with a nonmatched control group of 151 students. There was no statistically significant difference found between pretest and posttest scores as it relates to STM participation on the cross-cultural sensitivity of the participants. Interestingly however, those students who were more politically liberal, more experienced in international travel, female, and younger in age showed the greatest increase in cultural sensitivity. The qualitative element of the study indicated that "students were impacted by

[37] R. E. Lingle, "How Returning Short Term Missions Volunteers Impact the Local Church" (DMin diss., Covenant Theological Seminary, 2003).

contact with people (primarily host nationals), the ministry activity itself, moments of crisis (past and present), and exposure to injustice, including the differing cultural perspectives on women."[38] Blezien concludes that the participants experienced "increased cultural awareness and appreciation of personal and cultural values" as a result of their STM involvement.[39]

> Words can't express how much short-term mission trips mean to me. Every trip I have been on has been an unforgettable experience, and I would definitely say it has been worth all of the time, money, and effort that went into it. It's so funny because you go there expecting to give to others and change their lives, but I always end up getting so much more from the trip. Every place I have been, whether Russia, China, or Peru, people act as if they had everything to give, yet they have close to nothing. The Christians I've seen in other places are so full of joy that one cannot help but be encouraged by their example. It's really eye opening to go and see people who don't take their faith for granted. I wish I could convey to people just how amazing the trips are, but the only thing that is sufficient to explain it is to go on a trip and see it for oneself. I've seen miracles happen, lives have been changed, and God's word was spread in amazing ways. —Jillian

Cook (2005) interviewed 36 individuals who had participated in academically sponsored intercultural mission trips from 1968 to 2000. Some of the participants spent six to eight weeks on the field, while others spent 10–14 months overseas. It was Cook's purpose to examine the long-term effects of these experiences on the subsequent direction of participants' lives. He noted 10 factors discovered by his study, one of which was the acknowledgment by participants that their global perspective expanded as a result of their exposure in a cross-cultural setting.[40]

[38] P. Blezien, "The Impact of Summer International Short-Term Missions Experiences on the Cross-Cultural Sensitivity of Undergraduate College Student Participants" (EdD diss., Azusa Pacific University, 2004), 110. See also 113–17 for more discussion on the qualitative findings.

[39] Ibid., 110.

[40] C. A. Cook, "Assessing the Long-Term Impact of Intercultural Sojourns: Contributions of Canadian Bible College Intercultural Sojourns in Developing Global Awareness" (PhD diss., Trinity Evangelical Divinity School, 2005).

Fitzgerald (2005) found that participation in STM expanded the participants' worldview.[41] Swartzentruber (2008) conducted a case study that examined 14 high-school seniors who had participated in an international mission trip. Students noted substantial changes in their worldview. In particular, Swartzentruber noted that "poverty evoked much reflection on the host culture as well as the participant's home culture."[42]

Participant's Self-Awareness

Linhart (2004) conducted a study using a grounded theory approach to investigate how cross-cultural service projects provide opportunities for participants to explore their personal identities.[43] He worked with 10 North American high-school students who participated in a service project to Ecuador. Several months prior to the trip, he distributed microcassettes to the students so they could record their reflections during the training process, while in Ecuador, and for four months following their return home; this resulted in 19 hours of student recordings, in addition to 10 hours recorded by the researcher.

Linhart noted that "mission trip created an experience that resembled a psychological and spiritual 'stage' for identity growth with concrete beginning and ending points."[44] The students' encounters "were considered to have unusual (and spiritual) significance. These identity pursuits were not psychoanalytical or developmental, but existential as they considered their place in the world and their own culturally-shaped identities."[45] The participants reported recognizing the "consumeristic influences of their home culture" in their lives and how this focus on materialism promotes "an unauthentic way of living life."[46] They also acknowledged that interacting with and observing their hosts caused them to see their own lives as typically passionless in comparison with the passionate faith they experienced while being on the mission field.[47]

Linhart's study is helpful for those who view STM as a means to develop the participant holistically. His emphasis on the STM experience

[41] Fitzgerald, "The Student Missionary Experience and Its Impact on Young Adults."

[42] C. Swartzentruber, "The Effect of International Short-Term Mission Trips on Intercultural Sensitivity in Secondary Christian School Students" (EdD diss., Duquesne University, 2008).

[43] T. D. Linhart, "The Curricular Nature of Youth Group Short-Term Cross-Cultural Service Projects" (PhD diss., Purdue University, 2004).

[44] Linhart, "They Were So Alive!"

[45] Ibid., 452.

[46] Ibid., 452.

[47] Ibid., 452–53.

being an explorative event is insightful, as it reminds church leaders how STM can be used to shape teenagers' understandings of themselves and help them become what God desires them to be.

> Several years ago, during my high-school to college transition, I went on a 10-day mission trip to Peru. With all good intentions, I went to help change the lives of the Peruvians I would come into contact with along the Amazon River. What I didn't realize was that it was MY life that would be changed in a very significant way. As I served in the jungle and on the riverfront, I became acutely aware that I was one small person in a big world, and coming from a materialistic lifestyle, I was struck with the realization that this world did not revolve around me or my plans. Suddenly, God's work (and His desire for our participation in it) became supremely important to me—important enough to chart the direction of my life, my education, and the worldview that I would come to embrace. The week and a half of my life that I spent on a short-term missions trip allowed me to see God, His continuing purposing to save His own, and a proper perspective on who I am in light of who He is. —Travis

LEADERSHIP SKILLS

As a part of his study, Wilder (2004) examined youth ministry leaders and adult participants' perceptions of the usefulness of short-term mission experiences as a method to develop the leadership skills of participants. An essay question on the adult survey asked whether short-term missions have an impact on the development of new leadership skills and the reinforcement of known leadership skills among student participants.

The respondents acknowledged their perception that STM experiences do have a positive impact on the development of their students' leadership skills, with 93.4 percent answering yes to the question. The respondents answering yes were then asked to describe the leadership skills they saw being developed in their students. The researcher did not define the phrase "leadership skills," affording the respondents significant leeway in their answers. The respondents enumerated 13 different skills, including a willingness to lead (31.5 percent); spiritual leadership—the ability to pray out loud, lead group devotions, teach the Bible (18.5 percent); the ability to work well in a team construct (16.1 percent); evangelistic skills (15.3 percent); and personal confidence to lead (15.3 percent).

The student participants were asked if they had gained any new leadership skills from their participation in World Changers. The respondents answered yes, with 88.6 percent acknowledging that they had developed new skills during their mission experience. Here are the top five responses: confidence to lead (34.7 percent), evangelistic skills (27.3 percent), Christian character (18.2 percent), relational skills (17.0 percent), and communication skills (14.2 percent). One student, reflecting on his STM experiences, stated, "I was always a quiet and shy person. I have seen a great change over the 4 years I have been at World Changers (a STM program). I am more outspoken and able to lead because of my experience."[48]

These findings suggest that STM can be strategically used in a youth ministry context for the purpose of developing leadership skills among the student participants.[49]

I had the incredible opportunity to lead a church in their first mission trip in over a decade. Since such a trip had not been done in so long, there was no precedent for me to follow. My leadership skills were developed in ways that only experience can bring about. There was no budget, little interest among church members at first, and nobody else willing to help lead this endeavor. Through prayer, God led me through the process of raising an abundance of funds. The church became excited about the mission trip as the time grew closer to leave. In the end, it was a huge success. After this trip, I knew for sure God was calling me to lead His people in full-time ministry. —Chris

Mixed Messages

The section above was provided as a way to expose you to what some of the research describes as potential positive effects of STM involvement

[48] Wilder, "Short-Term Missions as a Strategic Component in Youth Ministry Programming," 121.

[49] Ibid.

on the participant. We use the word *potential* because other research exists that calls some of these results into question. A simple reminder is appropriate here: putting on bifocals means looking below the line with a measure of scrutiny at the current research; therefore, we proceed in the next section to evaluate honestly the way STM is being done. We will provide a brief overview of these studies as they make us question the lasting effects of STM participation as currently practiced. But we also remind you that we are staunch advocates of STM and believe that it is often a dynamic component in the transformation process.

Method Matters

Let us first take a moment and review some basic research principles. Social science research, like most other subjects, has philosophical foundations. Researchers usually have a dominant personal philosophy that prompts them to gravitate toward a closely aligned research method. For example, if a researcher embraces existentialism, then he will often choose a research method that reflects an emphasis on human individuality and personal experience—perhaps an ethnographic study.

Someone who is more pragmatic may look for research methods that allow him to examine the best practices in his focus area because he is interested in what actually works in an organization or among a group of people—perhaps a case study would be used.

Someone who is more idealistically committed may opt for studying the writings of great thinkers from the past—such a person would likely choose a historical or biographical text-based study.

Those who are more realistic will normally choose a research method designed to assess the situation accurately and fully. They desire to arrive at conclusions that can be further substantiated by replicating a series of quantitative studies—they may choose a quasiexperimental method. In addition to one's philosophical disposition playing a role in the selection of research methodology, the primary input is always dependent on the type of question is being asked.

Really, all of these approaches have a place at the table. We suggest that when studying a particular topic, it is most helpful for people with divergent perspectives and differing methodologies to investigate the research concern. When this is done well, we end up with a more accurate evaluation.

The second research principle worth noting relates to the maturity of the field being studied. When the first forays into investigating a research concern occur, they are often phenomenological; the early attempts simply focus on describing the phenomenon that is occurring. After a reasonable number of studies have been conducted in accordance with this method, a more precise methodology takes shape, which is intended to test the conclusions derived from the early studies. This is exactly what has been happening in recent STM research.

When we put these two research principles together, we have an explanation for the types of studies that have already been conducted. Thus, we can see more clearly the natural progression of studies over the past 20 years.

Conflicting Reports

Earlier we outlined five types of transformation that have been reported among STM participants: understanding of and commitment to biblical Christianity, openness to volunteer and vocational ministry service, expansion of one's global perspective, deepening of a participant's self-awareness, and the exercise and development of leadership skills. In the last few years several studies have questioned some of these results.

Let us begin with some studies related to STM involvement and financial giving. Robert Priest and a team of PhD students at Trinity Evangelical Seminary set out to answer the question, What has been the impact of short-term missions on the recruitment and support of career missionaries? In a 2006 journal article, they suggest that there are "two human elements essential to the career missionary enterprise: (1) a pool of individuals desiring to serve and (2) a support base of sustained funding for these individuals over the course of a lifetime. Both elements are essential."[50] Much of the research has indicated STM experiences produce greater openness to serve and greater funding for missions. As several researchers have noted, however, it is more difficult to measure accurately a participant's openness to a career-missions call (intangible result) than how much an individual gives toward missions (tangible result).

With this in mind, Priest and his colleagues surveyed 495 evangelical Christians (from college classrooms, seminary classrooms, and adult Sunday school classes) who were between the ages of 18 and 37. They asked (immediately following tax season) how much each individual gave to support missionaries in the preceding year. Their findings were suggestive: 18- to 22-year-olds gave $68.15; 23- to 27-year-olds gave $620.35; 28- to 32-year-olds gave $1,403.57; and 33- to 37-year-olds gave $3,603.57 to

[50] Priest et al., "Researching the Short-Term Mission Movement," 431–50.

support missionaries per year. Each five-year period showed more than a double increase in giving.[51]

Priest et al. used this study to call into question the results of Peterson and Peterson (1991) and McDonough and Peterson (1999), both of whom claimed that STM participation contributed to the doubling of annual contributions toward missions. As Priest correctly notes, the problem with this finding relates to methodology. The participants surveyed were asked to report retrospectively on how much they gave to missions prior to their STM experience and how much they give to missions now, several years later. The 1991 study, which provided age demographics, revealed that 83.5 percent of those surveyed were under 36—a time when annual income is typically increasing at a rapid pace. Consequently, Priest argues that "there is no reason to attribute increased giving to anything other than increased discretionary income associated with increased age."[52]

Another study that highlighted the relationship between STM participation and missions giving was Purvis (1993). In this study, 76 percent of the respondents claimed that their mission giving had increased as a result of their mission endeavors. Purvis then triangulated these responses with the missions giving by the 38 represented churches over the period when their state convention had coordinated efforts in Brazil and Kenya. The data showed that the churches had increased their giving by a total of 66.8 percent from 1981 to 1992. Though this seemed to support Purvis's findings, he had not adjusted for inflation. When adjusted, the results told a different story—giving increased merely 7 percent, or just under 0.68 percent per year.[53] Furthermore, Ver Beek notes that 89 percent of the participants had received some amount of subsidy for their trip, which would have come from the state convention's budget. He suggests that this may have even hindered the amount of money that was ultimately allocated toward career missions during the same timeframe.

Ver Beek (2006), as noted in the previous section, attempted to survey

---

[51] Ibid., 437. The authors note that in their sample 385 were between the ages of 18 and 22, 54 were between the ages of 23 and 27, 37 were between the ages of 28 and 32, and 19 were between the ages of 33 and 37. Moreover, they saw some evidence that upon marriage, individuals began to calculate their giving as a couple, reporting as individual giving what may actually be coming from two people. This factor may call into question a portion of the findings; nevertheless, it is helpful in pointing out that giving tends to increase proportionately with one's salary in an evangelical setting.

[52] Ibid., 436.

[53] K. Ver Beek, "Lessons from the Sapling," in *Effective Engagement in Short-Term Missions,* ed. Robert Priest (Pasadena, Calif: William Carey, 2008), 498, 501. See endnote 16 on page 501, which states that Tommy Purvis confirmed that he did not adjust for inflation. Ver Beek used an inflation calculator accessed at http://www1.jsc.nasa.gov/bu2/inflateCPI.html.

162 participants (127 responded) who had taken part in a short-term mission project to Honduras. Part of the study queried the participants about their financial support for the Honduran Christian organization with which they partnered in the mission trip. Approximately 10 percent responded that their financial support for this organization had increased significantly, and 49 percent stated that it had increased somewhat since their STM experience.

In an attempt to triangulate these results, Ver Beek examined the donor records and found that 75 percent of the 162 total participants did not send any direct donations to the organization in the two years after their trip. The total amount given to the organization increased 6 percent in the two years following the mission trip; if divided equally among all the participants, then giving per person would have increased from $31 to $33 per person per year. The number of actual donors increased from 21 before the trip to an average of 31 after the trip, with 14 new donors included. However, 10 participants who had given prior to the trip did not contribute financially following the trip, resulting in a net gain of four new donors. Ver Beek also examined the records of the 17 churches that sent groups to Honduras. He found that the annual giving from these churches to the organization increased approximately 1 percent per year, with six churches increasing their giving and 11 churches decreasing their contributions.[54]

Ver Beek concludes, "It appears that the participant's perceived/reported changes in giving after their experience in Honduras were much higher than their actual changes/actions."[55] Such a discrepancy, he suggests, calls into question the other positive results related to participants' transformation. His primary concern is that much of the research to date has rested upon self-reporting and therefore may be lacking in accuracy.

Priest et al. conducted two additional studies related to financial giving. In 2004, they surveyed 120 seminary students, asking them about their prior year's missions contributions. The researchers found no relationship between the amounts of time spent participating in STM and current giving—whether to missions or total charitable giving. In 2006, they surveyed 133 Sunday school attendees, 407 Christian college students, and 24 seminary students—664 total. In terms of missions giving, there was no statistically significant difference between those respondents who participated in STM and those who had not.[56] As Priest puts it, "No methodologically sound research we have discovered has yet demonstrated a significant average

[54] Ibid., 479–80. See also Ver Beek, "The Impact of Short-Term Missions," 477–95.

[55] Ibid., 480.

[56] Priest et al., "Researching the Short-Term Mission Movement," 431–50.

increase in giving by participants caused by STM experience. In short, one claim about STM, that it helps create higher levels of financial support for the career missionary enterprise, does not appear to be true."[57]

More Areas of Dissention

Other studies related to STM and areas such as ethnocentrism, materialism, and spiritual growth have failed to yield results supporting the notion of sustained transformation in the life of the participant. For example, Tuttle (1998) administered the belief and commitment scale to a group of college STM participants one month prior to an STM experience and approximately one month following. She also gave it to a control group of nonparticipants. In neither group did she find significant change along the scale.

Wilson (1999) used the FMS and administered the pretest and a posttest 45 days later. In terms of the scale as a whole, he did not find any significant changes.

Similarly, Beers (1999) used the FMS and the Growth in Mature Faith Index and found no significant differences between the pretest and posttest scores on either scale. Nor did he find any significant difference between the STM participants and the control group of non-STM participants (though he did find three positive results for the STM participants, as noted in the above sections).

Manitsas (2000) used the Spiritual Well-Being Scale and the Tennessee Self-Concept Scale when surveying 25 church members. Fourteen of them participated in a mission trip to Mexico (seven with no prior STM experience and seven with prior experience), while 11 served as a control group of non-STM participants. He administered the surveys before the trip, immediately following the trip and six months after. He did not find any significant difference on either scale between the STM participants and the non-STM participants. The only change that persisted at the six-month follow-up was that the STM participants were more likely to participate in future STM trips.[58]

As a part of his online *Christianity Today* dialogue with Robert Priest, Kurt Alan Ver Beek noted that "nearly every study which has applied pre- and post-trip tests to STM participants has found that there is little or no lasting change in areas like spiritual maturity, cross-cultural awareness, ethnocentrism, and other hoped-for results of STM."[59]

---

[57] Ibid.

[58] Manitsas, "Short Term Mission Trips."

[59] K. A. Ver Beek and R. Priest, "Are Short-Term Missions Good Stewardship?" *Christianity Today*

Well, there you have it—studies that report significant transformation among STM participants and studies that show little to no change. Studies used to support and studies used to refute. So where lies the truth in all of this research?

Saplings at Best

To this point we have attempted to look below the line of the bifocals with a measure of scrutiny concerning the existing research. And if you are asking the question, Does STM cause transformation in the lives of participants?, our answer would be yes and no. The answer is yes in the sense that some of the more controlled research does show positive change. Moreover, in most of the research, there is an initial indication of positive life transformation.

The answer is also no, however, because this initial indication of transformation is often merely temporary. It is what we might call good intentions. Likely, the participant has experienced dissonance and is attempting to alleviate it by making these initial commitments. While he has a desire to see the commitments come to full fruition in his life and even sets his mind in that direction, he often lacks the support and follow-through necessary to reinforce such decisions.

For this reason we believe STM must be seen as a strategic component in youth ministry programming. It cannot be a stand-alone event if it is to accomplish lasting transformation in the lives of those whom you have been called to shepherd. Rather, it should be a part of the larger discipleship process. Just as a youth camp or a leadership retreat, if done well, functions as part of an overarching strategy to grow students and adults, so must STM. In youth ministries where youth camps act as isolated events, students enjoy the euphoria of the mountaintop experience, only to return home to their old patterns of thinking and behaving. So it is with STM that are disconnected from the whole discipleship process.

Kurt Ver Beek, who serves as a professor of sociology at Calvin College and director of that institution's semester-abroad-in-Honduras program, perhaps has best captured what takes place on the STM field. He has described the participant as a sapling. While reporting on his 2006 Honduran study, he notes his prior assumption concerning the fragility and

(July 5–8, 2005). Online: http://www.christianitytoday.com/ct/article_print.html?id=34557. This was a Web-only article posted in a four-day discussion format.

vulnerability of the North American participant: "a one-week experience in Honduras could easily 'shake-up their world' and cause lasting changes in giving, prayer, and other areas."[60] He now questions that assumption:

> Rather than seeing communities and North Americans as easily changed entities, I wonder if they more closely resemble saplings, which can be bent and even held in one place for a week or more but once let loose quickly go back to growing vertically. Those saplings need to be held in place for a much longer period of time for the change in direction to become permanent. . . . It is very difficult to make lasting positive changes in our own lives or our neighbors.[61]

SAPLINGS OFTEN GROW UP TO BE STRONGLY ROOTED TREES

Let us digress momentarily from Ver Beek's saplings to take you on a mental road trip to Lampe, Missouri (just outside Branson), where Dogwood Canyon is located. It is a 2,200-acre nature park nestled in the Ozarks that is home to amazing deer, bison, elk, and trout as long as your arm. If you were to take the wildlife tour, your guide would show you many interesting things, including an Indian marker tree. This particular tree was used to mark the location of a cave and has a broad trunk with a lower limb about eight inches in diameter, bent at a 90-degree angle. The limb points directly at the entrance of a cave about 100 yards away.

The Indians would have taken the sapling tree, shaped it into place over time, and kept continual pressure on the limb to ensure that it was growing properly. What is even more intriguing is that at some point the Indians no longer traveled those pathways or tended that tree. The end of the limb began to grow in a perfect vertical direction toward the sun—when the steady reinforcement ceased, the tree returned to its normal pattern.

Ver Beek is correct in his description of STM participants. What excites us, however, is that with the right reinforcement mechanisms in place, the participants stand a greater chance of true life transformation. Churches must see STM as part of an ongoing and deliberate approach to discipleship. In the last section of this book, we will discuss further some principles for making STM a more successful transformation tool. These principles will

[60] Ver Beek, "The Impact of Short-Term Missions," 492.

[61] Ibid.

help effect lasting changes in the lives of participants. We have great confidence that saplings can be shaped and eventuate into strongly rooted trees.

Looking Through the Top of the Bifocals

As you can tell, we have begun peering above the line and looking into the "what will it look like if done well" distance. Before we propose these STM principles, we must first examine the biblical and theoretical foundations that undergird them. In the next several chapters, we will do just that as we examine the doctrine of sanctification and the tenants of cognitive dissonance theory.

Discussion Questions

1. Why is it important that students engage in service-type ministry?
2. What two metaphors do the authors use to describe STM? Do you see these as accurate descriptors? Why or why not?
3. What types of transformation are discussed in this chapter?
4. What are some of the "rosier" study results concerning the potentially transformative effects of STM?
5. What does the research say about the lasting effects of STM?
6. How does Ver Beek refer to the participant? Would you agree with his assessment?
7. If you have been involved in STM, then take a moment and write a paragraph summarizing the impact of STM on your life and spiritual development.

PART II

TRANSFORMATION IN PERSPECTIVE: EXAMINING THE PROCESS AND PRINCIPLES

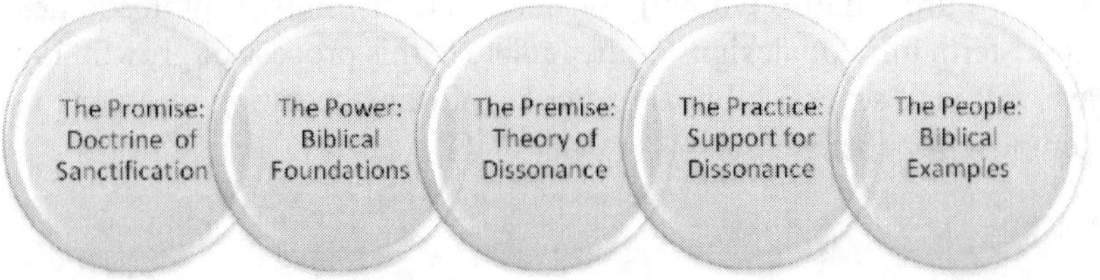

The Promise: Doctrine of Sanctification
The Power: Biblical Foundations
The Premise: Theory of Dissonance
The Practice: Support for Dissonance
The People: Biblical Examples

At Urbana 2000, the Operation Mobilization staff tried to identify the concerns about and hindrances to student involvement in mission in a unique way. Behind their display, they posted a 12-by-8 foot wall, on which students could record these fears and hurdles. By the end of the conference, there were over 700 handwritten notes on the wall. Concerns ranged from financial drawbacks, to safety, to lack of support by family members, to simply a desire to remain in relative comfort.

Operation Mobilization U.S.A. representative Kathy Hicks recorded and categorized these concerns in her book *Scaling the Wall.*[1] Hicks was concerned that these obstacles—this "wall" that was standing in the way of a generational group—be addressed honestly through scriptural reflection and engagement with the personal testimonies of others who had faced these same issues and found ways to overcome them. Having experienced, seasoned missionaries address concerns that they themselves had faced, so that the walls might be breached and today's students might find their place in the global work, is a crucial element of discipleship. As a result of this encouragement, one student offered this prayer of devotion: "My fear, pride, and ignorance plague me, Lord. But Your victory in life, death, and

[1] K. Hicks, *Scaling the Wall* (Waynesboro, GA: Authentic, 2003).

resurrection free me from their shackles. I love You, Jesus. I thank You for forgiving my lack of trust in these areas before. But here, now and in the future, I lay them at Your feet. Open my hands. And say, 'Here I am Lord. I have heard Your calling. Send me.'"[2] Stories such as this of movement from paralysis to complete abandonment to God always fascinate us. What happened in between the trepidation and the resolve to go wherever and whenever and to do whatever God ordains?

The process of students like this one making that transition, or transformation, from inconsistent and fearful to godly and unabashedly bold for His glory and gospel is what we examine next. We will investigate this transformation in terms of doctrinal understandings of sanctification and theoretical perspectives on the role of tension in bringing about resolution. Furthermore, we will consider student ministry philosophies and short-term mission designs as they relate to this process of growth. Finally, we will visit several biblical examples of transformation in order to see a template for change.

[2] Ibid., 198.

CHAPTER 5

OVERCOMING INCONSISTENCIES FOR A CHANGE: THE PROMISE

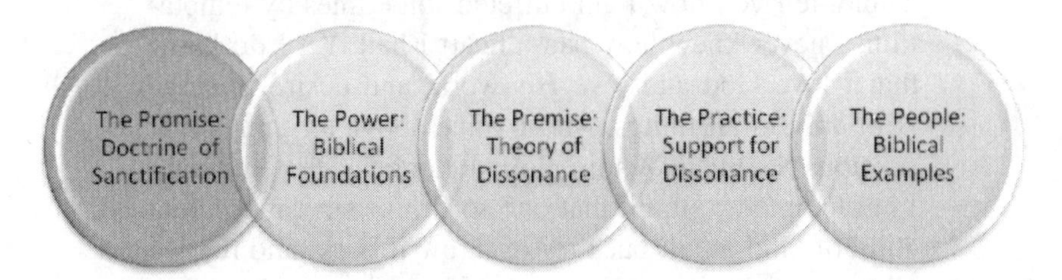

If we were to ask a group of believers about their experiences living the Christian life, surely we would entertain many different stories. We would hear about what led to their conversion and how they expressed the God-given faith necessary for salvation; we would hear about the joys that accompany the certainty of an eternal future in the presence of God; we would hear about the difficult days they have experienced because of the world's hatred toward them as children of God; and we would surely hear about successes in overcoming sin and temptations in their lives. But would we hear about the struggles they are having in their everyday lives?

Believers often feel like they must put on a good front, while on the inside each is wondering, "Why can't I overcome this particular sin issue in my life? Why am I getting angry, or why I am being so selfish with my time or resources?" The guilt and frustration begins to set in because they have been taught that salvation includes life transformation, but they do not seem to be experiencing daily victory.

J. Hudson Taylor, the great British missionary to inland China, would have categorized himself as one certain of his salvation in Christ but disappointed and wearied in his daily struggles with sin.[1] Taylor had become a believer in his childhood and in his teenage years sensed a call to the mission field of China. As a missionary in his early twenties, he was used in

[1] H. Taylor, *The Spiritual Secret of Hudson Taylor* (New Kensington, PA: Whitaker House, 1996), 16.

mighty ways among the people of China. Yet, like many others who serve the Lord faithfully, Taylor was struggling in his walk with the Lord. At the age of 37, he penned a long letter to his mother expressing his deepest desires concerning the things of the Lord:

> My own position becomes continually more and more responsible, and my need greater of special grace to fill it; but I have continually to mourn that I follow at such a distance and learn so slowly to imitate my precious Master. I cannot tell you how I am buffeted sometimes by temptation. I never knew how bad a heart I had. Yet I do know that I love God and love His work, and desire to serve Him only in all things. And I value above all things that precious Savior in Whom alone I can be accepted. Often I am tempted to think that one so full of sin cannot be a child of God at all; but I try to throw it back, and rejoice all the more in the preciousness of Jesus, and in the riches of that grace that has made us "accepted in the Beloved." Beloved He is of God; beloved He ought to be of us. But oh, how short I fall here again! May God help me to love Him more and serve Him better. Do pray for me. Pray that the Lord will keep me from sin, will sanctify me wholly, will use me more largely in His service.[2]

Sometime later, a fellow missionary by the name of John McCarthy wrote Taylor a letter. The letter reflected McCarthy's dependence upon his Savior for grace and power and was intended to encourage Taylor: "To let my loving Savior work in me His will, my sanctification is what I would live for by His grace. Abiding, not striving nor struggling; looking off onto him; trusting Him for present power; trusting Him to subdue all inward corruption; resting in the love of an Almighty Savior, and the conscious joy of a complete salvation."[3] This letter prompted in Taylor a new understanding of his salvation. A letter to his sister reflected his newfound joy. Attempting to explain the change, he declared that "there is nothing new or strange or wonderful—and yet, all is new!"[4] Indeed, Taylor's friends and family noted the difference in his life and demeanor.

---

[2] V. R. Edman, *They Found the Secret: 20 Transformed Lives That Reveal a Touch of Eternity* (Grand Rapids: Zondervan, 1984), 18.

[3] Ibid., 19.

[4] Ibid., 19–20.

In declaring "God has made me a new man! God has made me a new man!"[5] Hudson Taylor finally began to comprehend in his own life what Paul wrote in Rom 6:3–7:

> Or do you not know that all of us who have been baptized into Christ Jesus have been baptized into His death? Therefore we have been buried with Him through baptism into death, so that as Christ was raised from the dead through the glory of the Father, *so we too might walk in newness of life.* For if we have become united with Him in the likeness of His death, certainly we shall also be in the *likeness of His resurrection,* knowing this, that our old self was crucified with Him, in order that our body of sin might be done away with, so that we would no longer be slaves to sin; for he who has died is freed from sin. (italics mine)

Calvin suggests that in this passage Paul does not just encourage us to follow Christ as an exemplar but rather "announces a doctrine . . . [namely,] that the death of Christ is efficacious to destroy and demolish the depravity of our flesh, and his resurrection, to effect the renovation of a better nature."[6]

This idea—that the depravity with which we wrestle is defeated at the foot of the cross—produces in the believer a hope of living life with a renovated heart. A renovation which is received through Christ's abundant grace and predicated upon His atoning work at Calvary and His blessed resurrection. The difference that this truth has the potential to make in the everyday life of the believer is inexpressible. What we are talking about is life transformation by the only One who truly has the power to change us. What we are talking about is the power of God's grace effecting God's kind will toward His children. What we are talking about is the glorious promise of God that our lives will be forever changed as a result of God's working in us.

[5] R. A. Pyne and M. L. Blackmon, "A Critique of the Exchanged Life," *Bibliotheca Sacra* 163 (2006): 131–57.

[6] J. Calvin, *Commentary on Romans*, trans. John Owen (Grand Rapids: Eerdmans Publishing, 1948), 221.

GOOGLE THIS . . .

Those of us who live in the Christian community ought to recognize that the longing for a transformed life is not confined to Christianity but is common to all people. If you were to take a moment and google the word *spirituality*, you would discover around 56 million entries to explore. If you dig through the layers, you would also find that the majority of the references are not to "Christian spirituality" (only about 2.6 million directly relate). Though the secular beliefs about spirituality amount to heresy, they remind us that people in every nation, tribe, and tongue are in desperate need of hearing the gospel that is the power unto salvation. Just as there is a renewed interest in secular spirituality, there is also a renewed interest in Christian spirituality. This renewed interest demonstrates that believers desire to experience a transformed life and are searching for a clearer understanding of how to actuate it in their lives. To help meet this need, a generation of Christian writers and church leaders have set in motion an exploration of this life transformation process so as to better lead God's people in the life He intends. We would place our own work in this context because it is our heart that God's people live the new life they have been given. We desire that believers would be so oriented toward God's will that they fulfill His commandments and His commission, thereby bringing glory to Him and enjoying a transformed life. In the following section, we will address questions related to the life-transformation process and its biblical groundings.

WHAT IS LIFE TRANSFORMATION?

This is the right question to begin the discussion. Many terms are used currently to describe the process of transformation, such as "Christian spirituality, spiritual transformation, character formation, and spiritual theology."[7] Porter suggests that the terminology may be confusing; all of these terms reasonably equate to the doctrine of sanctification and refer to "the nature of spiritual maturation from the time of regeneration to the time of glorification."[8] For a variety of reasons we have chosen to use the

[7] S. L. Porter, "On the Renewal of Interest in the Doctrine of Sanctification: A Methodological Reminder," *Journal of the Evangelical Theological Society* 45 (2002): 416.

[8] Ibid.

term *life transformation* when referring to the doctrine of sanctification. Our goal is not to add to the confusion on the subject but rather to direct the discussion toward the *telos* of sanctification.

Historical Development of the Christian Community's Understanding of Life Transformation

When asked the question, What is life transformation? most will answer without regard to the historical development of the doctrine. However, it is important for every believer to be acquainted with some of the different views on this great doctrine, for it is one that affects the entirety of the Christian experience. We will briefly summarize several such views: Roman Catholic, Reformed, Wesleyan, Victorious Life, and Dispensational.

Roman Catholic. Roman Catholicism asserts that salvation comes through the practice of the sacraments *(a vehicle or means of grace)*. In the sacrament of baptism, God infuses a justifying grace that purifies the individual from original and actual sin, while imparting the habits of righteousness. Sanctification is the increase of justification in the life of the baptized, and the increase occurs through additional sacraments such as confirmation, Eucharist, penance, and extreme unction. Progress in sanctification not only requires good works but also complete obedience to God's commandments. If sanctification is not complete in this life, then the individual endures the cleansing work of purgatory until the process of sanctification is complete. In congruence with its doctrine of justification, Roman Catholicism espouses the belief that perseverance of the baptized is dependant upon continued obedience; therefore, certainty of salvation is impossible.[9]

Reformed. The reformed view of sanctification emphasizes the Sovereign's work in regenerating the heart of the elect. According to reformed theology, salvation is both God determined and God directed; it is also God initiated and God completed. What occurs in regeneration is both justification and sanctification: the elect are declared righteous and holy based upon Christ's atoning work. B. B. Warfield suggests that in "regeneration God recreates the governing dispositions of the regenerate man's

[9] G. R. Lewis and B. A. Demarest, *Integrative Theology* (Grand Rapids: Zondervan, 1994), 175–77. See also *Catholic Encyclopedia* at http//www.catholic.org/encyclopedia/view.php?id=10395 (accessed December 15, 2009).

heart holy (*sic*). Regeneration is therefore essentially the communication of a new spiritual life, and is properly called a 'new birth.'"[10]

Within the reformed understanding of salvation, positional or definitive sanctification and progressive sanctification are inextricably linked. A proponent of this view argues that because of the unity of justification and sanctification, one is able to avoid the common errors of cheap grace (salvation without necessary change) and works-righteousness (holiness primarily dependant on the individual rather than God).[11] For the reformed thinker, it is untenable to suggest that someone could be regenerate yet still exhibit a carnal lifestyle. From the moment of conversion, the believer is growing in his declared holiness. Anthony Hoekema reflects this view concerning the new self:

> The new self described in the New Testament, therefore, is not equivalent to sinless perfection; it is *genuinely* new, though not yet *totally* new. The newness of the new self is not static but dynamic, needing continual renewal, growth, and transformation. A believer deeply conscious of his or her shortcomings does not need to say, Because I am still a sinner, I cannot consider myself a new person. Rather, he or she should say, I am a new person, but I still have a lot of growing to do.[12]

The sanctification process includes mortification (God breaking the dominion of sin and weakening the carnal desires) and vivification (the Holy Spirit enabling the new self to perform works that are pleasing to God and to demonstrate the renewing of God's image).[13] Regarding the need for the new self to progress in sanctification, here is what Calvin writes:

> This restoration does not take place in one moment or one day or one year; but through continual and sometimes even slow advances God wipes out in his elect the corruptions of the flesh, cleanses them of guilt, consecrates them to himself as temples, renewing all their minds to true purity

[10] B. B. Warfield, "Regeneration," in *Selected Shorter Writings of Benjamin B. Warfield,* ed. J. E. Meeter (Nutley, NJ: Presbyterian and Reformed, 1973), 2:323.

[11] Lewis and Demarest, *Integrative Theology,* 184.

[12] A. Hoekema, "Reformed View," in *Five Views on Sanctification,* ed. S. Gundry (Grand Rapids: Zondervan, 1987), 81–82.

[13] Lewis and Demarest, *Integrative Theology,* 185.

> that they may practice repentance throughout their lives and know that this warfare will end only at death.[14]

God guarantees to accomplish this transformation process in the life of the believer. The reason for this guarantee is that sanctification has as its final goal, the glory of God (Eph 1:4–6,12,14; Phil 1:9–11), and as its proximate goal, the perfecting of God's people (1 John 3:2).[15] Not only is sanctification assured, but so is the perseverance of the saints. Therefore, the believer can be certain that he will reflect Christ's image and will ultimately spend eternity in God's presence—all to the glory of God.

Wesleyan. Adherents of Wesleyanism generally believe there are two works of grace that exist. The first is that of conversion, whereby the believer experiences justification, regeneration, reconciliation, and initial sanctification; resulting from this first work of grace is the forgiveness of actual sins. The second work of grace is often called the second blessing or entire sanctification; typically equated with the baptism of the Holy Spirit, it is thought to remove original sin, thereby eradicating the carnal nature and enabling the Christian to live life without willful sin. The Christian who has experienced this second blessing will be filled with a heart of agape love for God and for others.

The cornerstone of Wesleyan theology is the focus upon this second work of grace. Wesley understood the Christian life as process-crisis-process: new birth—second blessing—continued growth in holiness. Here's what Wesley writes in his book *A Plain Account of Christian Perfection:*

> To this day both my brother and I maintained—(1) That Christian perfection is that love of God and our neighbor which implies deliverance from all sin; (2) that this is received merely by faith; (3) that it is given instantaneously, in one moment; (4) that we are to expect it, not at death, but *every moment;* that *now* is the accepted time, *now* is the day of this salvation.[16]

Moreover, Wesley held that the perseverance of the believer is dependent on his continued obedience and faith. Necessitated by this position is the view that the second work of grace could be lost due to neglect and that

[14] John Calvin, *Institutes of the Christian Religion* 3.3.9.

[15] Hoekema, "Reformed View," 88–89.

[16] J. Wesley, *A Plain Account of Christian Perfectionism* (London: Epworth Press), 41.

the first work of grace could be lost due to outright rebellion against God's commands and the rejection of one's personal faith in Him.

Victorious Life. This position has its roots in the Higher Life Movement of the 1850s and the Keswick Movement of England that began in 1875. Often the terms *victorious life*, *higher life*, and *Keswick* are used interchangeably when discussing the idea that God has called Christians to live a victorious life reflecting empowerment from the indwelling Holy Spirit to resist known sin and choose to walk in obedience to the Spirit. Advocates of this position often speak in terms of the *normal* Christian experience, which consists of living a life that clearly reflects the attitude and behavior of Jesus Christ. This way of living is contrasted with *subnormal* Christianity, which is typified by self-interest and consistent yielding to temptation.[17] H. W. Webb-Peploe, a leader in the Keswick Movement, summed up this perspective while speaking at a convention in 1890: "Before I expected failure, and was astonished at deliverance; now I expect deliverance, and am astonished at failure."[18]

The victorious life position suggests that sanctification occurs in three phases: *positional sanctification* (accepting Christ as Savior), which is realized through forgiveness of sin, justification, and regeneration; *experiential sanctification,* which begins with the crisis event of full surrender to the lordship of Christ and continues as a process throughout life, resulting in victory over sin; and *permanent (*or *complete) sanctification,* which occurs when a believer is transformed into the likeness of Christ in the age to come—also known as glorification.[19]

Believers are either average Christians (subnormal) or spiritual Christians (normal), in this perspective. The average Christian lifestyle is represented by Christians who live a defeated life, while the spiritual Christian lifestyle is the experience of those who fully surrender to God's leadership and live obediently out of loving response to Him. This view obviously places heavy emphasis on the individual's willingness to cooperate with God's work within him, in order to be freed from the desire to sin and the power of sin.[20] The normal Christian does not experience the eradication of the old nature but is empowered by the Holy Spirit to counteract its influence. He will not reach a state of perfection in his earthly life but will

---

[17] J. R. McQuilkin, "Keswick View," in *Five Views on Sanctification,* ed. S. Gundry (Grand Rapids: Zondervan, 1987), 151–52.

[18] S. Barabas, *So Great Salvation: The History and Message of the Keswick Convention* (London: Marshall, Morgan & Scott, 1952), 99.

[19] Lewis and Demarest, *Integrative Theology,* 182.

[20] Ibid.

be enabled to enjoy the possibility of consistent success in resisting temptation. Since the victorious life position supports the view of positional sanctification, it necessarily affirms the eternal security of the believer.

Dispensational View. There is much agreement between the reformed view of sanctification and the dispensational view. They find common ground in the following ideas: salvation is God directed; justification and sanctification begin at the point of regeneration; sanctification is both a definitive act and a process; sanctification involves sovereign grace and human responsibility; the baptism of the Holy Spirit occurs at the point of justification, resulting in the placement of the believer into the body of Christ; the believer is assured of eternal security; and sinless perfection cannot be attained until one enters heaven.

The two perspectives differ on a few significant items. The dispensational view, for instance, suggests that the old and new nature of man coexist in postregeneration. Thus, one may truly be a Christian yet living a *carnal lifestyle.* The believer, in this case, must willingly yield his life to God. At this point of surrender to the lordship of Christ (postconversion), the believer is empowered by the Holy Spirit to live a *spiritual lifestyle.*[21]

Dispensationalists place great emphasis on the infilling of the Holy Spirit as a result of one's "yieldedness." This infilling, in turn, enables the believer to grow spiritually and realize a state of fruitfulness reflective of the image of Christ. Walvoord puts it thus:

> The believer who is filled with the Spirit does not get more of the Spirit quantitatively, but rather the Spirit is able to minister in an unhindered way in the believer and in a sense has all of the believer. Accordingly, the issue is not one of getting more of the presence of God but rather of realizing the power and ministry of God's presence in the believer's life.[22]

From the dispensational perspective, this combination of the lordship decision and the daily infilling of the Holy Spirit results in the sanctification of the believer.

---

[21] For further information regarding the dispensational view, please refer to J. Walvoord, "Augustinian-Dispensation View," in *Five Views on Sanctification,* ed. S. Gundry (Grand Rapids: Zondervan, 1987), 197–238, and R. Gleason, "B. B. Warfield and Lewis S. Chafer on Sanctification," *Journal of the Evangelical Theological Society* 40 (1997): 241–56.

[22] Walvoord, "Augustinian-Dispensation View," 216.

DEFINING LIFE TRANSFORMATION

We have taken a brief tour of some of the different views on sanctification. It may prove helpful at this point to look at some specific definitions of "life transformation" (i.e., sanctification). Here is a sampling of how various thinkers describe it:

> Sanctification is our growth in Christ-likeness. It is a progressive experience covering our entire Christian lives from salvation to glorification. (Jerry Bridges)[23]
>
> The continuing work of God in the life of the believer, making him or her actually holy. By "holy" here is meant "bearing an actual likeness to God." Sanctification is a process by which one's moral condition is brought into conformity with one's legal status before God. It is a continuation of what was begun in regeneration, when a newness of life was conferred upon and instilled with the believer. In particular, sanctification is the Holy Spirit's applying to the life of the believer the work done by Jesus Christ. (Millard Erickson)[24]
>
> Sanctification is a progressive work of God and man that makes us more and more free from sin and like Christ in our actual lives . . . a part of the application of redemption that is a progressive work that continues throughout our earthly lives. It is also a work in which God and man cooperate, each playing distinct roles. (Wayne Grudem)[25]
>
> Sanctification [is] that gracious operation of the Holy Spirit, involving our responsible participation, by which He delivers us as justified sinners from the pollution of sin, renews our entire nature according to the image of God, and enables us to live lives that are pleasing to Him. (Anthony Hoekema)[26]

[23] J. Bridges, *Transforming Grace: Living Confidently in God's Unfailing Love* (Colorado Springs, CO: NavPress, 1991), 19.

[24] M. J. Erickson, *Christian Theology* (Grand Rapids: Baker, 1983), 980.

[25] W. Grudem, *Systematic Theology: An Introduction to Biblical Doctrine* (Grand Rapids: Zondervan, 1994), 746.

[26] Hoekema, "Reformed View," 61.

> I. They, who are once effectually called, and regenerated, having a new heart, and a new spirit created in them, are further sanctified, really and personally, through the virtue of Christ's death and resurrection, by His Word and Spirit dwelling in them: the dominion of the whole body of sin is destroyed, and the several lusts thereof are more and more weakened and mortified; and they [are] more and more quickened and strengthened in all saving graces, to the practice of true holiness, without which no man shall see the Lord.
> II. This sanctification is throughout, in the whole man; yet imperfect in this life, there abiding still some remnants of corruption in every part; whence arises a continual and irreconcilable war, the flesh lusting against the Spirit, and the Spirit against the flesh.
> III. In which war, although the remaining corruption, for a time, may much prevail; yet, through the continual supply of strength from the sanctifying Spirit of Christ, the regenerate part does overcome; and so, the saints grow in grace, perfecting holiness in the fear of God. (Westminster Confession) [27]

Some Common Threads

Several common threads are woven into this series of historical views and definitions that are important to note. First, life transformation begins with regeneration. Second, it is progressive and affects the whole person. Third, it involves a sovereign work of grace in the life of the believer that, coupled with a level of effort on his own part, results in a changed life. And finally, the transformation process is not complete until the regenerate one is glorified in his eternal state.

What Is the "Telos" of Life Transformation?

As you continue reading, we want to remind you of the question we asked above: What is life transformation? In attempting to answer this question, we looked at some historical developments in thought, along with resulting definitions and common threads that run throughout. If we

[27] Westminster Confession, n.p. Online: http://www.graceonlinelibrary.org/articles/full.asp?id =43|68|746 (accessed March 10, 2008).

are truly to understand life transformation, however, we must first answer the question, What is the aim or *telos* of life transformation? We must know the *telos* in order to develop a road map of the maturation process; we must have the end in mind as we journey.

Our understanding of the "destination" plays a vital part in how much we choose to value the process.[28] One writer puts it this way: "Persons eager to get on with their spiritual journeys will be quickly disillusioned if the identifiable guides cannot simply state the ultimate end. For us, clarity on the *telos* of sanctification appears crucial. And yet it is on this precise issue that there seems to be extensive conceptual confusion."[29]

This is certainly an accurate statement. When we look at the works of those who write about the doctrine of sanctification, and discipleship more generally, we find a variety of responses to our question. Some see Christ-likeness as the aim, while others advocate a more relational perspective that highlights the love of and intimacy with God. Some see moral transformation as displayed in one's personal holiness and purity as the goal, while others understand it to be living the Spirit-filled life. A yet further position holds that ruling with God in His kingdom through service is the prize possession of the one who is completely transformed.[30]

Though there is an element of truth in each of these traditions, we submit to you that the *telos* of life transformation is the restoration of the image of God in the life of the believer. The word *restoration* implies a process, and the phrase *image of God* conveys an absolute standard by which a disciple can measure his life. In the following chapter we will demonstrate from Scripture that life transformation is about the restoration of God's image in our lives.

Discussion Questions

1. Compare and contrast the different views on sanctification discussed in this chapter.
2. Create your own definition of sanctification and develop a supporting argument for it.
3. What do you understand the *telos* of sanctification to be? Why?

[28] Porter, "On the Renewal of Interest in the Doctrine of Sanctification," 416.

[29] Ibid., 417.

[30] R. Foster, *Streams of Living Water: Celebrating the Great Traditions of Christian Faith* (New York: HarperSanFrancisco, 1998).

CHAPTER 6

OVERCOMING INCONSISTENCIES FOR A CHANGE: THE POWER

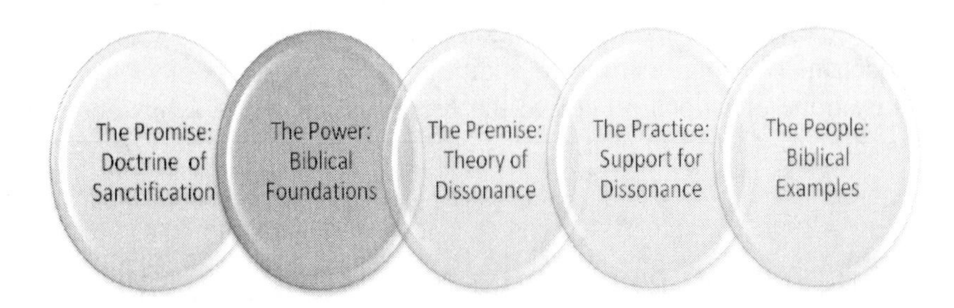

The writers and thinkers referred to in the previous chapter would certainly argue that their ideas about life transformation are founded upon Scripture. As you may guess, we would take exception with some of these views, yet it is not our objective to deconstruct each view or definition. We do believe, however, that it is important to discuss our understanding of the biblical foundations of life transformation.

When one begins to examine the doctrine of sanctification in Scripture, he discovers the concept of holiness. Truly, holiness lies at the center of life transformation. Upon careful thought, this makes perfect sense because holiness is God's crowning attribute.[1] As His children, we are being transformed into His likeness *(His holiness)* more fully each day. The Old Testament idea of holiness is, fundamentally, one of separation or consecration (the Hebrew noun *qōdeš* means "apartness," "holiness"; the verb *qādaš* means "to be consecrated," "to be holy"; and the adjective *qādôš* means "holy," "pure").[2] As Peterson puts it, "First and foremost, holiness in Scripture is a description of God and his character."[3] Countless passages speak of God as holy, and as the holy One, but Isa 57:15 says it particularly

[1] A. Pink, *The Attributes of God* (Grand Rapids: Baker, 1975), 41–42.

[2] G. R. Lewis and B. A. Demarest, *Integrative Theology* (Grand Rapids: Zondervan, 1994), 187.

[3] D. Peterson, *Possessed by God: A New Testament Theology of Sanctification and Holiness* (Downers Grove, IL: InterVarsity, 1995), 16.

well: "For thus says the high and exalted One who lives forever, whose name is Holy, 'I dwell on a high and holy place, and also with the contrite and lowly of spirit in order to revive the spirit of the lowly and to revive the heart of the contrite.'" His very name and nature are holy. In the Old Testament, the word *holiness* is applied to people, places, or objects that "are ceremonially holy because they are separate from what is profane and [are] devoted to God."[4] There is also a moral sense to holiness: God has called His children to be separate from what is evil or corrupt because He is holy and can tolerate nothing less (Lev 19:2). Indeed, God does call us to be holy as He is holy, yet is it truly possible to walk in perfect holiness on the earth? This vital question must be addressed as we discuss the doctrine of sanctification. In addition, in the sections below we will also examine questions related to the perseverance of the saints and the indwelling of the Holy Spirit.

SINLESS PERFECTION: IS THIS POSSIBLE?

The passage describing Isaiah's call to preach (Isaiah 6) is illustrative of both God's holiness and mercy. In this great text, Isaiah has a vision of the Lord sitting on His throne, encircled by seraphim (derived from the Hebrew *śārap,* meaning "to burn"). As the vision unfolds, the angelic beings cry out "Holy, Holy, Holy, is the LORD of hosts, the whole earth is full of His glory" (v. 3), and the temple begins to shake and fill with smoke. To these sights, Isaiah responds, "Woe is me, for I am ruined! Because I am a man of unclean lips, and I live among a people of unclean lips; for my eyes have seen the King, the LORD of hosts" (v. 5). In other words, in response to God's great holiness, Isaiah recognizes his great sinfulness.

Based on God's mercy and grace, one of the seraphim touches Isaiah's mouth with a burning coal and says, "Behold, this has touched your lips; and your iniquity is taken away and your sin is forgiven" (v. 7). The Lord then poses the question, "Whom shall I send, and who will go for Us?" (v. 8a). As one who has been made holy, both in position and purpose, Isaiah responds, "Here am I. Send me!" (v. 8b). In these verses God acts to judge that which is unholy, yet He also provides a means of cleansing and sanctification for the sinner.[5]

---

[4] Lewis and Demarest, *Integrative Theology,* 187.

[5] Peterson, *Possessed by God,* 19.

As we attempt to address the issue of sinless perfection, it is helpful to note others whom God called in the Old Testament—people like Noah, Abraham, Moses, and even the entire nation of Israel. In Gen 6:9, we read that Noah was a righteous man and blameless among the people, yet Gen 9:21 informs us that he was not free from sin (drunkenness and sexual immorality). Even Abraham, who was instructed to walk before God and be blameless (Gen 17:1), did not always display holiness (e.g., lying about Sarah being his sister [Gen 12:11–13; 20:6]; choosing a path of independence from God and conceiving a child with Hagar [Genesis 16]).

Then there is Moses, the chosen servant of God, who allowed his anger to consume him at Meribah and consequently was not allowed to enter the promised land (Num 20:24). This pattern of imperfection characterized the entire nation of Israel, as well. Through Israel, God had chosen to display His holiness so that the nations would know Him and glorify Him.[6] Yet, though holy in the sense that God had set her apart as an instrument of righteousness, morally Israel fell short.

King David poses the question, "LORD, who may dwell in your sanctuary? Who may live on your holy hill?" (Ps 15:1 NIV). He responds that it is the one who walks with integrity (*tāmîm*), demonstrates righteous behavior, speaks truth, and relates properly to others. In another psalm David asks, "Who may ascend into the hill of the LORD? And who may stand in His holy place?" (Ps 24:3). Again he answers his own question, saying that the one who has clean hands and a pure heart will worship the Lord and will receive righteousness from the God of his salvation. The emphasis in both passages is not on sinless perfection but on a life marked with integrity. These verses reveal "the life of the godly as one of progressive moral and spiritual development."[7]

Just as Israel was instructed to pursue holiness that would result in righteous living, so too are modern-day believers (Matt 5:6). What is most encouraging is that we are not left to seek holy living in our own power. We, like the Israelites, are reminded that the Lord sanctifies us in and through the power of His grace (Exod 31:13; John 17:17–19).

David himself is an excellent example of a child of God who desperately desired to walk in a manner pleasing to the Lord. He writes, "I will walk within my house in the integrity of my heart. I will set no worthless thing before my eyes. . . . A perverse heart shall depart from me; I will know no evil" (Ps 101:2–4). In another psalm, he writes, "I have hidden

[6] W. Kaiser, *Mission in the Old Testament* (Grand Rapids: Baker, 2000), 62–63.

[7] Lewis and Demarest, *Integrative Theology,* 189.

your word in my heart that I might not sin against you" (Ps 119:11 NIV). Yet we find David being confronted by Nathan about his adulterous acts with Bathsheba and the murder of Uriah.

According to Psalm 32, David resisted immediate confession of his sin before the Lord and was chastened physically and emotionally. In Psalm 51, he pleads with God, "Be gracious to me, O God, according to Your lovingkindness; According to the greatness of Your compassion blot out my transgressions. Wash me . . . and cleanse me from my sin. . . . Against You, You only, I have sinned, and done what is evil in Your sight, So that You are justified when You speak and blameless when You judge" (Ps 51:1–2,4). And then in Ps 32:5, we find the wonderful words of testimony: "I acknowledged my sin to You, and my iniquity I did not hide; I said, 'I will confess my transgressions to the LORD'; and You forgave the guilt of my sin." What glorious evidence of God's grace and mercy!

This sequence of passages may well represent the life pattern of the typical believer, who has been chosen by God and desires to live a holy life yet finds that rebellion and sin seem to persist.[8] It is refreshing however, to be reminded of the words spoken by the Lord about David: "I have found David the son of Jesse, a man after My heart, who will do all My will" (Acts 13:22). Though David did not always do the will of the Father perfectly, the Lord's words of affirmation to Solomon after David's death are significant: "And as for you, if you will walk before Me as your father David walked, in integrity of heart and uprightness" (1 Kgs 9:4b). The reality for the New Testament believer is the same as that for the Old Testament saint—sinless perfection is unattainable on earth, but continued transformation and perseverance are assured.

The writers of the New Testament clearly affirm the experience of those who lived under the old covenant. The absolute standard of holiness as measured by the character of God is beyond the reach of the believer. Remarkably, however, some argue that sinless perfection is indeed attainable during one's earthly sojourn. In making this argument, they often point to such passages as Matt 5:8, "Blessed are the pure in heart, for they shall see God," and v. 48, "Therefore you are to be perfect, as your heavenly Father is perfect." Yet the first of these verses refers to the believer encountering God in worship. Jesus is not requiring that the believer be absolutely holy to experience God richly in worship, but He is stating that the believer ought to be marked by the absence of deceit and false-

[8] K. Keathley, "The Doctrine of Salvation," in *A Theology for the Church*, ed. D. Akin (Nashville: B&H, 2007), 696.

hood (*katharos*—Lit., "clean," "clear," "pure") if he desires to enjoy God more fully. This beatitude is thus reminiscent of Psalms 15 and 24. The second verse from Matthew gives the often misunderstood directive "be perfect" (*teleios*). *Teleios* does not mean "sinless" but instead carries with it the idea of being complete or mature in growth and in mental and moral character. In the immediate context, the word *perfect* connotes the idea of maturity in love.[9]

We are also reminded of our propensity to sin in Matt 6:12 and Luke 11:4, where Jesus teaches the disciples how to pray. The inclusion of such phrases as "forgive us our debts" and "forgive us our sins" indicates that even the most committed disciples sin. Also communicating the reality of sin in the lives of God's children is the apostle John. In his first epistle he reminds us that we have an Advocate with the Father; this reality ensures that "if we confess our sins, He is faithful and righteous to forgive us our sins and to cleanse us from all unrighteousness" (1 John 1:9). Sinless perfection on earth would be wonderful, but biblical evidence does not seem to support this as a possibility.

Eternal Security: Once Saved, Always Saved?

The New Testament writers also affirm the perseverance of the saints. It is important to note that the issue of eternal security is part of the larger soteriological discussion. From a practical standpoint most Christians' perspective of salvation falls somewhere on a continuum between a man-centered approach and a God-centered approach. Those espousing a more synergistic approach argue that God has enabled humans to initiate the conversion experience by placing their own faith in Christ's finished work, while those on the monergistic end of the continuum deny any human initiation in the regeneration process.

You may be asking how this soteriological continuum applies to one's understanding of eternal security. On the one hand, those who believe they play a significant role in initiating a relationship with God (i.e., see themselves as the primary choosing agent in the salvific process) must also necessarily believe that they have the freedom to walk away from that same relationship. On the other hand, for those who believe that God is

[9] Lewis and Demarest, *Integrative Theology*, 190–91.

the primary choosing agent in the salvific process, it logically follows that the Christian does not have the freedom to renounce his relationship with God. In other words, if one's relationship with God is the result of human initiation, there can be no certainty of eternal security. Speaking to this issue, John tells readers that God does not desire His children to be uncertain about eternal life but rather desires that they would know it is a permanent relationship (1 John 5:11–12; John 10:28–29).

INDWELLING AND INFILLING OF THE HOLY SPIRIT

Another marker of the believer's permanent relationship with God is described by Paul in his letter to the church of Ephesus:

> In Him, you also, after listening to the message of truth, the gospel of your salvation—having also believed, you were sealed in Him with the Holy Spirit of promise, who is given as a pledge of our inheritance, with a view to the redemption of God's own possession, to the praise of His glory (Eph 1:13–14).

Paul speaks here of an event that occurs in tandem with one's conversion—the indwelling of the Holy Spirit. He uses the word "sealed" (*sphragizō*—lit., "to stamp [with a signet or private mark] for security or preservation") to indicate that the believer is the possession of God and is secure in His grace. The indwelling presence of the Holy Spirit is the believer's guarantee that his salvation is certain; it is also God's pledge that the salvation will be consummated.

Questions now arise pertaining to the essence of the Holy Spirit's indwelling presence: To what extent has the believer been indwelt? What is meant by the baptism of the Holy Spirit? Does Scripture (particularly Acts) indicate the need for or the availability of a second baptism? In order to answer these questions, we should begin with the promise that Jesus gave His disciples in Acts 1:5: "John baptized with water, but you will be baptized with the Holy Spirit not many days from now." *Baptism* here means "the outpouring of the Holy Spirit on believers."[10] Jesus' promise reflects John's words in Matt 3:11; Mark 1:8; Luke 3:16; and John 1:33,

[10] Ibid., 193.

but this baptism of the Holy Spirit was spoken of long before by the Old Testament prophets, as well (e.g., Ezek 36:27; 39:29; and Joel 2:28).

Is this outpouring of the Holy Spirit in the life of a believer a postconversion event, or is it simultaneous with conversion? Also, must one demonstrate pentecostal manifestations in order to be an authentic believer? In Acts 2, the disciples, though already believers, on the day of Pentecost receive the Holy Spirit and speak in tongues. In Acts 8, the Samaritans believe Phillip's message, after which the church in Jerusalem sends John and Peter to pray for them so that they might receive the Holy Spirit (there is no indication in this passage that they spoke in tongues). In Acts 10, Luke records Gentiles believing, receiving the Holy Spirit, and speaking in tongues prior to their water baptism. Finally, we read in Acts 19 how some of John the Baptist's disciples, hearing and believing Paul's proclamation of the gospel, are baptized, receive the Holy Spirit, and then speak in tongues and prophesy.

There are those who argue that what we see in Acts 2, 8, 10, 19—all accounts of the Holy Spirit being given to believers (accompanied by speaking in tongues in 2, 10, and 19)—is reflective of normative Christian practice and therefore proof that a second baptism of the Holy Spirit exists, with pentecostal manifestations present in most instances.[11] To refute this argument, one might point to the historical distinctiveness of each of these encounters as well as the descriptive, rather than prescriptive, nature of the book of Acts as a whole. At a minimum these accounts confirm that God was indeed accepting the Jews, Samaritans, Gentiles, and disciples of John into the Church on equal standing.[12]

We suggest that these accounts in Acts are indeed historically unique insofar as they mark the beginnings of the Church. The balance of the New Testament does not indicate a separation in time between believing and receiving the Holy Spirit. Also, most of the New Testament does not directly connect conversion and indwelling with pentecostal manifestations for all believers (e.g., 1 Cor 12:30).

The New Testament does, however, support the understanding that at conversion the new believer is indwelt fully with the Holy Spirit (Rom 6:3–4; Gal 3:27); it is not a partial indwelling, requiring a second work of grace or a "second blessing" at a later date. Paul asserts in 1 Cor 12:13,

[11] D. Smith, *A Handbook of Contemporary Theology* (Grand Rapids: Baker, 1992), 51–52.

[12] J. M. Hamilton, *God's Indwelling Presence: The Holy Spirit in the Old and New Testaments* (Nashville: B&H, 2006), 193. Also, see J. I. Packer, *Keep in Step with the Spirit: Finding Fullness in Our Walk with God* (Grand Rapids: Baker Books, 2005).

"For by one Spirit we were all baptized into one body . . . and we were all made to drink of one Spirit." In context, the apostle is describing the relationship among believers and how they function in service to God by using the spiritual gifts the Spirit has bestowed on them. In the above verse, he reminds the reader that the Spirit of God joins all believers to the body of Christ through the baptism of the Holy Spirit and, by necessary implication, through the regeneration of the individual. In this simultaneous moment with regeneration, God positionally sanctifies the new believer.

Paul writes in 1 Cor 6:11, "But you were washed, but you were sanctified, but you were justified in the name of the Lord Jesus Christ and in the Spirit of our God." Positional sanctification does not mean that new believers are sinlessly perfect, but it does mean that they are forgiven of their past sins and have perfect standing in God's holiness. Paul says as much when he greets the Corinthian believers: "To the church of God which is at Corinth, to those who have been sanctified in Christ Jesus, saints by calling" (1 Cor 1:2). At this moment of justification and positional sanctification, God fully forgives, fully accepts, fully indwells, and fully sets apart the believer for His glory and for use in His kingdom.

The New Testament also teaches the idea of experiential, or progressive, sanctification. This is the daily growth in the grace that God has bestowed in our lives as believers. It is the continual transformation of our lives to more accurately reflect God's image (Rom 8:29; Eph 1:4). It is our becoming in practice what God has purposed us to be. It is our fulfilling the good works that God has set out for us to accomplish in His power. This type of sanctification is a process rather than an instantaneous event.

Paul writes that we "are being transformed into the same image from one degree of glory to another" (2 Cor 3:18 ESV). In Eph 5:18 he issues the imperative, "be filled with the Spirit" (*plērousthe,* "be filled"; a present imperative, suggesting ongoing action). Though Scripture teaches a single baptism of the Holy Spirit (Eph 1:13; 4:30), it clearly affirms the ongoing filling of the Holy Spirit in the life of the believer. Millard Erickson explains:

> This is not so much a matter of our getting more of the Holy Spirit; presumably all of us possess the Spirit in his entirety. It is, rather, a matter of his possessing more of our lives. Each of us is to aspire to giving the Holy Spirit full control of our lives. When that happens, our lives will manifest whatever gifts God intends for us to have, along

with all the fruit and acts of his empowering that he wishes to display through us.[13]

A Closer Look in Acts

Another look at the book of Acts's witness to the presence of the Holy Spirit in the life of the believer would be helpful. In his record Luke describes "three distinct manifestations of the Spirit: the Spirit as the eschatological gift, the Christian life as characterized by the Spirit, and the particular fillings with the Spirit for inspired proclamation."[14] We have already discussed the Spirit as the eschatological gift in Acts 2; 8; 10; and 19. Elsewhere, particular Christians are characterized as being "full of the Spirit": Stephen ([*plērēs*] Acts 6:3,5; 7:55); Barnabas ([*plērēs*] Acts 11:24); and disciples ([*plēroō*] Acts 13:52). These individuals are, in other words, marked by the presence and fruit of the Spirit.

Luke also describes occasions of empowerment by the Holy Spirit. In Acts 2:4; 4:8,31; 9:17; and 13:9, he speaks of believers being "filled with the Holy Spirit" (*pimplēmi*). Each time someone is filled with the Spirit, great things occur—the powerful proclamation of the gospel, the restoration of Saul's sight and his ensuing proclamation, the bold rebuke and blinding of Elymas the magician. Seemingly, "Luke's use of the verb *pimplēmi* to describe a filling is reserved for temporary bursts of the Spirit's power."[15] In essence, he employs the term to depict the overwhelming power of the Holy Spirit at work in and through the life of the believer. This filling is temporary, repetitive, and distinct from the permanent indwelling of the Holy Spirit. To be clear, though, being filled with the Holy Spirit is not a second work of grace; it is simply the grace of God at work in the life of the individual who is surrendered to the Spirit's control.

The Battle Rages On in My Life!

The New Testament speaks clearly about the Holy Spirit's full indwelling presence in the life of the believer and the restoration process that He is accomplishing. The New Testament also affirms that the Spirit empowers believers to complete the good works that God has set out before them.

[13] M. J. Erickson, *Christian Theology* (Grand Rapids: Baker, 1983), 881–82.

[14] Hamilton, *God's Indwelling Presence,* 202.

[15] Ibid., 199.

For these scriptural truths we are thankful, yet many believers struggle daily with sin and with a lack of evidence of the transforming effects of sanctification.

Christians will often ask, "If I have been made new, then why am I battling my old habits?" This question is inevitable when discussing the believer's renewal. The answer lies in the "already–not yet dimension of Paul's eschatology."[16] As we have seen, the "already" refers to one's placement in the realm of the holy at conversion, based solely on Christ's substitutionary death and resurrection. The "not yet" of sinless life, however, awaits the consummation of one's salvation. Indeed, this interim period of time between conversion and consummation often causes the greatest amount of frustration in the life of the believer. Grudem reminds us that "sanctification is a progressive work of God and man that makes us more and more free from sin and like Christ in our actual lives."[17]

We want to make clear that God accomplishes this sanctifying work in the life of the believer, but we equally want to make plain that God expects the believer to participate fully in the process. Paul emphasizes this latter point in Rom 6:12–13: "Therefore do not let sin reign in your mortal body so that you obey its lusts and do not go on presenting the members of your body to sin as instruments of unrighteousness; but present yourselves to God as those alive from the dead, and your members as instruments of righteousness to God." Paul also urges believers to press on in the Christian life with the goal of full conformity, made possible by Christ's resurrection (Phil 3:9–15); here, the apostle was certainly looking "ahead to the completion of his salvation" and challenging other believers to do the same.[18] Paul also reminds the Colossians how they have laid aside the old self and put on the new self, which is being changed daily (Col 3:9–10). Likewise, the writer of Hebrews reminds us of those who have gone before as exemplars and challenges us to model similar behavior by laying "aside every encumbrance and the sin which so easily entangles us" (Heb 12:1a).

Peter is even more pointed about God's expectations: "As obedient children, do not be conformed to the former lusts which were yours in your ignorance, but like the Holy One who called you, be holy yourselves

---

[16] T. R. Schreiner, *New Testament Theology: Magnifying God in Christ* (Grand Rapids: Baker, 2008), 375.

[17] W. Grudem, *Systematic Theology: An Introduction to Biblical Doctrine* (Grand Rapids: Zondervan, 1994), 746.

[18] R. R. Melick, *Philippians, Colossians, Philemon*, NAC vol. 32 (Nashville: Broadman, 1991), 132.

also in all your behavior; because it is written, "YOU SHALL BE HOLY, FOR I AM HOLY" (1 Pet 1:14–16). It is only because we are children of God that we can have any hope of behaving in God-honoring ways. He is the One transforming us from the inside out and calling us to live holy lives while walking in the power of His grace. And as Paul reminds us, God is faithful in the believer's daily process of transformation: "No temptation has overtaken you but such as is common to man; and God is faithful, who will not allow you to be tempted beyond what you are able, but with the temptation will provide the way of escape also, so that you will be able to endure it" (1 Cor 10:13).

In our daily struggles with old sinful habits, we can be encouraged by the reality that "[we] are already holy in Christ," even though "the fullness of that holiness will not be [ours] until the day of redemption."[19] Today we stand humbly in the power of His amazing grace and wait with great expectation for what we will become.

The Restoration of the "Imago Dei"

Though none of us completely understands what it means, we do know that we will become like Christ. Ultimately, we will be fully restored so as to reflect perfectly the image of God.[20] Therefore, life transformation is the process of being restored to the *imago Dei* ("image of God") by means of the Holy Spirit's gracious and sanctifying work in the believer's life from regeneration through glorification. This definition assumes a change in one's behavior, thinking, passions, and motivations. Of course, the reality is that life transformation does not always occur in an invariant, sequential manner. In fact, it is often characterized by periods of positive change followed by apparent regression. This may be why, in part, Paul tells the Philippian church, "The things you have learned and received and heard and seen in me, *practice these things*, and the God of peace will be with you" (Phil 4:9, emphasis added). Growth in holiness never occurs by accident; it must be pursued.

Les Steele uses the anaology of a spiral to describe the formation process. Beginning with small circles at the base, the spiral moves in a deliberate manner that gradually encompasses a broader trajectory. This movement along the spiral is generally outward and upward, indicating a journey that delivers increasing spiritual growth, influence, and kingdom responsibility. Ultimately, Steele defines Christian formation as the "pro-

[19] Ibid., 375.

[20] A. Hoekema, *Created in God's Image* (Grand Rapids: Eerdmans, 1986), 31.

cess of becoming what we were first intended to be and are now allowed to be by the justifying work of the Holy Spirit."[21] Erickson's understanding of transformation is a similar idea; he writes that sanctification is the "continuing work of God in the life of the believer, making him or her actually holy. By 'holy' here is meant 'bearing actual likeness to God.'"[22]

In short, life transformation could be described as the soteriological process of being "remade" into the image of God (Rom 8:28–29; 2 Cor 3:18; Eph 4:23–24; Col 3:10). The believer is transformed, as Paul writes in Rom 12:2, involving a metamorphosis of the mind, indeed of the whole person;[23] the end result is something quite remarkable—Christlikeness. The writer of Hebrews says that Jesus Christ is an exact representation of the Father (Heb 1:3). It necessarily follows, then, that the believer is transformed to reflect more accurately Christ's image to a lost world, just as Christ reflects the Father and communicates His mercy plan to the nations.

How Do We Describe a Transformed Believer?

In the following section we examine select New Testament passages from the Gospels, the Pauline corpus, and the General Epistles that describe the qualities of a mature Christian, the process of maturation, and the impediments to Christian formation.

Life Transformation in the Gospels

The Gospels are the story of Jesus' incarnation, His earthly ministry, His death and resurrection. In this storyline, the believer finds comforting words on the one hand and disturbing words on the other. These words call Christians to forsake their former ways of living and demand full surrender to and worship of the only One who is worthy—Jesus Christ.

The Gospel of Matthew. Matthew emphasizes a lifestyle of obedience and righteousness. At the heart of his record is the Sermon on the Mount, wherein Jesus instructs the disciples on the actions and corresponding motivations of an ethical lifestyle. Christ addresses difficult life issues such

[21] L. Steele, *On the Way: A Practical Theology of Christian Formation* (Grand Rapids: Baker, 1990), 24.

[22] Erickson, *Christian Theology,* 967–68.

[23] Hoekema, *Created in God's Image,* 216.

as how one should respond to an enemy, deal with his thought life, value marriage commitments, maintain integrity in verbal agreements, handle financial resources, and act in interpersonal relationships. In Matt 6:33, Christ admonishes the maturing believer: "But seek first His kingdom and His righteousness, and all these things will be added to you." The believer responds to this command by prioritizing his life around the person and teaching of Christ, and what results is a lifestyle of obedience and righteousness.

The Gospel of Mark. One of the prominent themes relevant to Christian formation in the Gospel of Mark is suffering. Suffering is a necessary part of the restoration process. In suffering the Christian is forced to acknowledge a greater divine purpose than comfort. Mark records a pivotal conversation between Jesus and His disciples:

> And He began to teach them that the Son of Man must suffer many things and be rejected by the elders and the chief priests and the scribes, and be killed, and after three days rise again. And He was stating the matter plainly. And Peter took Him aside and began to rebuke Him. But turning around and seeing His disciples, He rebuked Peter and said, "Get behind Me, Satan; for you are not setting your mind on God's interests, but man's." (Mark 8:31–34)

In Jesus' rebuke of Peter, the reader finds a challenge to look at life, and particularly suffering, in a new way—a heavenly way. Jesus continues by addressing the entire crowd that has gathered and says, "If anyone wishes to come after Me, he must deny himself, and take up his cross and follow Me" (Mark 8:34). The maturing believer who issues a positive response to this radical invitation to join Christ in His sufferings is thereby enabled to grasp the sovereignty of God.[24]

The Gospel of Luke. Steele sees in Luke a focus on the believer's responsibility to act mercifully toward others: "To be about the business of God means to care for the uncared-for and to show mercy."[25]

Directly related to this idea is Luke's account of the parable of the Good Samaritan, which Jesus tells in response to a lawyer's question about receiving eternal life (Luke 10:24–37). This parable, and its subsequent interpretation, demonstrates that the authentic Christian will be marked by a sense of love and merciful actions toward others, especially toward

[24] J. Piper, *Let the Nations Be Glad* (Grand Rapids: Baker, 2003), 232.
[25] Steele, *On the Way,* 27.

the weakest and most defenseless portions of society. It also indicates that Jesus' gospel makes "no distinction" (Acts 15:9) between ethnicities and people of different social status.[26]

The Gospel of John. The first 12 chapters of John's Gospel record miraculous signs as evidence of Jesus being the Messiah. John then transitions Jesus' words to the disciples about living out the kingdom life. At the heart of this portion of John's writings is the Lord's Supper (John 13) and Christ's farewell discourse (John 14–17). Jesus discusses the role of the Holy Spirit in the believer's life, calls for total dependence on God; and admonishes believers to live in loving community with one another to demonstrate the character and nature of God.

Speaking to His disciples during their celebration of Passover, Jesus says, "A new commandment I give to you, that you love one another, even as I have loved you, that you also love one another. By this all men will know that you are My disciples, if you have love for one another" (John 13:34–35). Here there is an implicit call for believers to act and live within a community of faith, not for sectarian reasons but in order to attract unbelievers through such an observance of true Christianity. Moreover, within this community of faith, the believer is shaped, confronted, and conformed to a more accurate reflection of God's image. As Richards puts it, "We reach maturity as we bond with other believers, living together as Christ's church (Eph. 4:12–13)."[27]

According to the Gospels, Christians are called to live godly and righteous lives of self-denial, characterized by love and mercy toward others. This life should take place in Christian community, for God has designed the process of life transformation to occur within the context of relationships among believers. Rick Warren is right, therefore, when he says that "we need more than the Bible to grow; we need other believers. We grow faster and stronger by learning from each other and being accountable to each other."[28]

LIFE TRANSFORMATION IN THE PAULINE LETTERS

Paul's writings certainly focus on orthodoxy, that is, possessing right beliefs. However, his instruction does not allow a Christian to be merely theologically correct; a Christian must also live out his theological convictions. The book of Ephesians demonstrates Paul's approach. After spend-

[26] D. Bock, *Jesus According to Scripture* (Grand Rapids: Baker, 2002), 255–56.
[27] L. O. Richards, *A Practical Theology of Spirituality* (Grand Rapids: Baker, 1987), 23.
[28] R. Warren, *The Purpose Driven Life* (Grand Rapids: Zondervan, 2002), 134.

ing the first three chapters discussing right doctrine, in Eph 4:1 he writes, "Therefore I . . . implore you to walk in a manner worthy of the calling with which you have been called." In essence, Paul is saying that because one knows these right doctrines, he must make sure he is living in congruence with them. Orthodoxy is imperative but rather useless if it does not aid in producing orthopraxy in the Christian's life.

In Rom 12:2 Paul writes, "Do not be conformed to this world, but be transformed by the renewing of your mind, so that you may prove what the will of God is, that which is good and acceptable and perfect." As the believer allows the Holy Spirit to replace his false perspectives on life with godly thinking, his way of living and doing will change. When the Holy Spirit redeems and indwells a person, He begins the process of changing every part of that person's being.

Becoming Complete. One cannot examine the Pauline writings without noting the theme of becoming complete in Christ. In Col 2:9–10a, Paul writes, "For in Him all the fullness of Deity dwells in bodily form, and in Him you have been made complete." When conveying the purpose of his ministry to the Colossian church, Paul informs them, "We proclaim Him, admonishing every man and teaching every man with all wisdom, so that we may present every man complete in Christ. For this purpose also I labor, striving according to His power, which mightily works within me" (Col 1:28–29). Similarly, Paul describes his intercessions for the Corinthian church by writing, "This we also pray for, that you be made complete" (2 Cor 13:9b). Elsewhere, in Eph 4:11–15, Paul tells the church that God has given spiritual gifts and spiritual leaders to them in order to aid their individual and corporate spiritual growth. It was the apostle's desire that all believers become complete or mature in their faith—both in their beliefs and in their actions.[29]

Shared Responsibility. As already mentioned, Paul believed this life-transformation process must include the active participation of the believer. His admonition in 1 Thess 5:21–24 makes this point apparent:

> But examine everything carefully; hold fast to that which is good; abstain from every form of evil. Now may the God of peace Himself sanctify you entirely; and may your spirit and soul and body be preserved complete, without

[29] W. Klein, "Perfect, Mature," *Dictionary of Paul and His Letters,* ed. G. F. Hawthorne and R. P. Martin (Downers Grove: InterVarsity, 1993).

> blame at the coming of our Lord Jesus Christ. Faithful is He who calls you, and He also will bring it to pass.

Clearly detectable in Paul's instruction here is the assumption of individual responsibility. His directions include the tasks of personal reflection ("examine everything, hold fast to what is good") and self-discipline ("abstain from every form of evil"). He also promises his readers, though, that the Holy Spirit will bring about over time a more accurate reflection of God in their lives ("now may the God of peace Himself sanctify you entirely . . . at the coming of our Lord Jesus Christ"). Inherent in Paul's writings is a recognition of the complementary relationship between the wondrous work of the sanctifying Spirit of God and the responsibility of the child of God—"work out your salvation with fear and trembling" (Phil 2:12).[30]

God's intention before the foundation of the world was that His children be "holy and blameless before Him" (Eph 1:4). He guarantees by His very nature that this will eventually occur in a believer's life. In voicing his certainty that God will be faithful to complete that which He began in him, Paul affirms his confidence in this ultimate hope. Perhaps he summarizes it best in his first letter to the Corinthians: "For now we see in a mirror dimly, but then face to face; now I know in part, but then I will know fully just as I also have been fully known" (1 Cor 13:12).

LIFE TRANSFORMATION IN THE GENERAL EPISTLES

Pauline writings emphasize right beliefs, while the General Epistles focus to a greater degree on right practice. Certainly, biblically accurate thinking is important in the Christian formation process, as we are "transformed by the renewing of . . . [our] mind" (Rom 12:2); however, such thinking is useless without the corresponding actions and attitudes. For this reason, the writers of the General Epistles direct their attention to the living out of biblical teachings. The Holy Spirit even led Peter to use the word "behavior" five times in his first epistle (1 Pet 1:15; 2:12; 3:1–2,16).

The Writings of Peter. In 1 Pet 1:13–16, Peter bridges the chasm between the mind and actions of the believer:

> Therefore, prepare your minds for action, keep sober in spirit, fix your hope completely on the grace to be brought to you at the revelation of Jesus Christ. As obedient children, do not be conformed to the former lusts which were

[30] J. Piper, *Future Grace* (Sisters, OR: Multnomah, 1995), 291–92.

> yours in your ignorance, but like the Holy One who called you, be holy yourselves also in all your behavior; because it is written, "YOU SHALL BE HOLY, FOR I AM HOLY."

Peter readily accepted God's command to behave in a holy manner. In his admonition to wives, he even stressed that such holy behavior can be an evangelistic tool: "Be submissive to your own husbands so that even if any of them are disobedient to the word, they may be won without a word by the behavior of their wives, as they observe your chaste and respectful behavior" (1 Pet 3:1–2). It is apparent, then, that the theme of holy living as a result of the life-transformation process that takes place when one follows Jesus is paramount for Peter.[31]

The idea of holiness encompasses the radical transformation of the entire person: "In becoming sanctified and being sanctified, every facet, feature, attribute, and detail of a person is exposed and rejuvenated, rendered new."[32] Peter experienced what it meant to deny Christ; he felt the separation that resulted from his callous refusal to identify fully with Jesus. He also experienced the joy that follows the restoration of fellowship with Christ. These experiences must have sparked in Peter a passion to live a righteous lifestyle, to enjoy intimacy with the Father, to be used by the Master, and to reflect the glory of his Maker to a lost people.

The Letter to the Hebrews. The writer of Hebrews reinforces the idea that right living is the result of a supernatural work in the life of the believer by Jesus Christ, who is the superior sacrifice and the mediator of the new covenant. He portrays Christian formation as a believer's pilgrimage from life as a foreigner in a strange world to eternal dwelling in heaven, in the presence of the Lord. This pilgrimage includes difficulties, persecutions, temptations, and the traversing of unknown paths as one follows God's direction for his life. Luther writes that "we are always traveling and must leave behind us what we know and possess, and seek for that which we do not yet know and possess."[33] According to the author of Hebrews, this is exactly what Abraham's life was like:

> By faith Abraham, when he was called, obeyed by going out to a place which he was to receive for an inheritance; and he went out, not knowing where he was going. By

[31] R. Michaels, "1 Peter," *Dictionary of the Later New Testament and Its Developments,* ed. R. P. Martin and P. H. Davids (Downers Grove: InterVarsity, 1997).

[32] W. Stringfellow, *The Politics of Spirituality* (Philadelphia: Westminster, 1984), 41.

[33] G. Ebeling, *Luther: An Introduction to His Thoughts,* trans. R. A. Wilson (Philadelphia: Fortress, 1970), 162.

> faith he lived as an alien in the land of promise, as in a foreign *land,* dwelling in tents with Isaac and Jacob, fellow heirs of the same promise; for he was looking for the city which has foundations, whose architect and builder is God. (Heb 11:8–10)

Life transformation is indeed a pilgrimage with one's Maker through the adventure called life. It is a life lived with the assurance of complete restoration to the *imago dei* and the certainty of eternity in the presence of one's Creator.

The Writings of James. On examination of the General Epistles, James's letter stands out as perhaps the most practical text in the New Testament. In writing to the dispersed Jews, he begins by acknowledging that the Christian life is filled with various trials and difficulties. He instructs his readers to "consider it all joy, my brethren, when you encounter various trials, knowing that the testing of your faith produces endurance. And let endurance have its perfect result, so that you may be perfect and complete, lacking in nothing" (Jas 1:2–4). James understood that trials in one's life aid in the Christian formation process when one chooses to respond with a right attitude. In essence, these trials are catalytic events that can cause one to rethink his priorities, commitments, and even theology.

James gives the reader an excellent summation of how one's relationship to Christ should produce a change in his behavior:

> But prove yourselves doers of the word, and not merely hearers who delude themselves. For if anyone is a hearer of the word and not a doer, he is like a man who looks at his natural face in a mirror; for once he has looked at himself and gone away, he has immediately forgotten what kind of person he was. But one who looks intently at the perfect law, the law of liberty, and abides by it, not having become a forgetful hearer but an effectual doer, this man will be blessed in what he does. (Jas 1:22–25)

A maturing Christian, James says, will carry out the Word of God in his everyday life. Those who are immature will hold the Word as unimportant and fail to measure accurately their actions and attitudes against it; what results is a superficial form of Christianity. For James, true Christianity results in Christlike action and love toward those who cannot return the favor given to them (Jas 1:27).

James also makes clear that true faith is more than a set of beliefs or a way to make meaning out of life. True faith produces good works. After all, he asks, "What use is it, my brethren, if someone says he has faith but he has no works? Can that faith save him?" (Jas 2:14). The implication for Christian formation is that faith must produce a lifestyle that is reflective of Christ's lifestyle. James sums up this point by referencing the example of Abraham:

> Was not Abraham our father justified by works when he offered up Isaac his son on the altar? You see that faith was working with his works, and as a result of the works, faith was perfected; and the Scripture was fulfilled which says, "AND ABRAHAM BELIEVED GOD, AND IT WAS RECKONED TO HIM AS RIGHTEOUSNESS," and he was called the friend of God. You see that a man is justified by works and not by faith alone. (Jas 2:21–24)

James's use of the word *justify* in this context is different from Paul's use of the term in Rom 5:1, where it means "to declare a sinner righteous." Here, James uses the word "justify" to mean "to show to be righteous." In other words, one's faith in Christ's atoning work on the cross leads to a righteous standing in the sight of God, while the ensuing good works that derive from this new faith demonstrate that he is, indeed, righteous.[34]

The General Epistles paint a picture of life transformation as the believer's pilgrimage from infancy and immaturity in the faith to completeness in relationship with God and the living out of a Christlike lifestyle. It is a pilgrimage filled with challenges, difficulties, sufferings, joys, victories, opportunities, and, most of all, intimate interaction with one's Savior. It is a journey toward holiness and wholeness.

The Role of the Holy Spirit in Christian Formation

The underlying assumption in the passages presented above is that the Holy Spirit is well at work in the believer's life. According to John, the role of the Holy Spirit is to convict people of sin, righteousness, and judgment (John 16:8). He is also the One who guides people into all Truth (John 16:13) and exposes the lies of Satan. The Holy Spirit teaches the believer and calls to his remembrance the Word of God (John 14:26). The Holy Spirit trains him to discern between good and evil (Heb 5:14). And ultimately, according to John 8:32, He sets the believer free through the

[34] B. Demarest, *The Cross and Salvation* (Wheaton, IL: Crossway, 1997), 263–64.

Word: "You will know the truth and the truth will make you free." This means, among other things, freedom from erroneous ways of thinking about one's life, one's self, and one's future. It is important to remember that such transformation comes only through being justified by the imputation of Christ's righteousness.[35]

TWELVE MARKS OF CHRISTIAN TRANSFORMATION

Below is a list of twelve marks of life transformation characteristic of believers striving to reflect more accurately the image of God.[36]

Twelve Marks of Life Transformation

Accurately handles the Word of God	*2 Tim 2:15; 3:16–17*
Commits to living life in biblical community	*Matt 18:12–17; Acts 2:42–47*
Discerns God's will	*Rom 12:2, Matt 12:50*
Discovers and uses spiritual giftedness	*Romans 12; 1 Corinthians 12; Eph 4:11–16; 1 Pet 4:9–10*
Exhibits godly character	*1 Pet 1:15; Gal 2:20; 5:22–24*
Fulfills the Great Commission through active participation in personal evangelism and missions	*Matt 28:19–20; Acts 1:8*
Glorifies God through a lifestyle of worship	*Psalm 122, 150; Rom 12:1–2; Heb 10:25*
Displays a kingdom-minded lifestyle	*Matt 6:19–21; 1 Cor 3:11–15; 2 Cor 5:1–2,10*
Loves God wholeheartedly / Loves others compassionately	*Matt 22:36–39; 1 Corinthians 13*
Seeks and makes decisions based on wisdom	*Prov 4:7; Ps 111:10*
Practices spiritual discipline/training for godliness	*1 Tim 4:7; Matt 6:16–18; 1 Thess 5:16–18*
Willingly sacrifices for the sake of the gospel	*Acts 20:24; 2 Cor 11:23–28*

Though discussing the marks of life transformation is helpful, we cannot possibly be exhaustive in our description. We therefore prefer simply to describe Christian maturity as a regenerate person's act of living a life that

---

[35] J. Piper, *Counted Righteous in Christ* (Wheaton, IL: Crossway, 2002), 80.

[36] For the many conversations surrounding these ideas and the formulation of this list, we are much appreciative to Chip Evans.

more accurately reflects the glory and image of God in his behavior, thinking, passions, and motivations.

Life Transformation in the Trenches

It is one thing to discuss biblical truths with broad strokes, but if we do not answer the enduring question of how life transformation occurs in daily life, then we fail to achieve our purpose. Take the story of Billy, for example. He was 18 years old and beginning to walk with the Lord. He was emerging from the high school days characterized by weekend parties and sexually active relationships. He had become active in a college Bible study and was meeting with a mentor on a regular basis. As they met each Friday, the mentor would ask him a series of questions pertaining to his spiritual disciplines and his actions during the previous week. It eventually surfaced that Billy had been regularly viewing pornography. When Billy finally shared his struggle and his desire to change with his mentor, he was broken over his sin of lust. In the ensuing months he memorized Scripture and avoided the Internet—yet he still found himself struggling in this area of his life. He was so frustrated because he felt like it all rested on him to beat this sin, but he seemed to be losing the battle.

This story is not unique. It is, however, the story that is often untold when a believer shares his testimony. It is a story that contains confessions of struggle, sin, frustration, and confusion. So often believers are not certain what their role is in the life-transformation process and what the role of the Holy Spirit is. They are unsure how to live in the power of God's grace while also living with the reality that they play some part in their sanctification.

Wayne Grudem speaks directly to this issue when he writes, "The role that we play in sanctification is both a passive one in which we depend on God to sanctify us, and an active one in which we strive to obey and take steps that will increase our sanctification."[37] He goes on to describe sanctification as a process that may include advancement and retreat in various areas of our lives. He even states that a believer who "has bad teaching, lacks good Christian fellowship, and pays little attention to God's Word and prayer, may actually go for many years with very little progress."[38]

[37] Grudem, *Systematic Theology*, 754.
[38] Ibid., 750.

How is this possible? Simply because we fail to participate! We fail to have a heart for holy living.

This discussion conjures up a math formula from high school days—R x T = D (Rate x Time = Distance). Let us explain. We have seen people come to Christ who make what might be labeled an "all-out commitment." They begin to grow spiritually at a rapid pace and seem to surpass those who have been believers for years or even decades.

How is this possible? It's simple—they are growing at a rapid rate because they are choosing to saturate their minds with God's Word and are abstaining from that which is evil.

Their R (rate of spiritual growth) is almost mind boggling to those of us who have become accustomed to apathetic Christians. We do not expect rapid growth so we find ourselves surprised when we see it. Please understand that we are not trying to reduce life transformation to a human-driven formula, but we do want to stress our role in the growth process. One writer puts it into good perspective for us:

> A proper view of sanctification must mediate between God's initiative and man's response. To this end it might be helpful to distinguish between the certainty of spiritual growth and its degree. The former is guaranteed by the sovereign grace of God brought to bear by the indwelling Holy Spirit. The latter is determined by the believer in co-operation with dependence on the Spirit. Every Christian must experience some measure of spiritual growth . . . but the pace of this may be inconsistent and its degree widely varied from one person to the next.[39]

PHILIPPIANS 2:12–13

The apostle Paul gives us an even clearer picture in Phil 2:12–13, where he writes, "So then, my beloved, just as you have always obeyed, not as in my presence only, but now much more in my absence, work out your salvation with fear and trembling; for it is God who is at work in you, both to will and to work for His good pleasure." In this passage Paul does not contradict his words in Romans 5, which speak of one's salvation as the result of faith in Christ's atoning work. Here he clearly affirms that it is God who is at work, but he reminds the believer of the scriptural require-

[39] R. Gleason, "B. B. Warfield and Lewis S. Chafer on Sanctification," *Journal of the Evangelical Theological Society* 40 (1997): 255.

ment to cooperate with God in this transformation process (just consider all of the moral commands in the New Testament).

This idea of cooperation is echoed in Jas 2:24. There James states that "a man is justified [*dikaioō*—to show as just or innocent] by works and not by faith alone." James is reminding the believer that the way he chooses to live on a daily basis reflects the genuineness of his relationship with Christ. If one truly loves Him, then he will live a deliberate God-honoring life, made possible by the indwelling Holy Spirit and a willing human spirit.

Grudem notes that while believers do not share an equal role with God in sanctification, there is an expectation that the children of God will act in "ways that are appropriate to [their] status as God's creatures."[40] In other words, the Christian will live a life of loving obedience in accordance with God's precepts and commands. This is a daily, willful commitment to the authority of Christ in one's life. Such is the essence of working out one's salvation.

Romans 6

In Romans 6, Paul is more specific about how this deliberate living comes to pass for the Christian. In essence, he indicates that life transformation occurs through mortification of the old nature and vivification of the new nature.

Lewis and Demarest helpfully note that in this passage there is a "Godward aspect" and a "manward aspect."[41] In Rom 6:3–5, Paul writes that, in conversion, believers are united with Christ in both His death and resurrection:

> Or do you not know that all of us who have been baptized into Christ Jesus have been baptized into His death? Therefore we have been buried with Him through baptism into death, in order that as Christ was raised from the dead through the glory of the Father, so we too might walk in newness of life. For if we have become united with Him in the likeness of His death, certainly we shall also be in the likeness of His resurrection.

From a Godward aspect, "this means that Christians died to the old life of sin (vv. 6–8a); in its manward aspect it means that they must reckon

[40] Grudem, *Systematic Theology*, 753.
[41] Lewis and Demarest, *Integrative Theology*, 195.

themselves dead to sin (v. 11a) by allowing sin no place in their lives (vv. 12–14)."[42] This is what is meant by mortification—putting to death the old nature. But just as Christ did not remain in the grave without new life, neither do we remain without a new life—a new nature. From a Godward aspect, this means believers are united with Christ in His resurrection and consequently are made alive in Christ (Rom 6:8b). In "its manward aspect it signifies that they must reckon themselves alive to God (v. 11b) and become servants to righteousness (vv. 13b, 18b, 19b, 22)."[43]

Realistically, for a believer to resist sin and live righteously, he must make a daily and deliberate choice to deny himself, take up his cross, and follow Christ. From a practical perspective, this necessitates that the believer walk with the Lord and seek an intimate relationship with Him.

We are convinced that three streams of activity will feed this transformation process—practicing spiritual disciplines (such as worship, Bible study, prayer, meditation, fasting), living in biblical community, and serving as Christ's ambassador to the world. As believers are actively engaged in these activities, they will be shaped by the Holy Spirit through His Word, His people, and His service.

EXPANDING OUR SEARCH FOR UNDERSTANDING

We have devoted attention in the last two chapters to the biblical foundations of life transformation because we believe the Bible is the best source for understanding how God conforms us to His image. Though we have looked primarily at prescriptive passages, we also think that the narratives shed some light on how biblical characters were transformed. We will examine some of those stories in chapter 9.

As we have thought about the ways people are changed spiritually, cognitively, affectively, and behaviorally, our interest has been piqued by a simple question, asked from a human perspective: What experiences cause a person to make changes in their spirituality, thinking, emotions, and ways of acting?

In our pursuit of answering this question, we have examined numerous theories and poured over research and writings from various disciplines

---

[42] Ibid.

[43] Ibid., 195–96.

such as anthropology, sociology, biology, philosophy, and education. Several ideas emerged from these lines of inquiry, but the one that makes best sense and seems to align well with biblical teaching is a theory from the education field. It is known as cognitive dissonance theory. In the following chapter, we will examine this theory in detail and demonstrate its connection to how people change.

Moving forward, we invite you to join us in our expanding search for understanding what God uses to transform His people.

Discussion Questions

1. Compare your positions on sinless perfection, perseverance of the saints, indwelling and infilling of the Holy Spirit, and second works of grace with the positions described in this chapter.
2. Using the biblical texts, describe your understanding of what characterizes a mature believer. Develop your own marks-of-transformation chart.
3. What role does the Holy Spirit play in the sanctification process, and what role does the believer play?

CHAPTER 7

OVERCOMING INCONSISTENCIES FOR A CHANGE: THE PREMISE

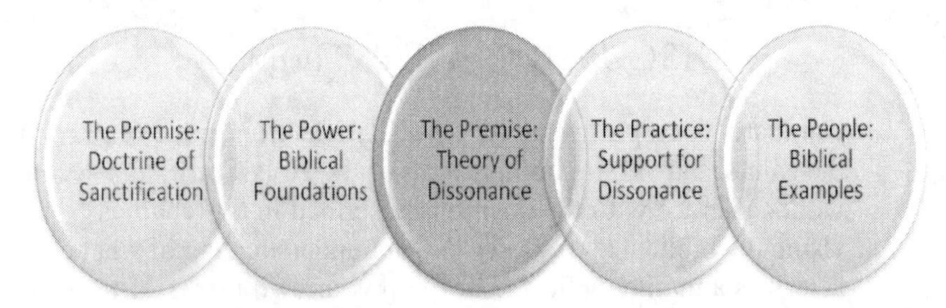

THE TENSION IN TAYLOR

He was just 16 years old when God changed his life forever. Fed up with the stagnant faith he had seen in those around him, he decided to move from the comfortable home where he lived with his parents in Yorkshire to the slums of Drainside. This place more than lived up to its name, with poverty and illness everywhere, affecting those whom society had largely, and in most cases gladly, forgotten. His time in Drainside served as a jarring realization of both the raw needs of people and the severity of living in a harsh, unforgiving environment.

The experience also prepared him for the eventual life of a missionary, engaged in taking the gospel where it had never been before—inland China. After years spent translating the Bible and pouring out his life for the Chinese people, this man, now seasoned in the realities of a life lived in sacrifice, returned to England for a visit. What he experienced at a church worship service horrified him. There was no desecration of the Bible, no compromise of key beliefs, no problem at all, according to those around him; however, he described the scene this way: "On Sunday, June 25th, 1865, unable to bear the sight of a congregation of a thousand or more Christian people rejoicing in their own security, while millions are perishing for lack of knowledge, I wandered out in the sands alone in great spiritual agony."[1] What Hudson Taylor, the founder of the China Inland Mission, could not bear to look on was the sight of hundreds celebrating God's grace in their own lives while doing little to nothing to see that same grace realized among those who had never heard the gospel.

Like so many of the students in our ministries, Taylor assumed that those who know Christ live to make Him known. When the actions of people fail to match what they say they believe, one can count on experiencing frustration and irritation, as Taylor did. Consistency must be achieved, but the matrix of a person's beliefs, attitudes, and actions is intricate. Our difficult job is to find a way to bring each of these areas into concert with one another, so that what is affirmed in the statements of believers is exhibited in their lives.

We usually say, "Live what you believe," but what if we switched it up? What if by getting them to live through the realities of challenging service, sacrifice, and mission, we could get students to gain the knowledge that Taylor acquired? What if, through experiences like these, students were forced to wrestle with their own convictions and life and consequently began to believe that such activities have immense value and are worth the whole of their lives?

We want to offer an approach that views student short-term mission offerings as one of the mechanisms that can be used to identify and confront these inconsistencies, while also serving as a directed discipleship method to facilitate student transformation.

Understanding the Tension

As we sat on the bench with the lake in view and loud students everywhere, Laura tried to help me understand her struggles. She said that if she was going to "live for Christ," she needed to stop coming up with "excuses," but she just could not figure out how that was going to happen. In a close echo of Paul's words in Rom 7:19, she said, "I know what I should be like, but I just can't seem to do it. I want to, but I can't."

If we are going to see growth take place in students like Laura, we have to begin by identifying how and why inconsistency like this happens. We could simply say that there is inconsistency because she and all the rest of us are sinners—and we heartily agree that this—and this alone is

[1] J. Pollock, *Hudson Taylor and Maria* (Grand Rapids: Zondervan, 1962), 127.

the root issue. At the same time, however, we must also recognize that the ways in which this "falleness" expresses itself in our day-to-day thinking, functional beliefs, and actions are numerous.

In our various ministry contexts, we all deal with this discrepancy between what people believe and what they do. With students and adults, "it is not at all unusual for them to attend church, hold conservative beliefs, and fail completely to develop attitudes, values, and behaviors which are not in harmony with the gospel."[2] Saying one thing and doing another is nothing new, but *how* does this happen? How do the most deeply rooted ideas—those most important—fail to influence how believers live? Answering these central questions will help us delineate how short-term mission experiences might play a part in forming consistent, mission-driven students.

POSSIBLE EXPLANATIONS FOR THE TENSION

Since the teenage years present so many opportunities to meet inconsistencies head-on, numerous proposals have focused on why adolescents, in particular, face such a struggle in maturing through these challenges in route to maturity.[3] In identifying the scope of developmental theories, Ted Ward notes that "the acceptability and utility of developmental theories derive largely from their relatedness to one another and their compatible fit within the larger picture."[4] Ward's "ecological" understanding of the value of these spheres of life indicates that in the "universe" of human thought, attitude, and action, each of these interdependent arenas (e.g., intellectual/cognitive, faith, moral) have bearing on the whole person.[5]

Therefore, even if one looks at these issues through the individual lenses, for example, of Jean Piaget's Genetic Epistemology, Lawrence Kohlberg's Moral Development paradigm, or James Fowler's Faith Development approach, he notices that each distinct perspective on growth shares some key traits with the others. As Duffy Robbins puts it, "In a sense, it is like reading from the journals of different expedition members

[2] L. Richards, *A Theology of Christian Education* (Grand Rapids: Zondervan, 1975), 63.

[3] For an integrative discussion of these approaches, see D. Robbins, *This Way to Youth Ministry* (Grand Rapids: Zondervan, 2004), 193–243.

[4] T. Ward, foreword to *Nurture That Is Christian,* ed. J. Wilhoit and J. Dettoni (Grand Rapids: Baker, 1995), 14.

[5] Ibid.

giving their personal accounts of the same adventure."[6] One of the common qualities, as Steven Patty has observed, is that adolescents try to make sense of life and what they encounter by developing "structured wholes," or consistent, integrated networks of understanding:

> These structures of understanding are coherent because developmentalists assume that each individual is naturally inclined to integrate the pieces of her understanding into a whole. Like Gestalt psychologists, developmentalists see an innate drive in people to fit the various pieces of life into larger, more inclusive ways of thinking, even if doing so changes the nature of the thinker.[7]

In order to make sense of all that they think, feel, do, and generally experience, adolescents go through a process of evaluating where new information and ideas should fit in the network of thought and life. According to Piaget's approach, for example, they will seek equilibration through assimilation or accommodation. In each of these theories, the impetus for successful transformation during this tension-resolution process is tied to the need to confront and resolve tension in thoughts, attitudes, and/or actions *through critical reflection*.

It seems, then, that a model of ministry intent on teenage development should, at least, include two key components. First, we need a holistic philosophy that recognizes the interconnectedness of the whole of the student; second, there must be a healthy emphasis on guiding students through a process of critical thinking and reflection.

THE NEED: AN APPROACH THAT INFLUENCES THE WHOLE STUDENT

We need an approach to the tension-resolution process and learning that seeks transformation of the whole student: his thinking, attitudes, and behavior. In *Transforming Worldviews*, the late anthropologist Paul Hiebert argues:

[6] Robbins, *This Way to Youth Ministry*, 193.

[7] S. Patty, "A Developmental Framework for Doing Youth Ministry," in *Reaching a Generation for Christ,* ed. R. Dunn and M. Senter (Chicago: Moody, 1997), 72.

> We need to return to a biblical view of transformation, which is both a point and a process; this transformation has simple beginnings (a person can turn wherever he or she is) but radical, lifelong consequences. It is not simply mental assent to a set of metaphysical beliefs, nor is it solely a positive feeling toward God. Rather it involves entering a life of discipleship and obedience in every area of our being and throughout the whole story of our lives.[8]

He goes on to offer the view that true spiritual transformation can only happen if the individual's worldview is transformed, which includes "the foundational cognitive, affective, and evaluative assumptions and frameworks a group of people makes about the nature of reality which they use to order their lives."[9] In this paradigm, all that a person experiences is filtered through these beliefs, feelings, and values (worldview), which then leads to behavioral expressions in keeping with the worldview. This "filter," therefore, dictates whether a person will act on truth or refuse to do so.

If student sanctification by worldview transformation is to take place, we must expend effort helping them think and reflect critically about "the deep, unexamined assumptions we have and thereby make explicit what is implicit."[10] Exposing students to other worldviews and cultures is another key piece in getting them to assess their own basic conceptions about reality.

We must also place emphasis on opportunities and approaches that intentionally promote critical thinking and evaluation. Considering how a student develops and shapes his thoughts, feelings, and evaluative criteria is crucial to helping him resolve the tension between what is said and what is lived, but just as important is the ability to guide that student in critical thought about the discord that exists in his heart and life in order to initiate eventual resolution. Therefore, we will explore an educational model that concentrates on the whole of thoughts, attitudes, beliefs, and actions, while placing the accent on bringing these areas into concert through focus on the area of tension and essential resolution.

[8] P. Hiebert, *Transforming Worldviews* (Grand Rapids: Baker, 2008), 310.

[9] Ibid., 25–26.

[10] Ibid., 319.

A Holistic Approach: Dealing with Dissonance

In his work *A Theory of Cognitive Dissonance*, the late Stanford University social psychologist Leon Festinger offered an approach to understanding disharmony among an individual's beliefs and the driving need to seek consistency. Festinger argued that when the "cognitions" asserted are accompanied by opposing cognitive or behavioral elements inconsistent with those cognitions, the result is an observable tension, which he labels "dissonance." The character of the tension between conflicting cognitions and the need for resolution prompted Festinger to look for an organizing structure in which to place these realities and a method to evaluate them.

Engaging What We Believe, Feel, and Do

A primary focus of Festinger's study was the relationship between "cognitions." He explains that these cognitions, which may be consistent or inconsistent in relationship to one another, should be given the title "knowledges":[11]

> These elements refer to what has been called cognition, that is, the things a person knows about himself, about his behavior, and about his surroundings. These elements, then, are "knowledges," if I may coin the plural form of the word. Some of these elements represent knowledge about oneself: what one does, what one feels, what one wants or desires, what one is, and the like. Other elements of knowledge concern the world in which one lives: what is where, what leads to what, what things are satisfying or painful or inconsequential or important.[12]

This understanding of "cognition," or "knowledges," makes clear that "cognition is not something discrete from attitudes, values, opinions, or feelings."[13] These individual cognitions compose the matrix of beliefs, values, and actions (see fig. 7.1); however, it is the nature and importance of

[11] L. Festinger, *A Theory of Cognitive Dissonance* (Stanford, CA: Stanford University Press,1957), 9.

[12] Ibid.

[13] M. Snapper, "Motivation for Learning Faith-Knowledge," in *Christian Approaches to Learning Theory,* ed. Norman DeJong (Lanham, MD: University Press of America, 1984), 161.

the relationship between these "knowledges" that is at the heart of the theory.

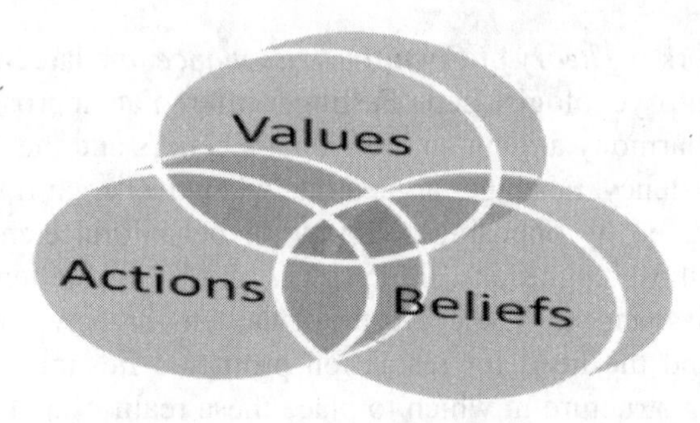

Figure 7.1: The Link Between Knowledges/Cognitions

In considering these relationships, Festinger submits three possible connections. First, two elements may be in congruent relationship with one another. This relationship is defined by Festinger as cognitive *consonance*. However, the nature of the relationship between cognitions might be *dissonant*. In this situation Festinger argues that the resulting "discomfort" will prompt the student to seek resolution and elimination of the dissonance. He likens this need for resolution to the self-preserving drive to satisfy hunger.[14] A third possible association between elements of knowledge may be *irrelevance*. Here one cognition has no direct bearing on the other. For example, a person may both know how long it takes mail to travel from New York to Paris and understand that a hot summer is a positive factor for Iowa's corn crop.[15] While each of these cognitions is held by the same person, they do not have a direct association. Figure 7.2 displays further examples of these three possible relationships between cognitions.

Of these three patterns, dissonance is of primary concern to Festinger. In order to understand it more clearly, he looked at the factors that determine the degree of the experienced dissonance.

THE DEGREE OF TENSION

Festinger found two primary dynamics that determine the magnitude of dissonance. First, the prominence of each belief is a determinant. Philip Zimbardo uses the illustration of a person who does not want to die prematurely but also smokes cigarettes. Zimbardo observes that the thought "'I don't want to die before my time' is dissonant with continuing to

[14] Festinger, *A Theory of Cognitive Dissonance*, 4.
[15] Ibid., 12.

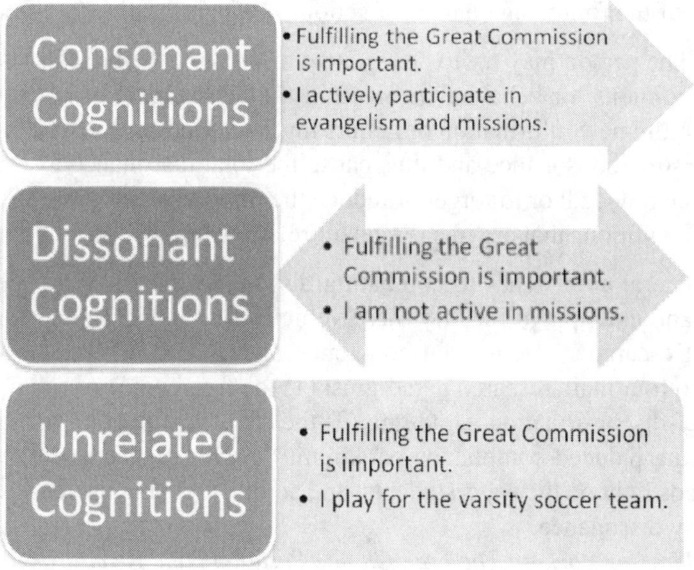

Consonant Cognitions
- Fulfilling the Great Commission is important.
- I actively participate in evangelism and missions.

Dissonant Cognitions
- Fulfilling the Great Commission is important.
- I am not active in missions.

Unrelated Cognitions
- Fulfilling the Great Commission is important.
- I play for the varsity soccer team.

Figure 7.2: Examples of Relationships Between Cognitions

smoke. But if it were not important to a smoker that he or she might die of lung cancer (because the person is 80 years old and has already lived a full life), then little dissonance would be produced by the two cognitions."[16] Here the amount of dissonance is directly tied to the importance of the cognitions.

The second factor that influences the degree of dissonance is the number of cognitions that are simultaneously discordant. In Zimbardo's illustration above, the smoker has only two cognitions in dissonant relationship. However, if he were to add the belief that his cigarettes "have less tar and nicotine," the consonant cognitions would outweigh those that are dissonant. Adding consonant cognitions should thus achieve the goal of alleviating dissonance.

How People Battle the Tension

Festinger observed three methods for alleviating dissonance, a provocative example of which appears in his work *When Prophecy Fails*. Focusing upon the phenomenon of increased devotion by "religious" groups

[16] P. Zimbardo and M. Leippe, *The Psychology of Attitude Change and Social Influence* (Philadelphia: Temple University Press, 1991), 108.

following an unfulfilled prophecy, he noted that members of these groups take one of the following courses of action:

> The person may try to change one or more of the beliefs, opinions, or behavior involved in the dissonance; to acquire new information or beliefs that will increase the existing consonance and thus cause the total dissonance to be reduced; or to forget or reduce the importance of those cognitions that are in a dissonant relationship.[17]

These general approaches to combating dissonance take several specific shapes, and attempts to identify these vehicles for alleviating tension are varied. Researchers Eddie Harmon-Jones and Judson Mills categorize them into four main research paradigms: (1) the free-choice paradigm, (2) the belief-disconfirmation paradigm, (3) the effort-justification paradigm, and (4) the induced-compliance paradigm.[18] Each of these research patterns sheds light on the ways students, and adults, try to handle the stresses caused by dissonance.

Looking for Backup: The Free-Choice Paradigm and Reassurance. The free-choice research perspective focuses on what takes place in the individual after he has made a decision. The theoretical basis for this approach is outlined by Harmon-Jones and Mills:

> Difficult decisions should arouse more dissonance than easy decisions, because there will be a greater proportion of dissonant cognitions after a difficult decision than there will be after an easy one. Because of this, there will be greater motivation to reduce the dissonance after a difficult decision. Dissonance following a decision can be reduced by removing negative aspects of the chosen alternative or positive aspects of the rejected alternative, and it can also be reduced by adding negative aspects to the rejected alternative. Altering the aspects of the decision alternatives to reduce dissonance will lead to viewing the chosen alternative as more desirable and the rejected alternative as less desirable. This effect has been termed

[17] L. Festinger, H. Riecken, and A. Schachter, *When Prophecy Fails* (New York: Harper & Row, 1956), 26.

[18] E. Harmon-Jones and J. Mills, *Cognitive Dissonance* (Washington, DC: American Psychological Association, 1999), 5–10.

> *spreading of alternatives,* and the experimental paradigm has been termed the *free-choice paradigm.*[19]

Festinger calls attention to the individual's need to feel that he has selected the proper alternative; to meet this need, he will seek *postdecision reassurance*. Festinger maintains a sharp distinction between the terms "conflict" and "dissonance," arguing that whereas before the choice is finalized, conflict is experienced as the person deliberates between two attractive options, after the choice is made, "he is now committed to the chosen course of action. It is only here that dissonance exists."[20] The manner in which this process takes place can be subdivided into three courses of action.

First, the individual may revoke the decision, psychologically. To pull this off, he must convince himself that, though having made a bad decision, he would choose another option if given the chance. Festinger also notes that the individual could deduce that "circumstances" forced him to select that original option. This revoking tactic is cyclical in that it reverts to conflict, which leads to eventual recurrent dissonance.

As a different course of action, the individual could change his beliefs about the alternatives decisions. Here the advantages of the chosen activity or the apparent deficiencies of the unselected option would join the cognition pool. This, again, is the idea of adding cognitions in the hope of alleviating dissonance.

Finally, the subject may pursue the establishment of what Festinger labels "cognitive overlap."[21] Here is how Jack Brehm and Arthur Cohen define the term: "The extent to which the alternatives have attributes in common. It is obvious that as the proportion of common attributes increases, the proportion that can be dissonant with the choice decreases. Therefore, the amount of dissonance created by the choice will decrease."[22] In order to ease postdecision dissonance, the individual may establish or contrive similar cognitions. The establishment of these similarities allows for traits to be discovered or invented for the chosen alternative. This provides reassurance that the chosen course is seen as the "proper" one.

In an effort to extend and clarify the idea of cognitive overlap, Brehm and Cohen wrote *Explorations in Cognitive Dissonance*. While agreeing with Festinger on the major premise of the theory and its findings, the psy-

---

[19] Ibid., 6.

[20] Festinger, *A Theory of Cognitive Dissonance*, 38.

[21] J. Brehm and A. Cohen, *Explorations in Cognitive Dissonance* (New York: John Wiley & Sons, 1962), 37.

[22] Ibid.

chologists wanted to specify certain decision-making factors that lead to the dissonance in the first place. Thus, they added two essential concepts to the theory, the first of which concerns the *role of commitment*:

> A person is committed when he has decided to do or not to do a certain thing, when he has chosen one (or more) alternatives and thereby rejected one (or more) alternatives, when he actively engages in a given behavior or has engaged in a given behavior. Any one or a combination of these behaviors can be considered a commitment.[23]

Once an individual has committed himself to a definite course of action, he must produce attitudes and behavior in keeping with that commitment.

Closely connected to the idea of commitment is the concept of *volition*—Brehm and Cohen's second addition to the theory. They contend that there is an essential link between the occurrence of tension and the ability, or perceived ability, to choose among alternatives. In fact, they observe that "the magnitude of dissonance resulting from a choice is directly proportional to the degree of volition in making the choice."[24] The import of Brehm and Cohen's two concepts can be observed in the following summative statement: "Commitment provides a specification of the conditions under which one cognition follows from the obverse of another. . . . The addition of the notion of volition may perhaps allow for the further provision of the exact point at which a dissonant relationship will create a psychological tension of some consequence."[25] These ideas help to elucidate how dissonance is provoked. From this perspective, the commitment of the individual, along with the ability to select an alternative course of action, creates the optimal environment for dissonance to occur and be resolved.

Struggling with Ideas: The Belief-Disconfirmation Paradigm. Tension in life and thought are also provoked when someone encounters information that does not mesh with what he believes to be true. Harmon-Jones and Mills encapsulate the possible reactions one might have to these new, incongruent ideas: "If the dissonance is not reduced by changing one's belief, the dissonance can lead to misperception or misinterpretation of the information, rejection or refutation of the information, seeking support from those who agree with one's belief, and attempting to persuade others

[23] Ibid., 7.
[24] Ibid., 210.
[25] Ibid., 300.

to accept one's belief."[26] The attempt to limit contact with adverse ideas, and people who hold to them, is aptly labeled *selective exposure*. Emory Griffin observes that "people avoid information that is likely to increase dissonance. Not only do we tend to select reading material and television programs that are consistent with our existing beliefs, we usually choose to be with people who are like us."[27] Avoidance and careful selection ensure that one rarely, if ever, finds himself in a situation that will foster dissonance. Furthermore, if he has altered beliefs, or added consonant beliefs in an effort to eradicate the tension, he may try to surround himself with people and ideas in league with these new beliefs and behaviors.

Social psychologists have labeled the attempt to maintain these convictions, and avoid "infiltration" of contrary ideas, "confirmation bias."[28] This bias manifests itself when people look at evidence that contradicts what they hold to be true and "find a way to criticize, distort, or dismiss it so that they maintain or even strengthen their existing belief."[29] In our student ministry context, we might call this the "whatever syndrome." We may try faithfully to offer a student the truth about the reality of their need for Christ, but because they are blinded to their need for Him, they may simply reply "whatever."

This is not simply a superficial rejection, as neuroscientists have discovered. Researcher Drew Westen, for example, examined the reaction of people to opposing political personalities and views during the 2004 U.S. presidential campaign. He monitored people by magnetic resonance imaging (MRI) while they were trying to process dissonant or consonant information about the candidates. The MRI results found that

> the reasoning areas of the brain virtually shut down when participants were confronted with dissonant information, and the emotion circuits of the brain lit up happily when consonance was restored. These mechanisms provide a neurological basis for the observation that once our minds are made up, it is hard to change them.[30]

Individuals such as these may attempt to surround themselves with persons and messages that affirm their decision and, in so doing, connect se-

[26] Harmon-Jones and Mills, *Cognitive Dissonance*, 6–7.

[27] E. Griffin, *A First Look at Communication Theory,* 2nd ed. (New York: McGraw-Hill, 1994), 486.

[28] C. Tavris and E. Aronson, *Mistakes Were Made* (Orlando, FL: Harcourt, 2007), 18.

[29] Ibid., 18.

[30] Ibid., 19.

lective exposure behavior with the need to seek post-decision reassurance, as outlined above.

Valuing Through Sacrifice: The Effort-Justification Paradigm. We have all heard, and probably said ourselves, "If you have to work hard to get something, you appreciate it more." The effort-justification approach to dissonance reduction, simply stated, argues just that. According to Cooper: "Voluntarily spending time, money, emotional, or physical effort arouses the uncomfortable tension state of dissonance, which can be reduced by enhancing the value of what the effort is for."[31] The connection between the magnitude of effort given to these "voluntary" activities and the alteration in attitudes is best conceptualized by Elliot Aronson's "justification of effort" theory, which resembles Festinger's work.

In his book *The Social Animal*, Aronson maintains that "if a person goes through a difficult or a painful experience in order to attain some goal or object, that goal or object becomes more attractive."[32] The degree of difficulty in attainment, therefore, is directly associated with the level of appreciation for the activity.

Believing Through Doing: The Induced-Compliance Paradigm. The induced-compliance paradigm explores the idea that "dissonance is aroused when a person does or says something that is contrary to a prior belief or attitude."[33] Closely connected is the dissonance-easing method called *minimal justification*. Aronson offers the following snapshot of minimal justification theory:

> Saying is believing. That is, dissonance theory predicts that we begin to believe our own lies—but only if there is not an abundance of external justification for making the statements that run counter to our original attitude. . . . If a person changes his attitudes because he makes a public statement for minimal external justification, that attitude change will be relatively permanent. . . . The individual is changing the attitudes because he has succeeded in *convincing himself* that his previous attitudes were incorrect.[34]

Here the tactic for attitude change diverges significantly from a behavioral approach, in that cognitive dissonance theory upholds a less-is-more ap-

[31] J. Cooper, *Cognitive Dissonance* (Los Angeles: SAGE, 2007), 165.

[32] E. Aronson *The Social Animal,* 3rd ed. (San Francisco: W. H. Freeman, 1980), 134–35.

[33] Harmon-Jones and Mills, *Cognitive Dissonance*, 8.

[34] Aronson, *The Social Animal*, 122.

proach to incentives and motivational rewards: the less incentive that is offered, the more the value that is placed on the action—rather than on the compensation received for doing it.

Festinger and James Carlsmith sought to substantiate this idea with their "$1/$20 Experiment." To do this, they enlisted 71 male subjects—referred to as *S*—who were students at Stanford University. Once in the lab, each subject was given a dull and tiring assignment to perform repeatedly.

After one hour the experimenter asked the subject to assist in an additional chore—telling a potential female subject of the supposedly fascinating nature of the task he had just performed. An incentive to perform this exercise in "counter-attitudinal advocacy" was offered to two distinct groups within this subject pool, with the third group functioning as a control. One of the experimental groups was given one dollar to tell the lie, while the other was offered twenty dollars to carry out the request. At the conclusion of the experiment, the researchers got some remarkable results:

> In short, when an *S* was induced, by offer of a reward, to say something contrary to his private opinion, this private opinion tended to change so as to correspond more closely with what he had said. The greater the reward offered (beyond what was necessary to elicit the behavior) the smaller was the effect.[35]

That is, they discovered that the subjects asked to lie about the "boring" task for this minimal amount of compensation (one dollar) did experience dissonance. However, dissonance reduction was achieved by altering one element to be consonant. In other words, by claiming to enjoy the task (public statement), the subject altered his view of the task in a favorable direction (private opinion).

The implication of these findings for those of us hoping to see students' perspectives change is that "if your ultimate goal is to get others to *like* or *agree with* the behavior you've compelled them to do, then the *less* inducement you need to gain behavioral compliance, the better. The less inducement, the more the private attitude will change in the direction of the induced compliant behavior."[36] Rather than support the idea that

---

[35] L. Festinger and J. Carlsmith, "Cognitive Consequences of Forced Compliance," *Journal of Abnormal and Social Psychology* 58 (1959): 208.

[36] Zimbardo and Leippe, *The Psychology of Attitude Change and Social Influence*, 110.

incentives will lead to lasting change, Festinger's findings indicate that unnecessary rewards may actually be detrimental to real transformation. A summary of distinctive elements found in each of these research paradigms is offered in figure 7.3.

Research Paradigm	Distinctive Activities	Alleviation Method
Free-Choice Paradigm	▶ Removing negative aspects of chosen alternative ▶ Removing positive aspects of rejected alternative	Post-Decision Reassurance
Belief-Disconfirmation Paradigm	▶ Avoiding ideas, or people, that conflict with chosen beliefs and actions ▶ Surrounding oneself with ideas, or people, that agree with chosen beliefs and actions	Selective Exposure
Effort-Justification Paradigm	▶ Voluntarily expending time, energy, or financial resources for something ▶ The greater degree of these that are expended, the higher degree of appreciation for the task and outcome	Justification of Effort
Induced-Compliance Paradigm	▶ Performed action can change belief ▶ Minimizing the degree of incentive offered to perform the action	Minimal Justification

Figure 7.3: Research Paradigms for Examining Alleviation Methods

Insights such as these about how those involved in our ministries experience and deal with tension should shape our thinking about how we, in turn, can help them through this struggle.

The Connections: A Bridge Between Theory and Practice

What form this thinking takes, as it influences our strategies, planning, curriculum, and discipleship efforts, will be the true test of its value. In the next chapter we will discuss some ways these ideas are already being put to use—in part, in youth ministry and short-term mission—while keeping in mind that our ultimate goal is an unshakeable consistency of life and character for our students and ourselves.[37] A Christlike character that lives to make His freedom known to the captives, for celebration of His glory among the nations (Isa 61:1; Luke 4:18).

Discussion Questions

1. Detail Festinger's understanding of how various cognitions or "knowledges" are related.
2. Discuss the four paradigms for alleviating dissonance presented in this chapter.
3. In your ministry, how do you see students process dissonance in their lives?

[37] T. Lane and P. Tripp, *How People Change* (Greensboro, NC: New Growth, 2006), 18.

CHAPTER 8

OVERCOMING INCONSISTENCIES FOR A CHANGE: THE PRACTICE

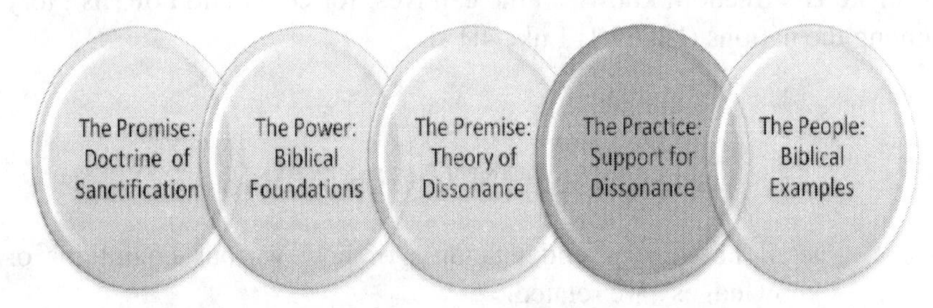

SUPPORT FOR THE PRACTICES

Conversing with a seasoned leader and researcher, we asked for confirmation of a relationship between short-term principles and dissonance theory. Without hesitating, he said, "Short-term mission *is* dissonance theory. That's what it's all about."[1] He elaborated that an approach focusing on life and perspective change—through coming to grips with the discrepancy between what should be and what is—needs to interact with ideas about dissonance. Thus, we set out to see if student ministry and short-term mission thinkers, as well as the relevant mobilizing ministers and agencies, showed any support for the concepts of dissonance theory.

MAKING THEM UNCOMFORTABLE: SUPPORT FOR STIRRING UP DISSONANCE

The need for students not only to struggle with concepts for themselves but also to seek a resolution through a directed critical thinking process is commonly noted in many youth ministry models. For example, Fernando

[1] From a casual conversation.

Arzola says that, particularly for urban youth, his Socratic "reflection-action praxis" directs students "through intentional dialogue and a progression of questions."[2] He argues that "this encourages and challenges youth to wrestle with the issue and seek the answer for themselves, instead of simply giving them an answer."[3] Confronting students with a distressing challenge through which to struggle is a "transformational" impetus in this approach.

In their work *The Godbearing Life*, Kenda Dean and Ron Foster note that it is crucial for students eventually to reach a point of consistency in their life with Christ. However, they emphasize that "discoveries" of greater cohesion between student actions and beliefs take place through a deliberate provocation of dissonance and disequilibrium:

> Typically these discoveries take place when I am a little off balance, a little uncertain, a little more punctured and vulnerable than I care to admit. Christian teaching artfully fosters this creative disequilibrium, seeking an intentional loss of footing for the sake of reorganizing the self's structure.[4]

The ability of the youth leader, or discipler, to nurture teenagers through this time of struggle is crucial because it is in this pivotal life-stage that will likely face their first large-scale "event" or crisis.[5]

The key to healthy development during this stage, as Byron Kehler sees it, is pushing students out of their "comfort zone" and into "challenge zones"; a leader's role is to encourage students to willingly "choose, and then stay, in their own challenge zone."[6] Likewise, Kehler offers a problem-posing, "stretching" educational aim that compels students to engage in activities and thought that they may not normally prefer, or choose, in order that they may experience the development or "growth" that only happens in this "challenge zone."[7]

Rick Lawrence also believes that these "crises" in a student's life are key to eventual maturity and writes about them in relation to outreach approaches:

---

[2] F. Arzola, *Toward a Prophetic Youth Ministry* (Downers Grove, IL: InterVarsity, 2008), 54–55.

[3] Ibid., 55.

[4] K. C. Dean and R. Foster, *The Godbearing Life* (Nashville: Upper Room Books, 1998), 160–61.

[5] Ibid., 167–68.

[6] B. Kehler, "Facilitating Experiential Learning," in *Impact: Student Ministry That Will Transform a Generation,* ed. S. Patty (Nashville: B&H, 2005), 134.

[7] Ibid.

> In practical terms, "as-we're-doing-it ministry" means scaring kids—in a good way. Jesus-centered outreach is all about asking them to do something scary: create something completely new (a worship service for the whole church?), serve in a setting far outside their comfort zone (a workcamp [*sic*]or missions trip?), or to reach out to people whose problems are beyond their ability to solve (not just feeding the homeless, but learning their stories?).[8]

He further suggests that, as youth pastors, we should infuse our ministries with "controlled crises," which he labels "Planned Direct Crisis Experiences." These "Planned Direct Crisis Experiences can include workcamps [*sic*], mission trips, service projects, retreats, and wilderness adventures. A new environment, challenging responsibilities, new relationships, and lots of time—that's a great equation for plunging kids into a crisis so they can embrace who they really are. And it really 'works.'"[9] From Lawrence's perception, outreach, mission, and service do a great deal to compel students to assess who they are and who they want to become. Crises of the types he describes can be the channels through which some of this assessment begins.

Another approach, targeted at STM in particular, is Terry Linhart's adaptation of Laura Joplin's experiential education paradigm. In his article "Planting Seeds: The Curricular Hope of Short-Term Mission Experiences in Youth Ministry," Linhart notes:

> Despite the diversity of perspectives, opinions, anecdotal observations, and theories regarding short-term mission trips, there remains little that we know about the effects (both on those who go and those host/receive) from these trips and experiences. Participants continue to report them as significant experiences (Rahn & Linhart, 2000), yet researchers have been unable to clearly describe the nature of the significance.[10]

Based on his survey of various studies dealing with both youth and involvement in short-term missions, Linhart attempts to "generate [a] substantive theory about what was happening on short-term mission trips and

[8] R. Lawrence, ed., *Jesus-Centered Youth Ministry* (Loveland, CO: Group, 2007), 117.

[9] Ibid.

[10] T. Linhart, "Planting Seeds: The Curricular Hope of Short-Term Mission Experiences in Youth Ministry," *Christian Education Journal* 2 (2005): 257.

avoid mere description," while also allowing "participants to freely depict the trip as they experienced or lived it."[11]

To accomplish his aim, Linhart embarked on a case study of the Northern Community Church short-term youth mission participants, hoping to observe emerging "categories and themes" found in the actions, writings, and statements of student participants. Some of these themes resemble the approaches and tenets of dissonance theory. The first such theme Linhart identified he labeled "focusing for passionate service."[12] To illustrate, he pointed to the preparatory schedule before the trip—seven months in length—that included accountability, homework assignments, and cultural training.

The second theme he labeled "acting in cross-cultural encounters." Linhart observes that "the students interfaced with people from a different culture, one which valued a new set of cultural practices, signs, symbols, gestures, and interpretations with which the students were not familiar (Hall, 1997). The exposure to the new culture created disequilibrium as the students tried to understand the cultural differences."[13] For the students, he argues, moving out of the so-called comfort zone "forced awareness of selfishness that they had never noticed before."[14]

A third theme Linhart observed and identified is the "support structure and feedback from adults." While the support and feedback on the field was daily and routine, "The moment the trip concluded, the support and feedback structures of the trip were removed from the students' lives."[15] Precisely for this reason the prolonged posttrip practices and structures are critical to producing sustained change and learning.

This is where the need for an approach like Joplin and Linhart's becomes evident. Here, in summary version, are the five steps of Linhart's model:

1. Focus: Anticipating the experience
2. Action-Reflection: Engaging in the experience
3. Support-Feedback: Sharing in the experience
4. Debrief: Dissecting the experience
5. Learning Transfer: Linking the experience with life[16]

[11] Ibid., 259–60.
[12] Ibid., 261.
[13] Ibid., 262.
[14] Ibid.
[15] Ibid., 265.
[16] See ibid. for Linhart's outline of these movements.

The emphasis of this approach is on guiding students through this ongoing "action-reflection" process that has as its goal "learning transfer"—integrating what has been learned, seen, reinforced, and assessed into daily life, for the purpose of transformation.[17] For this to happen, those around the student must link arms with him and walk him through the experience, offering positive selective exposure and reassurance.

SURROUNDING THEM: SUPPORT FOR SELECTIVE EXPOSURE

The pivotal issue here is that we all know students (and adults, for that matter) who avoid our calls for ministry involvement like the plague. Forget meeting the challenge or crisis; many times, they do not even want to know about it. Dissonance theory would designate this as an attempt to establish selective exposure. Sean Dunn paints an all-too-familiar picture of students who attempt to alleviate tension this way: "People may not be pleased with their sin and immaturity, but often they are too detached to put forth an honest effort to see those things change. Instead they isolate themselves from the people in their life who may challenge on these issues, and they work overtime to keep their relationships on shallow levels so that their sin is not discovered."[18] In this case the student is sure that isolation from these ideas and people will place him beyond the reach of any relationship that might remind him of his need for biblical awareness and action. Therefore, he will select and maintain relationships at a shallow level in order to avoid dissonance arousal and to find acceptance among those who already believe as he does.

This need for acceptance can be a key force behind students' carefully controlling their network of relationships. As Andy Stanley puts it:

> This is why some of our students can act so spiritual at youth group and live like the devil on the weekends. They want to fit in, and they are willing to adapt themselves to different environments in order to gain the acceptance they crave. Bottom line, their choice of friends has more to do with their desire to be accepted than a list of char-

[17] C. Clark and K. Powell, *Deep Justice in a Broken World* (Grand Rapids: Zondervan, 2007), 108–9.

[18] S. Dunn, *Bored with God* (Downers Grove, IL: InterVarsity, 2004), 50.

> acteristics they've drawn up. They don't choose their friends. They gravitate toward acceptance.[19]

According to Stanley, if students are surrounding themselves with unbelieving or disobedient adults and peers, then their own choice to "live like the devil" is going to be reinforced, not challenged.

For Doug Fields, concepts similar to selective exposure can, however, become a tool for positive student ministry—and specifically mission outcomes. If the student surrounds himself with those affirming of his desire to imitate Christ, then these same influences might serve as adult or peer models. If when choosing to participate in a mission event a student feels uncoerced, then he will look for others to affirm his decision. This is a prime opportunity for leaders to "model" missional attitudes and actions so that these relationships can help mold students' attitudes and subsequent preferred actions.[20]

Modeling has the potential to function in the parent-child, ministry leader–student, and peer-to-peer contexts.[21] Larry Richards maintains that there is a need within discipleship structures to engage the learner with "multiple models."[22] There is also a need for "group support" for ministry-engaged youth—"providing a supportive body relationship with other Christian kids who are committed to and personally active in sharing Christ themselves."[23] Richards goes on to argue that these groups serve as "*the* context for support and encouragement and stimulation to live Christ's life in the world."[24]

In support of this idea, the Association of Church Missions Committees observes that "youth are looking for a life to emulate. Youth leaders, teachers, parents, pastors, Christian nationals, and missionaries need to present integrated, authentic, consistent lives as world Christians for youth to emulate."[25] As Ronald Habermas and Klaus Issler strongly caution, "In the end, it comes down to modeling. It's not *whether* youth will emulate others; it's a question of *whom*."[26] Such patterns, visible both within peer

[19] A. Stanley and S. Hall, *The Seven Checkpoints for Youth Leaders* (West Monroe, LA: Howard, 2001), 114.

[20] D. Fields, *Purpose-Driven Youth Ministry* (Grand Rapids: Zondervan, 1998), 109.

[21] E. Pullman, "Life Span Development," in *Christian Education,* ed. M. J. Anthony (Grand Rapids: Baker, 2001), 71.

[22] L. Richards, *A Theology of Christian Education* (Grand Rapids: Zondervan, 1975), 46–47.

[23] L. Richards, *Youth Ministry: Its Renewal in the Local Church,* rev. ed. (Grand Rapids: Zondervan, 1985), 247.

[24] Ibid.

[25] P. Borthwick, *Organizing Your Youth Ministry* (Grand Rapids: Zondervan, 1988), 53.

[26] R. Habermas and K. Issler, *Teaching for Reconciliation* (Grand Rapids: Baker, 1992), 198.

relationships and through adult leadership, offer a potential remedy to isolation. They also, however, seem to foster spiritual growth, specifically, in moving students toward a ministry-driven lifestyle.

Mike King points out that one of the ways we secure relational environments for this modeling to take place is by ensuring that students and adults are together, not separated:

> Even though many churches pledge during infant dedications or baptisms to help raise a child as a community of believers, too often the next time the child is before the congregation is to honor them for graduating from high school. This is frighteningly dysfunctional and removes one of the most effective practices of spiritual formation, interaction between generations.[27]

King argues that this minimal, to nonexistent, interaction precludes the church from being a community that fulfills the influential modeling paradigm set out in Titus 2.[28] It is important to note that when church community functions well, when it helps guide students to dissonance resolution, it also provides a postdecision reassurance that encourages further commitment.

MAKING IT STICK: SUPPORT FOR POSTDECISION REASSURANCE

Rick Dunn's "pacing" model for youth discipleship and mentoring offers not only more modeling and influence ideas but also a way for us to see postdecision reassurance measures in action. He uses the example of one teenage couple to probe moral decision making. This couple had failed morally, and it was not because they failed to see at the outset that their sexual behavior was wrong; rather, over time they exchanged the cognition that it was wrong for a belief that "there was an exception for them" in the area of sexual purity.[29] This situation caused great "internal dissonance" but could have been avoided if certain steps had been taken earlier.

---

[27] M. King, *Presence-Centered Youth Ministry* (Downers Grove, IL: InterVarsity, 2006), 33.

[28] Ibid.

[29] R. Dunn, *Shaping the Spiritual Life of Students* (Downers Grove, IL: InterVarsity, 2001), 130.

A pacing approach would have positioned a consistent presence in the lives of the students:

> Ideally, a spiritual caregiver could have provided support and guidance to the young couple before they began to experience discontinuity between their moral commitments and moral choices. They lacked affirmation to strengthen their resistance to temptation and counsel on developing strategies for success in their moral purity.[30]

To help them keep their initial commitment to abstinence, the couple was in need of "support and guidance." Such reassurance typically provides much-needed direction and helps fortify student commitments.

This need for commitment reinforcement holds true during the entire STM process as well. Short-term strategist Floyd McClung pays particular attention to the posttrip process, seeing the participants as "stewards of experience" for the local church.[31] He notes that short-term missions "deepen the commitment to world evangelization" in the lives of participants.[32] In order for this to happen, however, there must be clearly denoted steps for recruitment, training, and the return home. The posttrip return is a crucial piece in the overall success of the experience if it is to be transformative. To maximize the value of the posttrip process, he offers several key elements that should be included in the posttrip plan.

First, the participants should be able to "talk it out" with those around them. This includes discussing their experiences and feelings about the trip with those who will be open to respond and affirm them, specifically those who "have a positive view toward the church and missions."[33]

Additionally, the church must offer "challenging" service opportunities for participants upon their return: "It is also important for the local church to have programs that challenge the young people and other short-term workers for constructive service once they come back to the local church. When the short-term workers come back fired up, but find no opportunity for service, they can become disillusioned and disappointed."[34]

Finally, there needs to be a detailed plan for "feedback" from church leadership and mission agency professionals. This "positive, objective

---

[30] Ibid., 134.

[31] F. McClung, "Short-Term Missions and the Local Church," in *Re-Entry,* ed. Peter Jordan (Seattle, WA: YWAM, 1992), 145.

[32] Ibid., 143.

[33] Ibid., 148.

[34] Ibid.

feedback" will assist the student in honest assessment and improvement, while fostering greater mission sensitivity and involvement; it should be offered by both the sending agency and the local church as a "long-range re-entry process."[35] McClung's suggested avenues of affirmation and direction, as well as involvement in further service with other short-term participants, are designed to encourage some degree of intentional exposure to those who will foster the mission-focused mind-set.[36]

The need for a deliberate postdecision framework can be seen in positive choices that require assurance: choosing to go, choosing to enjoy service, and eventually choosing to return on either a short-term or career basis. Borthwick addresses the role of leaders in the lives of students who are years away from additional service but are assessing career options, advising that "youth leaders, missions committee members, and other leaders can do their best to affirm, support, counsel, and encourage those who are hearing (or think that they are hearing) God's call to cross-cultural ministry."[37] We usually call this "follow-up," and its practice ensures that the proper perspective is maintained.

David Forward contends that mission participants should be warned about the response of others who will not be reassuring about their possible newfound perspective and desire to see the nations reached with the gospel. He writes:

> After arriving home from a mission trip, experiencing a letdown feeling is usual for the individuals. Team leaders can help participants combat those anticlimactic emotions. The first step is to address them up front. Tell the team that they may experience the missionary's equivalent of buyer's regret once the excitement and adventure of the trip have passed. Warn them not to expect their family and friends to be as excited about their mission experience as they are.[38]

Student participants may return home expecting a pat on the back from those closest to them; however, they may not encounter so much as a thumbs-up.

If they do not get this affirmation, the students will seek support through reassessing, and maybe reprioritizing, their "cognitions." A student may, for example, devalue the experience as "just another summer trip." This

[35] Ibid., 149.

[36] Ibid.

[37] P. Borthwick, *Youth and Mission* (Waynesboro, GA: OM, 1988), 224.

[38] D. Forward, *The Essential Guide to the Short Term Mission Trip* (Chicago: Moody, 1998), 182.

allows him to view the event as beneficial, which he really wants to do, while limiting the extent to which it has influenced him—thus keeping pace with those around him (who do not share his enthusiasm).

One way to contest participants' tendency toward this sort of resolution is through a "mission presentation service." Jim Burns argues that an opportunity for youth to share their experiences before their congregations is "essential for students' spiritual growth."[39] Ridge Burns goes even further, observing that "after planning several mission trips, I have discovered that as students' appetites are whetted for missionary service, I need to provide year-round opportunities to satisfy that hunger."[40] The motivation to gain reassurance drives students to seek more experiences and deeper relationships, which in turn helps reinforce their mission values.

Rewarding by Doing: Support for Justification Concepts

Minimal justification theory supports the idea that motivation must come, as much as possible, from participation itself, rather than from extrinsic rewards.[41] This type of method for casting off tension appears to be operative in the stated objectives of many short-term student trips. Stan May, commenting on the benefit and intent of these trips for the ministerial leadership, observes that "many pastors who ought to be on the field catch 'the bug' of missions while on these trips and begin applying for international missions once they return home."[42] He recounts the story of a pastor who was "divided" about missionary service; however, after participating in a trip, "his heart was stirred" and he "caught the missions spirit."[43]

The dissonance this pastor experienced between his belief that missions are crucial and his own lack of participation prompted a change of behavior so as to reduce the dissonance. This behavior change enabled his actions to cohere with his stated emphasis on world missions. Serving as the greenhouse for growing this change was a short-term mission experience.

[39] J. Burns and M. DeVries, *The Youth Builder* (Ventura, CA: Gospel Light, 2001), 155.

[40] R. Burns, "How to Plan and Lead a Student Mission Trip," in *The Complete Book of Youth Ministry*, ed. W. Benson and M. Senter (Chicago: Moody, 1987), 402.

[41] P. Zimbardo and M. Leippe, *The Psychology of Attitude Change and Social Influence* (Philadelphia: Temple University Press, 1991), 110.

[42] S. May, "Short-Term Mission Trips Are Great If . . . ," *Evangelical Missions Quarterly* 36 (2000): 446.

[43] Ibid.

Dissonance theorists advocate exposure to a preferred activity as a change agent in both the outward behavior and the inner attitude from which it results. So, if a student's stated value of mission and his patterns of living are going to agree, he must be exposed to mission realities. This idea is not novel, of course; it is already alive in many student mission approaches.

For instance, Andrew Atkins likes to use the label "taste and see teams." His reason for the title is simple: "Since our long-term goal is to strengthen this generation's involvement in world missions, our short-term objective should be to allow North Americans to 'taste and see' what cross-cultural ministry is all about."[44] This view of student mission proposes that exposure to the realities of the global task, by living it for a brief time, should strengthen the participant's determination to stay involved.

Missiologist Richard Slimbach also offers a long-range strategy, one which is focused on the participant as learner: "Organizing for learning rather than for teaching means that we take a long view of short terms: We affirm that earnest young people with limited life experience and intercultural ability can be developed into valuable resources in Christ's church if they refuse to settle for simply being 'tourists for Jesus' or unaffected 'soul savers.'"[45] He notes that exposure to mission contexts and service should lead to a realistic awareness of the student's role in missions, as well as a working knowledge of the significance of cross-cultural ministry. The key is that "cognitive information" must be tied to "*doing* the things of the faith," in order to provide an environment that is ripe for transformation.[46]

The final element in a minimal justification strategy for dissonance alleviation is, perhaps, the most vital. In this approach the participant must not be lavishly "rewarded" in a behavioral, stimulus-response manner.[47] Imagine, for example, that a youth ministry requires participation in a spring break mission trip in order to be eligible for the beach retreat that summer. The potential problem here is that the mission participant may simply convince himself that he participated, not because he now values the importance of the global initiative but because he "had to do it" in order to get the "reward" of the beach trip.

So the beach retreat, in becoming the means by which the student justifies his mission involvement, actually hinders his understanding of the

[44] A. Atkins, "Work Teams? No, 'Taste and See' Teams," *Evangelical Missions Quarterly* 27 (1991): 387.

[45] R. Slimbach, "First, Do No Harm," *Evangelical Missions Quarterly* 36 (2000): 439.

[46] T. Ward, *With an Eye on the Future* (Monrovia, CA: MARC Publications, 1996), 23.

[47] Zimbardo and Leippe, *The Psychology of Attitude Change and Social Influence*, 110–11.

value of participation in cross-cultural ministry. A youth mission philosophy in keeping with dissonance theory recognizes the "spiritual growth" and "new enthusiasm" gained as a result of the short-term mission experience *as* the reward.[48]

Borthwick, with his nine "training requirements" for participation in youth mission teams, provides an example of this philosophy. These requirements range from mandatory meetings with the missions committee to reading a missions text. He believes that "zeal seems to directly relate to the severity of our demands. If youth face tough requirements, they will value the project much more."[49] Together with these requirements Borthwick also offers objectives for the short-term experience, which include eventual career missions service, missions promotion at home, and the development of relationships with missionaries.

Andy Stanley offers a similar approach incorporating training and requirements for students involved in short-term experiences:

> That is why mission trips and other service-oriented efforts are such powerful events in their lives. Students make a conscious choice to serve God and others. They discipline their time to spend weeks and months in preparation. Often they work to earn the money to cover their costs. In that process they say no to many activities that would normally keep them distracted and instead focus their gifts and abilities on service. The trip or event itself is very impacting, but a large part of that impact is due to the investment made beforehand.[50]

While the idea of minimal justification seems evident in their approaches, both Borthwick and Stanley also offer ideas that dissonance advocates would see as similar to justification of effort. They realize, for example, that when one works hard for something, he tends to appreciate it more. General trends in youth service—student ministry outreach, in particular—bear out this principle.

Merton Strommen observes that data collected during the "Effective Christian Education" study demonstrated "that as the number of hours increase that youth give to 'helping people in one's town or city,' the percent-

[48] R. Peterson, G. Aeschliman, and W. Sneed, *Maximum Impact Short-Term Mission* (Minneapolis: STEM, 2003), 236.

[49] P. Borthwick, "Short-Term Youth Teams: Are They Worth It?," *Evangelical Missions Quarterly* 32 (1996): 404.

[50] Stanley and Hall, *The Seven Checkpoints for Youth Leaders*, 197–98.

ages increased *[sic]* of those strongly agreeing that 'their church means a great deal to them.'"[51] In other words, the effort exerted had a direct correlation to the level of appreciation for, and allegiance to, the group with which the student performed this activity.

The Thoughts of Student Pastors and Sending Agency Professionals

Having briefly looked at what some thinkers have suggested are the best practices for service and short-term mission, we wanted to explore whether some of these ideas offered in print have made their way into the practices of those mobilizing students. To do this, we performed semi-structured interviews with a small sample of youth pastors and short-term sending agency heads and personnel tasked with mobilizing students, and we sought to uncover what they believed to be the most vital principles and practices in a participant-oriented approach.[52] Their responses included several significant thematic categories of STM philosophy and praxis.

The Predominant Motive: Transformation

Youth pastors and agency personnel alike consistently mentioned as hopeful outcomes concepts related to development and transformation. Here are several excerpts from interview transcripts that focus on the intention in short-term mobilization of students:

> I mean, we want these young people to come and we pray over every one of these groups, "Lord, would you just irreparably change and impact these young people for mission." It's not so much the project that they're going to do with us for the one week. It's not that they're with us over two weeks or whatever. We are looking so much more long-term than that, and the statistics will bear out that most of the missionaries that are being launched, ca-

[51] M. Strommen, K. Jones, and D. Rahn, *Youth Ministry That Transforms* (Grand Rapids: Zondervan, 2001), 186.

[52] The interviews were performed as part of a larger qualitative content analysis of short-term youth mission attitudes and perceptions among those mobilizing students. These interviews were performed and analyzed between November 1, 2006 and January 30, 2007. For the full study, see S. Parker, "Cognitive Dissonance Theory and Adolescent Short-Term Mission Methodology" (PhD diss., The Southern Baptist Theological Seminary, 2007).

> reer-wise, had some sort of a positive short-term mission experience.
>
> It [the short-term mission experience] is to broaden their horizons and their worldview, while at the same time, helping them to make an impact on the kingdom.
>
> I think that an objective, one of the major ones, is discipleship, mentoring, and expansion of the participant's understanding of God's kingdom.
>
> We [Americans] tend to think we do everything right. That's part of human nature, and so we grow up in one small little area and we're more prone to it [ethnocentric thinking] than any other culture, just because of our position as a world power. We just think we're right on every level. When we expose young people to what's out there, I think it helps them broaden their perspective. We see that happen, not just in their thinking, but also their experience. We want to see lives changed.
>
> We've really focused on exposing students to the needs of those in third world countries and getting them to think beyond their culture.[53]

While each of these perspectives is unique, there is nevertheless a commonality in the stated desire to see God "irreparably change and impact" students through "exposure" and catalytic "experiences," which have the potential to broaden "their horizons" or "their perspective" (thinking and experience). Holistic transformation of the students, through these events, was a fundamental initiative in the outcome sets of those interviewed.

The Predominant Means: Challenge and Critical Thinking

While those interviewed consistently stressed the goal of transformation, they perceived that in order to facilitate such transformation, they must consciously adopt a structured approach to placing students in environments and situations that force them to process the realities, value, and consequences of authentic mission support and involvement. Even more prominent in the interview transcripts than transformational aims is the stated means to reach these goals—challenges and critical thinking. The

[53] Ibid.

orientation of these opportunities toward challenges and critical thinking can be seen in statements like these:

> When it makes a difference in their lives and other people's lives, it changes your thinking. When you see God working and active and see the reality of these things, it does change your thinking.
>
> We plan to create situations where they're going to experience these things, and we do that by not allowing our teams to come back and sleep in Motel 6, by not allowing them to come back and sleep in air-conditioned situations and eat food that they're comfortable with. You want them to sort of unpack their underwear, so to speak. You want them to be there long enough where they can shift their thinking away from American things to the cross-cultural thinking.
>
> They must be consistently confronted with these realities, and you know, these trips need to challenge and really frighten them on some level. They need to be shocked by what they see and experience.
>
> I think, in one way, a cross-cultural experience, by definition, is going to raise more questions than it answers. That individual's response to the questions that are raised is what is going to enhance or enable them to grow. It's going to raise doubts, in all honesty. That's largely dependent on their response to the Holy Spirit's initiative to teach them in that experience. It's a startling instance, when they realize that people really do think differently than me and have a different experience than what they had growing up. That encounter, with any reflection at all, is going to raise that issue and challenge a person's position.[54]

Challenges to the thinking, values, and even the actions of student participants, in turn, ushers in the need for critical thinking.

THE PREDOMINANT MOVEMENTS: PATHWAYS TO RESOLUTION

Those interviewed not only offered insight into the value, as a means of transformation, of facing these challenges and responding to them with

[54] Ibid.

critical reflection. They also provided several ideas about how, with specific practices employed or strategic movements made by those designing and executing the experience, this evaluation process can be a positive tool in the student's life transformation.

Connections to Minimal Justification. When discussing the desire to see student participants changed, one issue that arose was that of motivational incentives, which includes any reward or incentive offered as part of the short-term experience. Two of the interviewees imparted these perspectives:

> They won't be talking about mission, they'll be doing missions. The incentive for groups that are coming is that they'll experience this challenge. We have received e-mails from students who have surrendered to missions because of their involvement in a trip, and that's one of our goals is to see the students not only experience it, but to be so caught up in the experience that they'll be challenged to make mission an integral part of their life. Some of them are responding by being called to the mission field.
>
> If the church just says, "Okay. I'll pay for you to go." There is no sacrifice. Churches can offer to help them get there, but there still should be sacrifice on everybody's part to do something that costs them. I won't do that which costs me nothing. I won't give that which costs me nothing. It's not just what you give on the field, but it's what did I give back home. *[sic]* Sacrifice is the best incentive that you can get.[55]

Both of these interviewees spoke about the motivational drive of student missionaries, as this may affect the value of the experience itself and its tie to the development of a more thorough global ministry mind-set. The suggestion here is that, in order to maximize the impact of the trip, the motivation for going should be the value of the trip itself—as participation in mission—rather than other extraneous rewards. This idea bears remarkable similarity to the dissonance concept of minimal justification. Moreover, the second quote carries an apparent connection to the concept of the justification of effort; the mentality that team members must "do something that costs them" for the experience to be worthwhile is comparable to the effort-justification paradigm.

[55] Ibid.

Connections to Justification of Effort. The idea that preparation, experience, and follow-up should be difficult, so that the participant appreciates the experience, was also emphasized in the interview responses, especially in reference to the extent and difficulty of pretrip requirements. One interviewee said that "on any trip, the more preparation you have, the more meaningful the field experience is going to be."[56] This is true, one response indicated, not just because of the degree of cross-cultural preparation but also for another reason: "The multiple pre-trip requirements foster within that individual that they are being asked to be responsible. They are making a commitment. They are contributing in a valid way, and if they are not, it becomes evident as well. There is some teaching, in that sense, of responsibility."[57] Several research participants addressed the need for the on-field experience to be strenuous. Here are two examples of such responses:

The effort or trip must be difficult. It must challenge and stretch them.

> For us, one of the first things that we do, we make sure that we don't sugarcoat mission. We don't soften it up and make it easy and go out of our way to create comfort. And we don't want to make them suffer either. And so when we go into Mexico, even on the border, we could come back and sleep in a motel and we make sure that we don't do that. We sleep in shacks and we sleep in tents. We sleep on the floors of the houses of our friends and we eat Mexican food, mostly. We try to integrate as much as we can into the lives of the people we work with. We play soccer with them or go fishing with the men or our wives and young girls talk and participate in cooking. We are trying, even for a week, to get into the lives of our people. We are not saying that the little day trip projects are not legitimate. Or that they're not fulfilling a purpose. They are completing a project, but a lot of times these kids work in that way and are eating hamburgers and sleeping in nice hotels. And if they go home thinking that this is what mission is, they get the wrong idea and in the bigger context of career missionaries, there is an incredibly high failure rate of missionaries. Why are they failing? There are many reasons,

[56] Ibid.
[57] Ibid.

> but one reason is that they go out with wrong with unrealistic expectations in the first place. So, through the short-term missions, we are going to give them a healthy dose of the hardships of cross-cultural mission.[58]

Indeed, the short-term experience should in no way "sugarcoat" or "soften" the reality of the authentic missionary experience, so that the students gain "a healthy dose of the hardship of cross-cultural mission." This communication of reality is significant for the development and recruitment of potential career missionaries, but it is also instrumental in helping participants to value rightly this authentic life and calling, rather than an "unrealistic" facsimile.

Connections to Selective Exposure. Interviewees also placed a high premium on the social component of pre-, mid-, and posttrip relationship dynamics and leadership personnel as they have the potential to influence transformation:

> If you have a whole team of people who are not excited, but you have one person on the team who is getting people pumped up to see how God's going to use them, that one person's individual attitude and beliefs can affect the whole team. If they're so focused on what God has for them, the one person can change the whole team's perspective for a day. Students have a major, major effect on each other for each day and on each student. When they return, it depends on the relationship that is built on the field. If we are talking about the same group of people that were on the field together, I've seen students who are go-getters and constantly reminding of what God did and how God used a team. We are continually challenging the students. Then students will call out other students that may never be willing to share their faith at their school Bible study, but go to another culture and get the opportunity to practice sharing their faith. When they come home, they have greater confidence, and students are seeing that and so they'll say, "I've seen you do that. I know that you can do it."
>
> Teenagers are social animals. They will be linked together, in some way. Call it tribal security, or whatever you

[58] Ibid.

> like. You know, many times we focus so much on making sure that students are individuals and are different from everyone, but we aren't designed to be on an island. We are part of the Body of Christ, and we need each other.
>
> The key really for the adults on a short-term mission, and when they return, is that students aren't looking for a buddy. They want to see a level of competency in the adults. They want to see that there is something that they can teach them. One of the most beloved teachers at one of our schools just died. This was a guy who would not round up a final grade. What you had was what you got, but this was also the guy, that if you had tried your best on a project and were struggling, he would come to your house to help you. These students loved him for that. That's what students want. They want adults that know what they are doing and show that they care about the students. These types of adults have an incredible effect.[59]

These excerpts clearly indicate that both peer and leader relationships are significant to the effectiveness of the experience. The nature of these relationships, whether meaningful or superficial, has great bearing on how trip participants are influenced, as they will take cues from those around them.

Connections to Postdecision Commitment and Reassurance. Once a student has made the decision to participate in the trip, goes through with the preparation, invests on the field, and makes it back home, the true test begins—in the estimation of several interviewees. Posttrip "debriefing" and "ongoing service" are two of the practices championed here:

> The old saying is, "Out of sight out of mind." If all it's been was a mission trip, and then there's not a significant change, it was just a date on the calendar, if it was just one activity in your year. But if it's a work inside of the Spirit of God, at work in your heart and your mind, that you see the fruit of, then wherever you are, you can be a different person. You, as a different person are living, thinking, acting differently, wherever you are.
>
> Collectively, it's the idea of placing into perspective the events and following through with commitments that

[59] Ibid.

may have been made. Of these individual elements, the debriefing party is significant. Something not so positive may have happened, and someone might be holding grudges and developing a pattern of not forgiving. Reaching out to an individual, and the team having to face the situation from a group perspective, hopefully, would give them a chance to put it in a better perspective. One of the benefits of that to the individual is that they do stop after they've gotten into that busy pace again to get reflective and perhaps the Holy Spirit has one more chance to grow that individual in whatever the Spirit was trying to do, and it gives another opportunity to reconfirm that God was at work, in my heart, and I do remember what I committed to, and it may increase their resolve. It gives a chance to reinforce that commitment.

The debriefing is helping the young people to interpret the mission experience. You are helping them to really understand what they experienced, and sometimes it's a very tearful and very emotional time, because, again, they're coming back and you should allow students to begin talking about the poverty of the people. They have so little and we have so much. In a longer trip, when they come back, the issue is the guilt. A lot of times young people begin to feel guilty about all that they have. And so we have to deal with them about materialism. We've had to teach them that it's not what you have; it's what you do with what you have. It is not a sin to live in your nice home and drive a nice car. Don't feel guilty about the blessings that God is giving you, but be inspired to use that to bless others. Don't begin thinking irrationally because of the intensity of the experience you've had with these poor people. Debriefing deals with all of these issues.

They may not share things with the parents, but to the church, or to a share group, they may share these things, and that's where you see the most fruit. You see where that change has happened. Also post-trip, you need to give them the opportunity to do some of the things that they did on the field. For instance, if every day he shared his story but has never done that at your church on Wednesday

> night, you give him the opportunity to do that. He will be more willing to do that at school with his friends. So, some of the things that they've learned and become familiar with . . . we have to give them opportunity to do that back in the states *[sic]*.[60]

"Debriefing" and granting students "opportunities" for similar service at home provide a framework within which ideas similar to postdecision reassurance and commitment can be put to practice.

COMPLETING THE PUZZLE: WORKING TOWARD TRANSFORMISSION

Although some of the pieces to the puzzle of an approach emphasizing holistic transformation through critical reflection are on the table, the synthesis of these and other components into a unified portrait remains to be completed. We have seen so far that transformational emphases in student short-term mission experiences, carried out through critical reflection in key areas, seem to be necessary to fostering life change. In the next chapter we will relate biblical examples of this type of "transformation through tension resolution," which will provide the additional puzzle pieces necessary to move from theoretical to functional dimensions of student STM.

DISCUSSION QUESTIONS

1. Describe how you have seen selective exposure occur in your youth ministry.
2. What mechanisms might you use in a youth ministry setting to support the positive decisions and commitments your students have made?
3. Should you use reward systems to entice student involvement in missions? Why or why not?
4. What did youth ministers and mission agency personnel say was their primary objective pertaining to students?

[60] Ibid.

CHAPTER 9

OVERCOMING INCONSISTENCIES FOR A CHANGE: THE PEOPLE

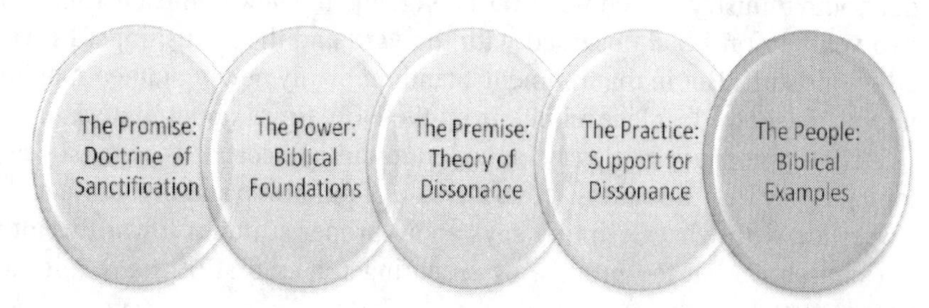

If you have not yet picked up on the fact that we believe strongly that God has called His children, throughout all generations, to make His name known among the nations, then let us plainly state it here. We serve the one true God who has created all of humanity in His image and who is seeking to transform those who will believe on the name of the Lord Jesus Christ for their salvation. We respond to Christ, who has commissioned His children to travel across the street and to the ends of the earth to proclaim His merciful plan to those who have not yet heard of His love and grace, His holiness and righteousness, or His judgment and wrath. We walk according to the Spirit who is empowering us to fulfill His commandments and His commission with the certainty that as we are obedient, we are conformed.

God has called us to be ministers of reconciliation among all people groups. We know that as the people of God engage in this mission, they are forever changed. God, in His infinite wisdom, has always known that as His children encounter people with overwhelming needs, places too horrific to describe, and pagan belief systems, they will be challenged in their thoughts, feelings, beliefs, and actions. He knows that the Great Commission will lead not only to mission advance but also to the life transformation of those who fully participate in its directives.

MICHAEL AND MOSCOW

My own life is filled with these experiences. God has used my mission encounters not only to spread the truth of the gospel but also to reshape my way of living.

It was fall, and I was strolling across my backyard, admiring the brilliant colors of the leaves while examining my landscaping. Truthfully, I was gloating. Life was great: I was enjoying my wife and three daughters; our youth ministry, which was flourishing; and my new home, custom built two years prior. I had obsessed with the yard and the furnishings. I loved all of our stuff. But in that moment, standing by my newly planted magnolia tree, I received a clear rebuke from the Holy Spirit about materialism.

That moment is so clearly etched in my mind because it began a year-long journey that ultimately led to the sale of our home and my new car. As I wrestled with what Scripture says about proper attitudes toward wealth, our church was in the process of preparing for its first of many mission trips to Russia.

Spring break had finally arrived, and our team was entering the customs area of the Atlanta International Airport. The students and adult leaders were electrified with anticipation. The trunks were packed with resources, our team had been prepared for the new culture they were about to encounter, and our hearts were surrendered.

By the fourth day of the mission, all had gone well. We were beginning to establish a long-term relationship with a regional church, and our team was embracing the vision of partnership with this church to reach hurting and hopeless people with the good news of Christ. Indeed, all was going well for me on a personal basis until we arrived at one of the orphanages with which our newly adopted Russian church works. As we arrived and disembarked from the bus, we were greeted by a host of orphanage workers and orphans dressed in traditional Russian clothes representative of the formal attire of the eighteenth century. The director of the orphanage held in her hand what I can only call "showbread." It was a large round, handcrafted artisan loaf decorated with wheat stalks made from dough. Glossy and perfect, it sat atop an embroidered piece of white lace material. We were quickly told by our interpreters that this was a centuries-old tradition and indicated great honor and respect.

As we made our introductions, we were overwhelmed by the generosity and kindness of the orphanage personnel. This sense of being overwhelmed, however, gave way to dismay when we were escorted into their dining room. I vividly remember a table that would seat 35 with platters of food at its center. We were invited to take a seat and were immediately served. While the food was not exquisite, it was plentiful. Each of us was well aware that this was one of the poorest orphanages in the area and that their food supplies were limited. As the platters of food were passed from person to person, our team members were faced with a dilemma: if we ate the food, many orphans would surely go hungry in the coming week, but if we did not eat the food, our hosts would almost certainly be insulted.

At this point our team's lead interpreter, seated to my right, leaned toward my ear and with a smile said, "This is their gift of hospitality; receive it with joy." For the next 30 minutes I considered the sacrifice made so that we could enjoy this unexpected meal; these were not people to hoard the little bit they had. In that instant, the Holy Spirit brought to fruition all of the teachings he had been impressing on me in the previous six months. Though I was one who valued generosity, I also valued my pleasures and possessions. In that moment of dissonance, I made the decision that something must change in my life.

Affirmation of my decision came as we were preparing to leave the orphanage that day. Two children approached with smiles on their faces, possessing a crudely cut piece of wood that provided the canvas for a painting of a brightly colored teapot. With great joy these two children gave me the gift they had made. My heart melted away—here were two children who had no parents and no money but possessed an abundant love for people. To this day that crude painting occupies a special place on the bookcase in my den and reminds me of a group of people who, despite having little, are content.

If space permitted, I would tell you of the Russian lives that were changed in that and subsequent years through our partnership with this Russian church. What I will tell you is that five months after returning home, we sold our house and my new car. My beliefs and my behavior regarding the use of wealth were finally coming into alignment with the biblical standard.

Making the Connection

As should be obvious from this testimony, STM changes participants' lives. It certainly has ours. But we do not consider a handful of testimonies to be an adequate foundation on which to build a thoroughgoing approach to personal transformation and discipleship. Such is the reason in earlier chapters we examined the doctrine of sanctification and the theory of cognitive dissonance. In this section of the book, we began with Scripture since the Bible is the primary source of the divine revelation that directs our faith and practice. Any acceptable approach to ministry must be based on its truth.

We have also sought to understand better the transformation process by examining a particular educational theory. Some may question the inclusion of such material in this volume, espousing that the Bible is sufficient for understanding human behavior and development. Though we will be the first to argue that the Bible does accurately describe human nature, human behavior, the necessity of salvation in Christ, and the ongoing sanctification process, we would also suggest that it is beneficial to investigate further these issues from a cognitive perspective. Paul is clear that we are transformed by the renewing of our mind. One's attitudes and beliefs directly affect one's behavior. In this spirit we have attempted to address the mechanism(s) God is using to eliminate the inconsistency between biblical beliefs and behavior in the lives of believers. Part of the answer, as we have discussed, lies in the believer experiencing cognitive dissonance. This dissonance occurs when there is a disharmonious relationship between what one believes and how he is behaving. A significant tension arises as a result of this incongruence, and human beings naturally attempt to resolve the presenting conflict and alleviate any dissonance associated with their decisions. Though this theory is certainly insufficient by itself to explain life transformation from a Christian perspective, it does provide an additional layer of understanding into how a believer's mind is renewed.

DISORIENTING DAYS

Our goal for the balance of this chapter is to highlight a few biblical characters who experienced much dissonance as a result of various life events. Often these disorienting experiences were initiated by God's call in their lives. Sometimes they were the direct result of the individual responding obediently to the Father's will. In any case the evidence suggests that God used these moments to grow the saints. As Steve Fortosis writes, "Christian growth takes place most readily when it is spurred by dissonance. That is, in our encounters with new information and situations that throw us off balance, we attempt to understand and adjust to them and, *[sic]* thus resolve the dissonance."[1]

Before we look at several narratives below, a couple points of clarification are in order. First, we do not see these biblical illustrations as normative for today's believers. The passages are instead descriptive of the personal experiences of biblical characters in their specific historical period and setting. In other words, God works in different ways in different periods of history, so we do not expect that He will appear to us in a burning bush or commission a big fish to swallow us alive—now that would cause incredible dissonance! Moreover, it is not our intent to provide proof-texts for the tenants of dissonance theory. Instead, we are simply recognizing that these biblical examples of dissonance are similar in principle to what we see in the experience of every believer, as he encounters challenges of varying degrees.

Gideon the Intimidated

We pick up the story of Gideon in Judges 6. The nation of Israel is in a "downward spiral" toward intensifying degrees of sinfulness.[2] The cycles in this progressive deterioration follow this pattern: Israel serves the Lord—Israel falls into sin—Israel is enslaved—Israel seeks God—God raises up a judge—Israel is delivered, and then the cycle begins anew.[3]

During this particular cycle, Israel is oppressed by the Midianites for seven years because of their evil before the Lord. Out of fear the Israelites

> made for themselves the dens which were in the mountains and the caves and the strongholds. For it was when Israel had sown, that the Midianites would come up with the Amalekites and the sons of the east and go against them. So they would camp against them and destroy the produce of the earth as far as Gaza, and leave no sustenance in Israel as well as no sheep, ox, or donkey. (Judg 6:2–4)

[1] S Fortosis, "A Developmental Model for Stages of Growth in Christian Formation," *Religious Education* (Spring 1992): 295.

[2] R. Dillard and T. Longman, *An Introduction to the Old Testament* (Grand Rapids: Zondervan, 1994), 125.

[3] G. Archer, *A Survey of Old Testament Introduction* (Chicago: Moody, 1994), 299.

The narrative goes on to record that "Israel was brought very low because of Midian, and the sons of Israel cried to the LORD" (v. 6). Clearly, the entire population was fearful for its life and well-being.

The Lord then sent a prophet to rebuke Israel and to remind of their historical deliverance from Egyptian captivity and possession of Canaan. In a theophany the Angel of the Lord—who is later said to be the Lord Himself (6:14)—appeared to Gideon in Ophrah, where he was beating out wheat in a wine press,[4] true evidence of his fear and desperation.

The Lord's first words to Gideon must have shaken him—"The LORD is with you, O valiant warrior" (6:12). Picture that: here is a young man hiding out from enemy raiders, and he hears his Lord call him a valiant warrior. Doubtlessly, Gideon did not feel much like a warrior at that moment; instead, he felt insecure and uncertain of God's plan. He was truly struggling with what he believed about *Yahweh*. Gideon even questioned the angel directly, saying, "O my lord, if the LORD is with us, why then has all this happened to us? And where are all His miracles which our fathers told us about?" (v. 13). Gideon even went on to accuse the Lord of abandoning Israel!

To say that this moment was a disorienting event for Gideon is a bit of an understatement. He had always believed that God was able to work wonders among His chosen people, but his experience of the last seven years was beginning to call this belief into question. Gideon found himself not living in accordance with his belief in God's miracle-working power. Instead, he was living daily without any true sense of peace. He was experiencing dissonance.

The Lord looked at Gideon and said, "Go in this your strength and deliver Israel from the hand of Midian. Have I not sent you?" (v. 14). Gideon's response included excuses about his family's insignificant status, but the Lord reassured him of success in defeating Midian. Hearing this, Gideon then asked for, and received, a sign that convinced him it was indeed the Lord directing him. After accepting Gideon's offering and blessing him with a "Peace to you," the Lord instructed Gideon to pull down the altar to Baal and cut down the Asherah that stood beside, both of which belonged to his father.[5]

This situation forced Gideon to decide whether to adjust his actions to fit his beliefs. Would he actually carry out the Lord's directive? At that moment, he was certainly experiencing conflict that arose from compet-

[4] H. Wolf, *Judges,* Expositor's Bible Commentary 3 (Grand Rapids: Zondervan, 1990), 420.
[5] Ibid.

ing commitments to his father and to his Lord and was exacerbated by his spirit of fear and cowardice.[6] Gideon ultimately made the decision to be obedient and consequently found success in his task.

This was only one in a series of disequilibrating experiences in Gideon's life that God used to strengthen his faith. Gideon was called to trust that God would deliver the whole Midianite army into his hands. He sought reassurance of his decision to follow God's course of action by conducting the "fleece test"—twice. He was then instructed to battle Midian with only 300 men and enjoyed victory.

Gideon is a great example of how God creates a sense of dissonance within His followers for the purpose of their transformation. Gideon emerged from the wine press as "Gideon the Intimidated," only to become "Gideon the Valiant Warrior."

Esther the Commoner

The story of Esther is one that every young Christian girl loves to hear and read about. It is the story of a young commoner, a peasant girl of sorts, who becomes queen of the world. What is not to like about it? But there is much more to the story than the rags-to-riches plotline. Ultimately, it is about God's providential work to deliver His people through the struggle and resulting courage of Esther.[7]

We find the heart of the story in Esther 3–4. Evil Haman had decided to annihilate the Jews throughout the world due to his personal jealousy of the Jew Mordecai. Queen Esther, because of her position, was in a unique position to influence this situation. Living in the king's palace and removed from her kinship, she was seemingly protected from Haman's murderous plot. Her cousin Mordecai, recognizing this, informed her of the intended harm by way of her servant Hathach and petitioned her to appeal to the king on behalf of the protection of her people.

Now imagine if you were in Esther's shoes at that moment. What would you do? Countless peoples' lives were at stake in light of Haman's murderous intentions, but so was hers if she were to approach the king without an invitation. Having been raised by Mordecai before entering the palace, she was taught the Jewish law. This law clearly taught that one is to value human life because all humanity was created in the image of God. Esther found herself in an extremely disorienting experience: her

[6] Dillard and Longman, *Introduction to the Old Testament*, 125.

[7] W. McClarty, "Esther," in *A Complete Literary Guide to the Bible,* ed. L. Ryken and T. Longman (Grand Rapids: Zondervan, 1993), 218.

inclination was self-preservation, but she knew that her responsibility was to protect her people.

This is one of those moments when one's beliefs and one's actions collide. You can imagine that God must have used this moment to cause Esther to consider what was right in His sight. At that moment she did not yield but sent Mordecai a message informing him of appearing before the king uninvited (Esth 4:11). Her cousin's reply was pointed:

> Do not imagine that you in the king's palace can escape any more than all the Jews. For if you remain silent at this time, relief and deliverance will arise for the Jews from another place and you and your father's house will perish. And who knows whether you have not attained royalty for such a time as this? (Esth 4:13–14).

Faced with great conflict in her spirit, the tension had to be increasing for Esther.

Esther made her decision. She chose to stand with her people at the risk of losing her own life, realizing that the need to fulfill God's will was more important than self-preservation.[8] She called the Jews in Susa to prayer and fasting. Three days later Esther put on her royal robe and entered the inner court of the king's palace—in front of the throne room. Remarkably, she received the king's favor and was permitted to speak to him (Esth 5:2).

From this point the story takes many more twists and turns, with the final outcome being the salvation of the Jews through Esther's boldness and God's gracious hand. This story is full of many disorienting days, to say the least. Reading it, we have the benefit of peering over Esther's shoulders as she processes events and is forced to push through her personal conflict and the dissonance that ensues as a result of her decisions. "Esther the Commoner" emerges as "Esther the Royal Rescuer." What a great story of providential redemption; what a transformed life!

Peter the Pious

Maybe you are like us. When you scan the pages of the New Testament, you find yourself identifying with many of its characters. One of those characters with which countless believers tend to identify readily is Simon Peter. He was certainly the leader ("first") of the apostles, as

[8] B. Arnold and B. Beyer, *Encountering the Old Testament* (Grand Rapids: Baker, 1999), 273.

we see in Matt 10:2, but he often spoke out of turn.[9] He seemed to be the life of the party. He was fickle and uncommitted at times. Peter was just being Peter. The writers of the New Testament recorded many of his life events—walking on water (Matt 14:27–29), confessing Jesus as the Christ (Matt 16:15–17), wielding a sword in the garden (John 18:9–11), fearing a teenage girl (Mark 14:66–68), denying Christ (Mark 14:66–72), preaching at Pentecost (Acts 2:14–41), and the list goes on.

Perhaps one of the greatest New Testament accounts of Peter's experiences is found in Acts 10. This passage features an example of dissonance in the context of mission advance. The story begins with Peter staying for many days in Joppa with a tanner named Simon—a curious fact since a person who worked with the skins of dead animals would have been considered unclean (Lev 11:24–40). Meanwhile, a Roman centurion by the name of Cornelius, who was devout and God-fearing, experienced a vision instructing him to send for Peter (Acts 10:4–5). As Cornelius's men were about to arrive in Joppa, Peter was on the rooftop praying. He fell into a trance and saw a vision of the sky opening and an object like a great sheet coming down. On the sheet were "all kinds of four-footed animals and crawling creatures of the earth and birds of the air." Peter then heard a voice saying, "Get up, Peter, kill and eat!" (vv. 12–13).

Because he did not want to violate the dietary restrictions outlined in Leviticus 11, Peter responded to this voice: "By no means, Lord, for I have never eaten anything unholy and unclean" (v. 14). For this response, God rebuked Peter, telling him, "What God has cleansed, no longer consider unholy" (v. 15). Not only did the vision repeal these dietary restrictions for Christians, but it signaled for Peter that his attitude toward Gentile inclusion needed to be checked and indeed changed.[10] Three times the object was lowered and immediately taken up into the sky. While Peter was still reflecting on his vision, the men from Cornelius arrived. The Spirit instructed Peter to go with these Gentile men without any reservation.

Peter's reaction to the words spoken in the vision is somewhat understandable. He had faithfully maintained his separation from the Gentiles. In fact, Peter's reaction to the extension of the gospel to the Gentiles appears representative of the overall Jewish-Christian aversion at this point.[11] Seemingly, the early church resisted the idea of evangelizing Gentiles di-

[9] M. Wilkins, "Disciples," *Dictionary of Jesus and the Gospels*, ed. J. B. Green and S. McKnight (Downers Grove, 1992).

[10] R. Longenecker, *Acts,* Expository's Bible Commentary 9 (Grand Rapids: Zondervan, 1990), 388.

[11] G. Ladd, *A Theology of the New Testament* (Grand Rapids: Eerdmans, 1993), 383–84.

rectly or accepting them into the Christian fellowship without their first becoming Jewish proselytes (see Acts 10:14,28; 11:2–3,8). If this attitude were to change, it makes sense that a seminal leader in the development of the church would have to change first.[12] It was ultimately God who introduced Gentiles into the Church and miraculously showed His approval of their inclusion (see Acts 10:3,11–16,19–20,22,30–33,44–46; 11:5–10,13,15–18).[13]

The initial discomfort experienced by Peter proved significant regarding the inclusion of Gentiles into the Church. He certainly faced a moment filled with dissonant cognitions evidenced by the great tension that existed between his application of the law and the new information received in his vision. Peter's apparent resolution of the dissonance and the subsequent inclusion of Gentiles into the first-century Church appear to possess what Köstenberger and O'Brien label "paradigmatic and normative" significance for contemporary mission ideology and emphasis.[14]

Peter was confronted with the reality that God intended to extend the gospel call to the nations. From this disorienting experience, "Peter the Pious" emerged as "Peter the Proclaimer"—the man whom God had chosen to initiate the gospel's expansion to the nations. We must be ever mindful of Peter's obedience in this passage, which led to Cornelius and his whole household coming to a saving knowledge of Christ.

Though we have limited our discussion to three examples in this chapter, we could have easily included stories such as Noah and the flood (Genesis 6–9); Abraham and his covenant with God (Genesis 12); Joseph and his journey to Egyptian power (Genesis 37–50); Moses and the emancipation of the Israelites (Exodus 2–15); Joshua and the conquering of Canaan (Joshua 1–12); David and Bathsheba (2 Samuel 11), including Nathan's confrontation (2 Samuel 12), and David's repentant cry (Psalm 51); the calling and training of the twelve (e.g., Matt 4:18–22; 9:9–12; 10:1–42); and Paul's conversion (Acts 9) and missionary journeys (Acts 13:1–14:28; 15:36–18:21; 18:22–21:16). The Bible is filled with examples of biblical characters like these experiencing disorienting events, which often result in life transformation.

Hopefully, through the examples of Gideon, Esther, and Peter, it is clearer how the Holy Spirit works in the lives of believers to bring about

---

[12] Ibid., 384.

[13] A. Köstenberger and P. T. O'Brien, *Salvation to the Ends of the Earth: A Biblical Theology of Mission* (Downers Grove, IL: InterVarsity, 2001), 143–45.

[14] Ibid., 145.

this transformation. We believe that God is still working today through disorienting events. Indeed, we believe that STM experiences are one of the beneficial methods He is using to confront inconsistencies between what our students profess to believe and the way in which they are actually living their lives.

It is imperative, then, that we recognize STM as a catalyst for Christian formation. If our goal is to develop mature, global-minded disciples who accurately reflect Christ's image, then STM must become part of this larger discipleship process. In the following chapters we will present our I.D.E.A. of how to integrate and use STM as a strategic component in the student discipleship plan.

Discussion Questions

1. Describe a time when you faced a disorienting event that God used to clarify your thinking and your behavior.
2. Select a story from a biblical text related to Paul's life and missionary journeys and think through the dissonance and the resolution exhibited in the passage.

PART III

THE TRANSFORMISSIONAL DIMENSIONS OF SHORT-TERM MISSION: GETTING THE I.D.E.A.

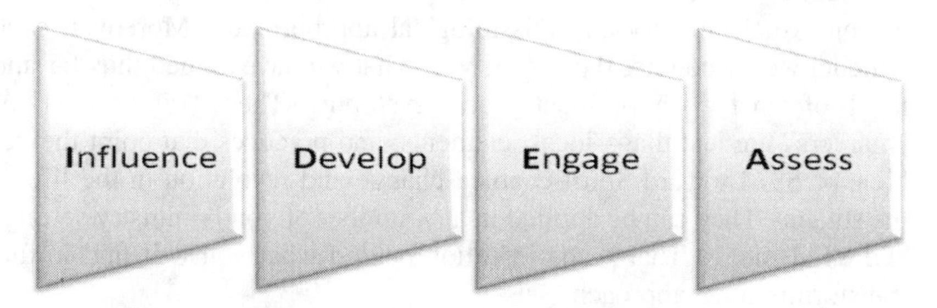

FIRST THINGS FIRST: CASTING STM IN A DISCIPLESHIP MOLD

Most texts dealing with STM seem to start with the idea that they are valuable in and of themselves and then move to show why that is the case. We, however, are starting from another vantage point: we see STM as having little value for long-term initiatives and intentions of the Church and kingdom unless they occur, primarily, as *an* element in the discipleship process of all who go. Starting with discipleship is crucial because it provides for the integration of the various dimensions of a transformissional STM process within the overarching growth plan and curriculum that is guiding your ministry to students and families.

Four dimensions form the I.D.E.A. of a transforming approach to STM:

1. **I**nfluence: Surround them with relationships.
2. **D**evelop: Shape them through process.
3. **E**ngage: Mobilize them for challenge.
4. **A**ssess: Evaluate them to change.

These parts of the transformission I.D.E.A. are not disconnected from one another. In fact, there is a great deal of overlap, as you will see. We make these distinctions in order to probe the nature of the associated activities. These dimensions converge on the student's life concurrently from different sources and angles, but each plays a key role in the discipleship of the STM participant.

Important to note, before we enter this section, is that we are not presenting herein a full-orbed short-term mission *model*. Though it sounds enticing, a "trip in a box" is nearly impossible to offer due to the nuances of contextual ministry and missiological appropriation. Moreover, such a model would counter the majority of what we have argued thus far and much of what we have spent years developing. These "dimensions" or "markers" are just that—ideas, elements, and practices that point the vehicle of STM toward Spirit-enabled change and revolution in the life of the student. They can be applied in any number of youth ministry settings and STM molds. That is the intention behind what you will find in this transformissional approach.

Chapter 10

Influence: Surround Them with Relationships

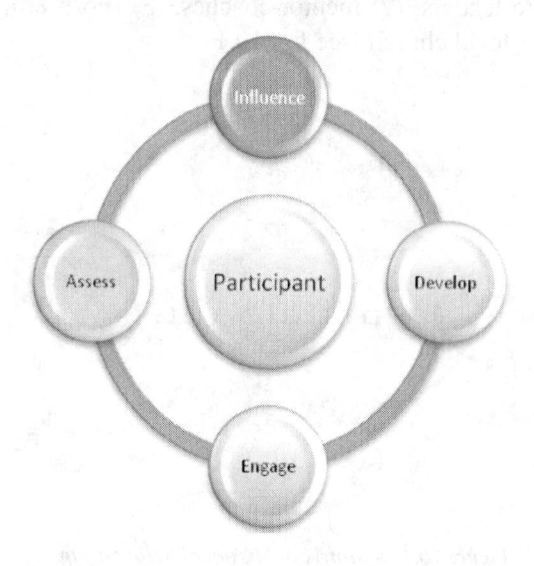

Nowhere to Run: Surrounded by Relationships

Having one person you can count on is great. Having one person you can always count on is fantasy. Even our spouses will eventually let us down or be absent at a critical moment, even if it is no fault of their own. It happens to us, and it happens to your students, too. If your students are to experience change of beliefs, attitudes, and actions, then they will need constant reminders from every possible angle, from multiple people. Without this wall of relationships, they will likely avoid the one or two people they do not want to see and consequently miss an opportunity to have thinking and behavior reinforced. Even the most devoted advisor, friend, or guide cannot always be there, and when such an individual is going to hold the student's feet to the fire, he may not be welcome anyway.[1]

Doing everything you can to safeguard your students from unwise decisions, while maximizing their ability to envision their role in discipleship and mission, starts with surrounding them with positive *key* relationships. Although each connection by itself can develop into a more prominent role, depending on time and place, a continuing convergence of several on the student's life is best. We will examine these key relationship partners: (1) life leaders, (2) mentor-coaches, (3) short-term team members, and (4) the local church (see fig. 10.1).

Figure 10.1: A Matrix of Missional Relationships

LIFE LEADERS: PARENTS OR GUARDIANS

While we are often inundated with the notion that students want to get away from parents and only spend time with their peers, this does not seem to be an accurate picture. Chap Clark calls this "the separation myth." He advises parents:

> Underneath their words and behavior, kids are desperate for their parents—*both* parents—to care enough to stay

[1] C. Clark and K. Powell, *Deep Ministry in a Shallow World* (Grand Rapids: Zondervan, 2006), 109. Powell points toward a "constellation of mentors" as the cure for any isolationist or avoidance tendencies that a student might demonstrate.

> close to them. What is perhaps even more surprising is that this is true even for those kids who send the exact opposite message—the "I don't need you or want you" message. But please be assured, your child innately longs for you to actively and intently care about them. The key is *how* we as parents show we care, how genuinely and on what basis our love is dispensed, and how consistently our message of love and engaged compassion is presented.[2]

In fact, when students are asked who the greatest influences are on their lives, they indicate their parents. For example, when Rick Lawrence surveyed 10,000 students that took part in Group's work camps during the summer of 2003, he found that the number one reason students said their faith had deepened was because their *parents* influenced them to grow.[3]

Steve Keels points out that there are three practical reasons parents are in a unique, and primary, position to mentor and influence their teenagers. First, they have an unparalleled, "indescribable" *love* for their children. He reminds parents: "The bottom line is this: No one loves your kids the way you do. Others can appreciate your children, good people will take the time to coach them, and some will even go out of their way to help them. But no one loves your children as you do. It's this radical, self-denying, all-consuming love that qualifies you to be a major influence in their lives."[4]

In addition to this unrivaled love, parents also *know* their children better than anyone else. Clark notes that the increasing connection to friends is apparent in almost every teenager's social development but sees a potential perceptual problem. Parents and other adults (including youth ministers), observing these other relationships increase in significance, often conclude falsely that the parental influence naturally tapers off at this stage. While friends may have known each other for a few years, their time together has been spent primarily in controlled and guarded environments, much like an extended first date. Parents, by contrast, see students when their hair and teeth have not been brushed, when their attitudes and actions are not

[2] C. Clark and D. Clark, *Disconnected: Parenting Teens in a MySpace World* (Grand Rapids: Baker, 2007), 36.

[3] R. Lawrence, ed., *Jesus-Centered Youth Ministry* (Loveland, CO: Group, 2007), 117.

[4] S. Keels and D. Vorm, *Transparenting: Mentoring the Next Generation* (Nashville: B&H, 2006), 73.

as tightly reined in, and with their full history in view (even if they may not know who their favorite pop star is this week).

Third, children have been entrusted to their parents for the *purpose* of influence. Children are a stewardship from God that we, as parents and youth leaders, must seek to influence in godliness and obedience to His Word (Ps 127:3–5). [5] Many teenagers seem to understand innately this social and biblical pattern of influence, as they consistently point to the primary weight of parental modeling on their lives.[6] The issue is not whether parents will function as an influence, but rather the *type* influence they will be.

COME TOGETHER: EQUIPPING AND MOBILIZING FAMILIES

Merton Strommen and Richard Hardel offer several thoughts on how to strengthen parents as influencers by equipping parents to develop more solid relationships with God *within and through the family*:

1. Becoming gospel-oriented parents
2. Communicating moral values
3. Being involved in service activities
4. Sharing faith at home[7]

The nature of each of these contributors to greater faith in youth is summarized in figure 10.2.

These are predominately "ought-tos," which are so much easier to pinpoint than "how-tos." But if we look more closely at the basic implications of these traits, we see that modeling through involvement in mission and service is a key way that life leaders (parents or guardians) can demonstrate dynamic faith to and live it out with their students.

In fact, living life on mission allows parents to show that they are gospel oriented, morally intent, and authentically living by faith in Jesus. These areas are linked to one another. And as Keels points out, while effective mentoring influences your kids toward mission involvement, even greater influence can come through going together. He notes that a STM provides "focused ministry" and a "shared experience" that have the po-

[5] Ibid., 10–15.

[6] M. DeVries, *Family-Based Youth Ministry* (Downers Grove, IL: InterVarsity, 2004), 61–62.

[7] M. Strommen and R. Hardel, *Passing on the Faith: A Radical New Model for Youth and Family Ministry* (Winona, MN: Saint Mary's, 2000), 81.

tential to help galvanize the relationship and direct ongoing conversation and thinking about life and mission.[8]

Gospel-Oriented Living	Communicating Morals	Involvement in Service	Sharing Faith at Home
Marks of these parents: ▶ Value a spiritual dimension to life ▶ Know a personal, caring God ▶ Are relatively certain of their faith ▶ Are biblically oriented ▶ Consider their faith to be important ▶ Take a positive attitude toward life and death ▶ Reject the idea of salvation by works	***Example moral values:*** ▶ Care for your family ▶ Do good to others ▶ Protect the powerless ▶ Show generosity and mercy ▶ Keep promises ▶ Postpone gratification ***Motivations for these values:*** An ethic of responsible love Concern for others Personal faith	***Service is tied to:*** ▶ Faith maturity in children and youth ▶ Bonding of youth to the church ▶ Youth avoiding at-risk behaviors ▶ Countering self-centeredness ▶ Entertaining service professions as viable vocational options ▶ Critical thinking and service-learning	***Characteristics of committed youth (modeled by parents):*** ▶ Trust in a personal Christ ▶ Understand and live in grace ▶ Commune with God regularly ▶ Demonstrate moral responsibility ▶ Accept responsibility in a congregation ▶ Accept authority and be personally responsible ▶ Have a hopeful and positive attitude ▶ Engage in mission and service

Figure 10.2: Summary of Strommen and Hardel's Family Contributors to Faith[9]

Often it is difficult for us to perceive the priority of parents because we see so many examples of unhealthy parent-child relationships. That is precisely why our ministries, and our churches as a whole, must find ways not only to raise expectations to the level of a more biblically grounded parental discipleship but also to help families meet that standard. Greg Ogden offers a model for "parental empowerment," which he outlines for use in "multiplying" discipleship triads.[10] We have adapted and modified it

[8] Keels and Vorm, *Transparenting*, 73.
[9] Ibid.
[10] G. Ogden, *Transforming Discipleship* (Downers Grove, IL: InterVarsity, 2003), 105–17.

here because of its specific implications for parents wanting to understand how to connect better with their children (see fig. 10.3).

Life Stage	Life Stage Need	Disciple's Role	Parent's Role
Infancy	Modeling and direction	Imitation	Model
Childhood	Unconditional love and protection	Identification	Hero
Adolescence	Increased freedom and identity formation	Exhortation	Coach
Adulthood	Mutuality and reciprocity	Participation	Peer

Figure 10.3: Adaptation of "Paul's Empowerment Model" (Ogden)[11]

Much of this approach is about understanding relational needs, as determined by a child's life stage as well as maturational rate. The parent who understands that he needs to adjust his particular *style* of relating to and maintaining authority over his child—while still maintaining that guiding authority influence—will be assisted in his ability to parent well.

After more than 20 years in student ministry, and now a parent of teenagers himself, Steve Wright has come to this realization about his ability to influence students: "In the long run it is best to do everything we can to encourage the relationship with mom and dad since they have a much greater influence today and in the future than we will ever have. To ensure the advice they are giving their children is biblical, our church must teach and disciple parents."[12] The student minister's role is not so much training parents to have myriad specific skills as it is offering general support and encouragement for family structure and relationships.[13] In establishing relational connections for STM, do not overlook the existing connection of parent to youth. When parents are not connected to your church or ministry, explore how you can get them plugged in. Moreover, connect each

[11] Ibid., 105. In Ogden's model, the final column, which we have labeled "parent's role," is labeled "Paul's role." The outline of these stages, and the connected actions of both the disciple and the discipler, is derived from Pauline epistolary themes: "imitation" of a model (1 Cor 4:16; 1 Thess 2:7—"identification" with the mentor); "exhortation" to live faithfully (2 Tim 4:5); and "participation" in partnership with the disciple (Rom 1:11–12).

[12] S. Wright and C. Graves, *Rethink* (Wake Forest, NC: Inquest, 2007), 153.

[13] M. Strommen, K. Jones, and D. Rahn, *Youth Ministry That Transforms* (Grand Rapids: Zondervan, 2001), 292.

of your students to a qualified and trained mentor-coach. For those with absentee or unmotivated parents, mentor-coaches can stand in the gap.

Mentor-Coaches: Focused Leaders

When we hear the word *coach,* images of a has-been athlete, donning a collared shirt that is tucked in, shorts, a whistle, and striped knee-high tube socks flood into our minds. If you grew up in the seventies and eighties, you know exactly what we are talking about. The coaches that we have in mind here are different. They still provide direction and skill development, but they also provide a relationship that encourages Christ-centered growth.

Though the concept of relational coaching has been defined in varying ways, there are some common points of agreement:

> Coaching helps people go from where they are to where they want to be. It is an action-oriented partnership that helps people stay focused on the results they want to achieve.[14]
>
> Coaching is the art and practice of guiding a person or group from where they are toward the greater competence and fulfillment that they desire.[15]
>
> Coaching is the practice of believing in people in order to empower them to change.[16]
>
> Christian coaching is a focused Christ-centered relationship that cultivates a person's sustained growth and action.[17]
>
> Coaching is an incarnational relationship between one leader and another that is intended to empower his or her life and ministry.[18]

---

[14] T. Hawkins, "Coaching, Pastoral Counseling, and Ministry," *Quarterly Review* 25 (2005): 297.
[15] G. Collins, *Christian Coaching* (Colorado Springs, CO: NavPress, 2001), 16.
[16] T. Stoltzfus, *Leadership Coaching* (Virginia Beach, VA: BookSurge, 2005), 7.
[17] L. Miller and C. Hall, *Coaching for Christian Leaders* (St. Louis, MO: Chalice Press, 2007), 10.
[18] S. Ogne and T. Roehl, *TransforMissional Coaching* (Nashville: B&H, 2008), 26.

Terms like *partnership, empower, competence,* and *action* indicate a skill-development orientation to coaching that may also be present in some forms of mentoring; however, Bill Hull clarifies the need for distinction between these two roles:

> At first glance, coaching and mentoring seem to be two words that describe the same process. Yet the difference is meaningful. While coaching focuses on skills and equipping, mentoring helps others make sense of their lives. More specifically, spiritual mentoring helps an individual gain awareness of his personhood as he lives under God. A godly mentor can help us emerge from the limits of self-fulfillment and narcissism to discover the joy of living for others.[19]

This distinction is the reason we need mentor-coaches for our students (see fig. 10.4). We want to help them as they gain a biblical perspective on life and the world (mentoring) and as they develop the skills necessary to act in keeping with what they uncover in their study (coaching).

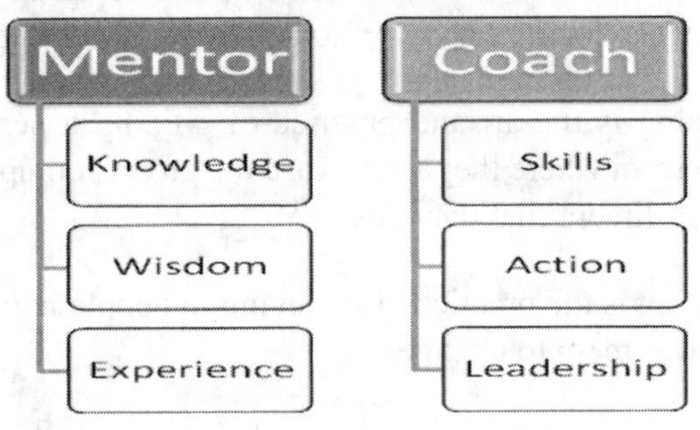

Figure 10.4: Example Benefits Provided by Mentors and Coaches

As a result of this relationship, the student has both an ongoing source of wisdom and direction as well as skilled guidance to help him discern how critically to assess similar circumstances in the future.

A mentor-coach can be trained to ask the right questions. In a coaching paradigm, questions are one of the essential "tools" used by the coach to "focus a conversation, foster exploration, push the client to dig deeper and reach higher, and ensure commitment."[20] Miller and Hall place "fo-

[19] B. Hull, *The Complete Book of Discipleship* (Colorado Springs, CO: NavPress, 2006), 214.

[20] Stoltzfus, *Leadership Coaching*, 177.

cused listening" and "asking precise questions" at the core of their body of crucial coaching skills.[21] The intent in both listening to the student's processing of challenges, concerns, and convictions, and in asking pointed and exacting questions, is to move the student to "intentional action" based on this evaluation.[22]

Larry Ambrose adds that exemplary mentors ask three primary types of questions: (1) *investigative*—probing questions seeking basic types of information; (2) *discovery*—perspective-taking, probing questions that assess experiences; and (3) *empowering*—questions that target objectives and map the course by which to achieve these aims (see fig. 10.5).[23] Questions like these push the student, and mentor, to assess fundamental issues and concerns in reference to mission and life in general.[24]

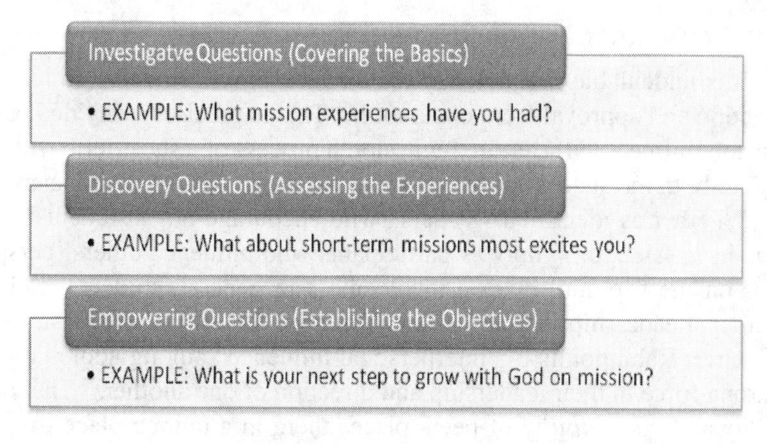

Figure 10.5: Question Types and Examples for Coaching

The mentor-coach also provides support. This support is, in optimal expression, a constant in the mentor-coach's approach. It involves the aforementioned skillful precision in asking questions (and actively listening), as well as an open and responsive relationship with the student, and an unwavering commitment to his development through "experiential" and "relational" support structures.[25] A mentor-coach gives students a living example that can "show" them what it means to persevere in godliness

[21] Miller and Hall, *Coaching for Christian Leaders*, 22–23.

[22] Ibid., 32.

[23] L. Ambrose, *A Mentor's Companion* (Chicago: Perrone-Ambrose Associates, 1998), 12–14.

[24] J. Lottes, "Jesus as Mentor: Biblical Reflections for Ministry with Young Adults," *Currents in Theology and Mission* 32 (2005): 129.

[25] J. Umidi, *Transformational Coaching* (Longwood, FL: Xulon Press, 2005), 93–96.

and growth, while asking them challenging questions to push them toward resolving their own struggles (dissonance) that come with the raw experience of mission.[26]

TEAM: MEMBERS AND LEADERS

Short-term team building holds great possibilities for the formation of new relationships or the deepening of existing ones. It is natural, then, that other student and adult short-term team members possess huge influence potential.

THE POWER OF PEERS

It is undeniable that socially focused teenagers are going to look for direction and approval from one another. That is precisely why dedication and commitment to the entire multimonth process of a short-term trip is so vital to both the success of the mission and the dynamics of the team.

Whether as identified "leaders" who encourage other students to engage in mission, or simply as participants who influence others' perspectives on the trip and mission involvement in general, students lead one another. Leadership, as many have observed, is, at its most basic level, influence. Rahn points to "interpersonal influence" among adolescents as a strong force in their leadership and direction of one another.[27] The *availability* and *accessibility* of peers places them in a unique place to informally and formally influence one another for mission.

Years of experience in youth ministry and mission have shaped Paul Borthwick's suggestions for recognizing and facilitating leadership in students who have a passion for mission. First, he suggests that we *affirm* their experience and interest. Doing this both privately and publicly can encourage the student and others to begin to view him as a resource and an example in mission.

Second, we should *moderate* the degree of leadership required. For some of us, it is rare to see a student commit wholeheartedly to mission. So when we see interest, we can tend to overload that individual with STM

[26] D. Rahn, "Restoring Adolescents: Essentials of Worldwide Ministry," in *Introduction to Christian Education and Formation,* ed. R. Habermas (Grand Rapids: Zondervan, 2008), 166.

[27] D. Rahn, "Focusing Youth Ministry Through Student Leadership," in *Starting Right,* ed. K. C. Dean, C. Clark, and D. Rahn (Grand Rapids: Zondervan, 2001), 170.

leadership responsibilities. Exercising some patience—and realism—about his abilities, time availability, and maturity can temper this tendency.

Third, we should emphasize *teamwork* as a developmental tool that can shape their initiative. Teaming the motivated students up with those less motivated can serve each student's growth. The leader can do this, for example, during STM preparation, on-field prayer and debriefing, and post-field service. In each of these phases, students can influence one another's understanding and practice.

Finally, Borthwick advocates that we give *special treatment* to those who have cross-cultural experience. The goal is not to elevate these individuals above the other students, but, as with the affirmation mentioned above, by recognizing their achievements and interest as exceptional to make them less so. In other words, the more commonplace these recognitions become, the more potential there is for students to see cross-cultural experience as a normative part of thinking and living.[28]

THE LIVES OF LEADERS

Some will recoil at the idea of student or adult leaders "influencing" students. They will say that this implies intrusiveness and fails to imitate Jesus' own incarnational model for relational ministry. However, the difficulty with associating the *nature* of our ministry too closely with Jesus' unique and perfect taking on of flesh, rather than his *practice*, is not only that it is theologically tenuous but also that it presents a false dilemma. Namely, this argument suggests that one must choose between being with students *or* influencing them.

The idea that Jesus was driven primarily to be with His disciples, rather than to influence them, flies in the face of passages that detail His call for absolute commitment (Matt 16:24–26) and His mandate to summon others to this same life-changing allegiance (Matt 28:18–20).

We would like to see a *representational* approach to youth mentorship lived out. In this model we are representatives of the King and His kingdom to those whom we lead and engage with the life-changing truth of the incarnate Son of God. Being "present" with our students through every twist and turn of life is a necessary component of being a diligent representative (incarnational *practice*). It is not the end itself, of course; rather, our walking with them (representational *nature*) is the means to their transformation (the end).

[28] P. Borthwick, *Youth and Mission* (Waynesboro, GA: OM, 1988), 83–87.

While parents, mentor-coaches, and peers each have the ability to be these types of representatives, other leaders involved in your student ministry also have the ability to influence students. Their opportunity springs from their role in participating along with the students in this challenging experience while also maintaining what should be a further-developed sense of the import of mission involvement. This will not always be the case, though, as many students will have the greater effect on adult leaders, as they exercise boldness in service. Our point is that your team development should include the placement of adult leaders who can offer perspective and experience to the insights and observations of your students.

Church: Driving Force, Greenhouse, and Launching Pad

The vision statement for one church where I served was simple and concise: "Developing Ministries Throughout the World." This statement hung on the wall in our worship center beside a map detailing the locations where we sent our own members as missionaries. The statement also hung on the wall of our youth facility, so that our leaders and students would consistently ask this question: "Is what we are doing right now going to develop disciples and ministries around the world?" The reason we could ask this question was because our leaders, members, and even those visiting knew that this was what we lived to do, *as a church*. Mission was not merely an element of what the church was about; it was our main expression of worship.

After evaluating scores of churches across the United States, Tom Telford identified nine marks of a "top-notch" mission-focused church:

1. The church must have an outward focus and strategy.
2. At least 30 percent of the church's budget must go to missions.
3. The church must have an ongoing training program for missionary candidates.
4. Missions education must be integrated into all the programs of the church.
5. The church must send its own people.
6. The church must be concerned about and pray for the lost.
7. The church must have a pastor that leads them in vision and outreach.

8. The church must be interested in helping other churches in missions.
9. The church must have a strong evangelism program focusing on its community.[29]

Church leaders and members of congregations like these direct their strategy, focus, and budget toward training programs, integrated missions education, launch of its own people, prayer for the lost, help for other churches involved in missions, and evangelism in the community. They "bleed" mission.

These are environments where relationships and initiatives are all focused on transformation that ripples out to the ends of the earth. These are churches that understand their *foundational* role in mission and live to see it happen. A crucial way these strategies can coalesce around the development of students is through heeding the admonition of Terry Hulbert to grow missionaries, as recounted by Borthwick:

> One of the greatest contributions the local church can make to worldwide evangelization is not just by giving money, but by growing missionaries. By modeling, teaching, training, motivating, counseling, encouraging, informing, and challenging people from their early years into the teens right through college, the church can move them right up to the launching pad from which they are propelled into the orbit of cross-cultural ministry.[30]

The activities can be championed by the church, enacted by the aforementioned personal influences, and facilitated through mission education and STM experience with students.

Influencing toward Transformation

In order for these influences to function in concert, there must also be a developmental plan in place. Ed Stetzer and David Putman see becoming a "missional" disciple as a process that looks similar to what is represented in figure 10.6.

[29] T. Telford, *All-Star Missions Churches* (Grand Rapids: Baker, 2001), 133–34.

[30] T. Hulbert, *Discipling Leaders with a Vision for the World* (Coral Gables, FL: Worldteam, 1984), 7.

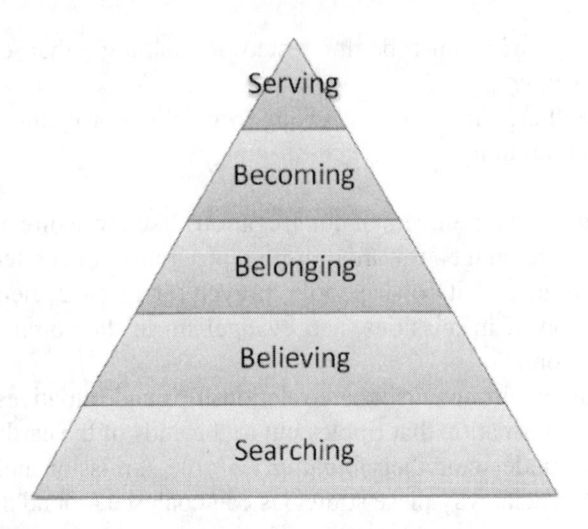

Figure 10.6: Developmental Process, Adapted from Stetzer and Putman[31]

Although this is not a lockstep progression, whereby the disciple always moves forward, it is a basic transforming progression that ultimately matures into active service. In order for a process like this one to unfold in a student's life, there must be directed relationships supporting his development. The influences are, as they participate in the process, walking with the student toward transformation. The plan to develop students through a process like this one is the subject of our next chapter.

DISCUSSION QUESTIONS

1. Discuss the role each of the following have in influencing students: life leaders, mentor-coaches, short-term team members, and the local church.
2. How would you intentionally develop this relational context in your youth ministry?
3. Which of the four relationships mentioned in this chapter had the greatest influence on your Christian formation?

[31] E. Stetzer and D. Putman, *Breaking the Missional Code* (Nashville: B&H, 2006), 128.

CHAPTER 11

DEVELOP: SHAPE THEM THROUGH PROCESS

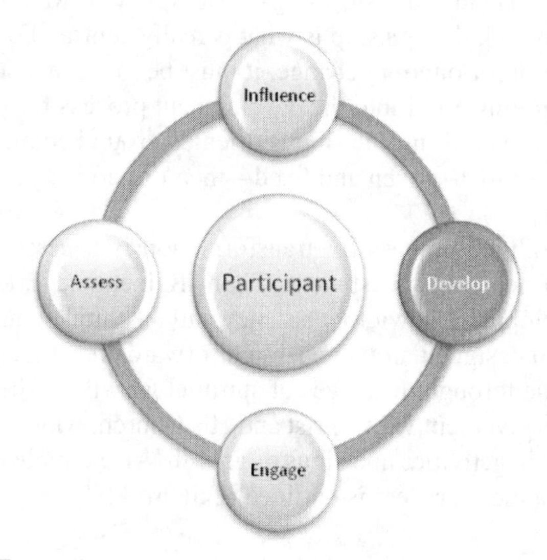

THE MAKING OF SKYWALKER

Becoming a Jedi knight like Luke Skywalker is largely about influence through relationships. Anyone who has watched the *Star Wars* saga knows that there is a master like Yoda (teacher) and a padawan like Luke (learner). The learner watches and emulates his master, completing certain tasks and trials, until he himself becomes a Jedi master and takes on a protégé of his own. The value of the relationship is tied to the method of tutoring the potential Jedi in the ways of the force. Without the system the relationship has no certain goal at which to aim.

In much the same way, influence toward obedience in mission may be relational, but it must also be methodological. If surrounding students with meaningful connections represents a fight against selective exposure, then the developmental discipleship process and curriculum is the battlefield on which this fight unfolds. It forms the parameters and constraints within which STM thought and practice are developed. In our view each of these influential relationship types plays a role in discipling students.

SEAMLESS ONGOING DEVELOPMENT

When STM is purely a onetime event, there is no reason to believe that it will be consistently transforming—that is why STM is not the heart of the issue. Instead, discipleship is what is really central. For STM to act as a catalytic tool for ongoing change, it must be more than an event or program.[1] Integrating STM into the development process for your students is not easy; however, if discipleship is oriented around communicating truth through the Word—spoken and lived—then mission experiences can help facilitate this.

A streamlined process for transformation is necessary to gauge the discipleship needs of the student. Thom Rainer and Eric Geiger refine church development down to what they call a "simple church," that is, "a congregation designed around a straightforward and strategic process that moves people through the stages of spiritual growth."[2] These "stages" are phases of involvement with Christ and His Church, which are distinguishable by certain activities and signs of growth. An example of a straightforward development process is outlined in figure 11.1.

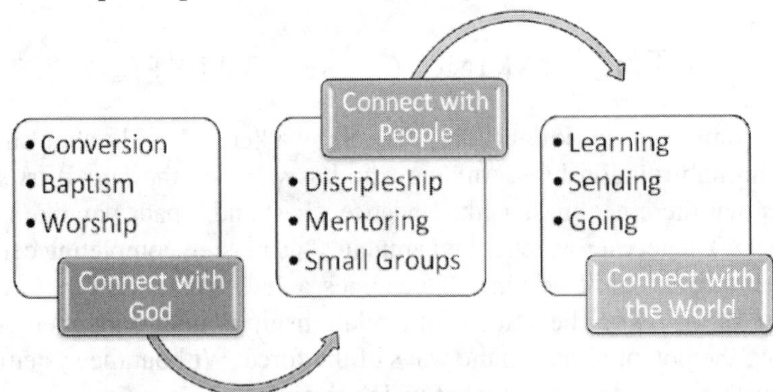

Figure 11.1: Example Discipleship Process

[1] D. Robbins, *This Way to Youth Ministry* (Grand Rapids: Zondervan, 2004), 448–49.

[2] T. Rainer and E. Geiger, *Simple Church* (Nashville: B&H, 2006), 60.

In this process the individual first comes into relationship with God (*Connect with God*), then is connected with the church and its other members (*Connect with People*), and finally joins hands with those other believers to engage the community and the world with the same truth that has transformed them (*Connect with the World*).

In this approach the student ministry also uses the same process to guide students to become more fully engaged in the church and with its global mission. Short-term trips fit into the last stage; however, students' influential relationships with parents, leaders, mentor-coaches, and those in their small group could, and should, begin before they are a part of a short-term team. In fact, God will most likely use these relationships to drive students toward STM participation. Such is the design and intent of a process like this.

What approach is taken to discipling students will be determined by what type of disciple we leaders want to see God produce.[3] The weekly, monthly, quarterly, and even annual planning we do will be informed and constrained by what a disciple should look like. A basic definition of a disciple is "a learner or follower of Jesus Christ."[4] While this is an accurate description of *what* a disciple is, *how* they "learn" and "follow" is another matter: What should they learn, and how do they learn it? What does it look like to follow Jesus, and how do students learn to do that? If you are still holding this book, our assumption is that you at least believe that learning to live out mission is part of what it means for students to become more mature disciples.

Learning and Following: Curriculum for the Process

When we speak about curriculum, we do not merely mean a classroom educational plan, or set of teaching outlines. In the truest sense of the term, a curriculum encompasses the whole of one's development to maturity; it refers to the *people*, *environments*, *content*, and *activities* that play a role in the growth of the follower-learner.

---

[3] Ibid., 115.

[4] B. Waggoner, *The Shape of Faith to Come* (Nashville: B&H, 2008), 14.

TRANSFORMISSIONAL PEOPLE

The influences mentioned above are the people who will influence students to embody mission on a daily basis and through short-term mobilization. A process approach allows each influence to understand his role, both in terms of where the student is in the process and in reference to the other active leaders involved. This, in turn, permits the content of discipleship to be offered within multiple deepening relationships and in differing manners. Although there are primary pathways to content delivery for each of those in relationship with the student, these pathways are fairly fluid and can be accentuated by other means of instruction (see fig. 11.2).

Figure 11.2: Some Transformissional Influence Types in the Development Process

The relational bonds that are formed through this approach can permit greater depth of study and dialogue, which many times fosters even deeper ties. This reciprocal pattern seems to be an organic display of what it means to walk with students and develop influential, mission-focused relationships.[5]

TRANSFORMISSIONAL ENVIRONMENTS

We are not purely a by-product of our environment, but extended presence in a particular setting has an undeniable bearing on whom we become. The more normative global awareness and service are in the *home*, the more likely they will be grafted into the worldview of a student. Sur-

[5] D. Putman, *Breaking the Discipleship Code* (Nashville: B&H, 2008), 81.

rounding children and youth with the sights (e.g., decorations, artifacts, videos), smells (e.g., indigenous fairly traded teas, spices, and food), tastes (food), issues (e.g., unreached areas, poverty, slavery), and people (e.g., international friends and missionaries on home assignment as dinner and house guests) that are a part of the larger world in which they live will help them comprehend that the scope of their reality is bigger than their school, town, state, or nation.[6]

The *church* can not only help life leaders appropriate and model these attitudes in the home; they can make the church "home" a place that models a mission-minded atmosphere. Through cultivating a deliberate ethos of mission, a church can make great strides toward growing students who relish the opportunity of living a life on the edge for Jesus throughout the whole world. To create this ethos, Hulbert and Kenneth Mulholland suggest that the church focus not only on conducting mission conferences and worship series but also on providing a steady diet of education (which we will discuss in more detail below); identifying and preparing their own missionaries; caring for missionaries on home assignment (e.g., through funding, housing, relational support); and financially supporting mission personnel, agencies, and movements.[7]

Employing these practices—in addition to becoming a multicultural church through intentional cross-cultural ministry in the immediate community—can create a tenor of missional living. Jim Estep reminds us that "curriculum is not something that can simply be purchased. When taken seriously, curriculum is the expression of the congregation's educational ministry and even culture."[8] Expressing a culture of mission is an approach to developing people that is, itself, mission focused.

In an approach to *student ministry* that sees its principles and functions as tied inseparably to those of the church, the process of creating an environment is heavily influenced by the body. There are exceptions to this general rule, as the young may be the channel through which the church as a whole becomes mission focused, which has occurred at times in the past. In this case, deference to pastoral leadership and a team approach to charting a global direction for your students is the mark of wise leadership. Student ministry leaders must patiently and methodically communicate the biblical and philosophical reasons for a mission concentration in

[6] P. Borthwick, *Youth and Mission* (Waynesboro, GA: OM, 1988), 76–80.

[7] T. Hulbert and K. Mulholland, *World Missions Today* (Wheaton, IL: Evangelical Training Association, 1990), 47–51.

[8] J. Estep, M. Anthony, and G. Allison, *A Theology for Christian Education* (Nashville: B&H, 2008), 282.

student ministry, to ensure that they bring other church members along in this change, rather than alienate them from the process. In any case, exposure to cross-cultural issues and experiences, especially through multigenerational STMs, can sometimes be the stimulant for creating a mission environment, just as much as it is resultant from such an environment.

Transformissional Content

Much of the existing curriculum for students—aside from the occasional multiweek study on missions or preparatory STM studies—does not reflect a cross-cultural mission priority. This is not a knock on student curriculum. Much of what is produced has some real disciple-making potential. Yet our concern is not for a "curriculum content piece" but an integrated mission emphasis that prevents students from ducking and dodging their global responsibility. This integration must be observed in what we say and do, and it needs to be arranged around three primary content spheres: (1) *biblical-theological*, (2) *historical-philosophical*, (3) and *cultural-anthropological* (see fig. 11.3).

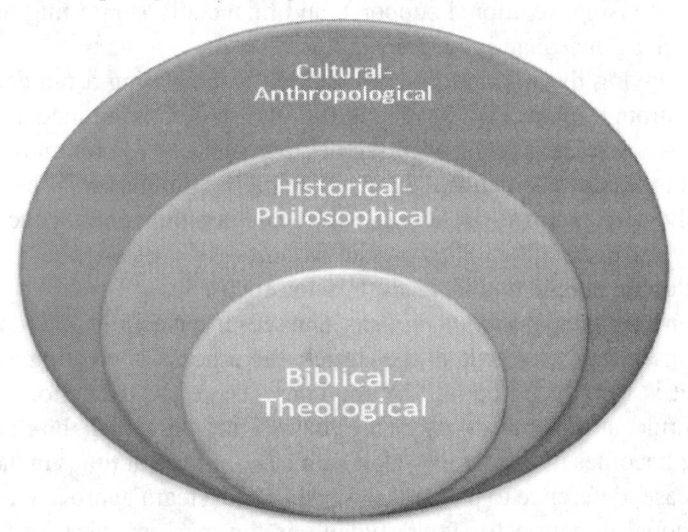

Figure 11.3: Spheres of Student Mission Curriculum

Sphere 1: Biblical-Theological. A steady diet of biblical teaching and preaching, which includes intense times of parental-, mentor-coach–, and small group–based dialogue and discovery learning exercises, is crucial in preparing for short-term mission trips and enhancing their long-term impact on student lives. This sphere must be first in priority and time allotment because Scripture is the rule and standard by which we judge all other experiences and realities.

As I am writing this, Christmas is just a few weeks away, and I have begun one of my annual traditions (warning: this is going to lose me a lot of "cool points" with some of you): reading Charles Dickens's *A Christmas Carol*. Dickens is my favorite author, by far. He is such an engaging storyteller, who paints remarkably vivid pictures of his various settings and characters; and Ebenezer Scrooge's journey from detestable creature to one that "knew how to keep Christmas well" has got to be one of the greatest pictures of literary redemption ever painted.

Scrooge's interaction with a pack of holiday spirits commences with a visit from his seven-years dead partner, Jacob Marley. When Scrooge evinces doubt about the real existence of Marley's ghost, the chain-clad spirit asks Ebenezer why he chooses to disbelieve "his senses." Scrooge replies, "Because a little thing affects them. A slight disorder of the stomach makes them cheats. You may be an undigested bit of beef, a blot of mustard, a crumb of cheese, a fragment of an underdone potato. There's more of gravy than of grave about you, whatever you are!"[9] Scrooge's defense of doubt serves as an illustration of the importance of a solid foundation for interpreting experience. Because what students see is filtered through their senses and their existing view of reality, we must ensure that their epistemological basis is scripturally forged. Once this is achieved, we can then develop a biblically driven perspective on historical and cultural issues in mission, rather than starting with the issues of culture and historical interpretation.

This is not to suggest that one cannot teach the other spheres concurrently with the biblical material. In fact, this is often the best way to communicate. For example, you may be teaching your students Psalm 67 (ESV), which reads:

> May God be gracious to us and bless us and make his face to shine upon us, that your way may be known on earth, your saving power among all nations.
>
> Let the peoples praise you, O God; let all the peoples praise you! Let the nations be glad and sing for joy, for you judge the peoples with equity and guide the nations upon earth. Let the peoples praise you, O God; let all the

[9] C. Dickens, *A Christmas Carol* (1843; repr., New York: Simon & Schuster, 1967), 43.

> peoples praise you! The earth has yielded its increase; God, our God, shall bless us. God shall bless us; let all the ends of the earth fear him!

If you emphasize, as the ultimate objective of mission and life, this prayer's hope in God for the peoples of the earth to worship and glorify Him, you can also show students snapshot markers that demonstrate this theme throughout the canon of Scripture (e.g., Isa 43:6–7; Jer 13:11; John 12:27–28; 17:24; Rom 3:25–26; Eph 1:4–6; Rev 21:23).[10]

Since the "nations" here are the people groups that we looked at in the opening chapter, you might also describe to students what it means for these ethno-linguistic groups to be without the gospel, giving details about their population numbers and dwelling places in the world. Doing this helps students see where the exclusivity of Jesus and the state of sinful humanity come to bear on their view of reality (worldview). Leaders can get the most recent statistics on these groups from www.joshuaproject.net and zero in on one as an example. Moreover, consider providing living or past examples of those who have poured out their lives reaching one of these people groups. Interviewing a missionary on Skype, for example, could be a great way to get firsthand cultural realities in front of your students.

In this example, we started with the biblical text and offered students a thematic sketch of the main thrust. We then explored with them the nature of concepts and how these connect with their worldview, while at the same time illuminating contemporary cultural examples, as well as a living example of what it means to connect with these groups. The point is that we were able to cover all three spheres, in one teaching session, while still sifting everything through the foundational grid of the Bible.

Sphere 2: Historical-Philosophical. Considering how the Church has understood and expressed cross-cultural mission through the centuries can both challenge and inform students. Expecting disciples to have a "global vision" is by no means a new standard; rather, growth in this essential area has merely been highlighted, and helped, by the recent trends in globalization.[11] People like David Brainerd, William Carey, Adoniram Judson, Amy Carmichael, David Livingstone, and many others have made a lasting impression on our thinking about life and mission. They all have something important in common—they are all dead. This is important because

[10] See J. Piper, *Let the Nations Be Glad* (Grand Rapids: Baker, 2003), 22–27, for a more extensive listing of texts outlining God's intention that all mission be for His glory.

[11] D. Wells, "Christian Discipleship in a Postmodern World," *Journal of the Evangelical Theological Society* 51 (2008): 32.

often we can only determine the measure and contribution—including the flaws—of someone's life after we have observed the results for a season.

Lives that have proven to inspire, challenge, and caution believers in general, and would-be missionaries in particular, can benefit your students and their families. For example, you might speak about the life of abolitionist William Wilberforce, and then challenge students to think about the fact that "today, 27 million people are enslaved, which is more than were enslaved during four centuries of the transatlantic slave trade."[12] This realization creates significant dissonance that in turn requires action—either to avoid the plight of these people or do something about it.

Zach Hunter heard about the life of Wilberforce and the grim reality of modern-day slavery. What did he do with this new knowledge and the dissonance it caused in his life? He became a modern-day abolitionist and is now a spokesman for the Amazing Change Campaign, which works to free slaves.[13] By the way, he is only 16, which tells us several things.

First, those that say young people are not influenced by biographies are misinformed. Granted, not every student becomes an abolitionist after watching *Amazing Grace*, but Zach points to parental influences as key to cultivating this determination to make a difference.[14] Independent of and isolated from other influences pushing a Christ-consumed mission in life and thought, little will probably come of reading or viewing works. Coupled with ongoing relational influences, however, these historical and living examples of mission-saturated lives have the potential to inspire believers at any age.

Second, observing living (even once-living) examples of mission-driven individuals allows our students to test their own value system and worldview against those who have made a significant contribution to the kingdom. This assessment process serves as an excellent educational tool for creating and resolving dissonance through critical thinking, as students are pushed to consider what they would do when faced with the same challenges and successes.

Sphere 3: Cultural-Anthropological. Understanding how and why people live, act, and interact as they do within their culture is the fundamental task of anthropology. Therefore, youth leaders are cultural anthropologists—at least they should be seen this way. We do not mean, of

[12] H. Dodson, "Slavery in the Twenty-first Century," *UN Chronicle* 42 (September 2005): n.p. Cited 12 December 2008. Online:http://www.un.org/Pubs/chronicle/2005/issue3/0305p28.html.

[13] See http://www.theamazingchange.com for details on the campaign and its structured aims (accessed August 17, 2008).

[14] Z. Hunter, *Be the Change* (Grand Rapids: Zondervan, 2007), 16–17.

course, that you should stop serving students to go back to school yourself in order to change careers. Anthropology is not your full-time vocation, but it should be an abiding concern. For there is a pressing need to better understand and serve students who live in a specific cultural setting or context.[15]

This is not only a need for your own immediate ministry—as you seek to understand and assimilate students from various cultural enclaves—but it is also of paramount importance in your training of the next generation to take right action based on biblical and philosophical foundations. Viewing anthropology this way takes it back to its roots, since it was originally conceived as a way to "understand people from a theological perspective," which is key to effective cross-cultural ministry.[16]

A holistic approach to training students, and yourself, to be prepared to cross cultures effectively is Dave Livermore's cultural intelligence (CQ) evaluation. Hoping to classify the chief areas of cross-cultural understanding and practice, specifically as they relate to STM, Livermore identified these four types of CQ:

> **Knowledge CQ: Understanding Cross-Cultural Differences**
> Knowledge CQ, or cognitive CQ as it is called in the original research, measures our level of knowledge about and *understanding* of cross-cultural differences.
>
> **Interpretive CQ: Interpreting Cues**
> Interpretive CQ, or meta-cognitive CQ as it is called in the original research, measures our ability to *interpret* accurately cues we receive as we engage cross-culturally.
>
> **Perseverance CQ: Persevering Through Cross-Cultural Conflict**
> Perseverance CQ, or motivational CQ as it is called in the original research, measures our degree of interest in *persevering* through cross-cultural conflict.

[15] W. Mueller, *Engaging the Soul of Youth Culture* (Downers Grove, IL: InterVarsity, 2006), 11.
[16] P. Hiebert, *Cultural Anthropology* (Grand Rapids: Baker, 1983), xvi.

> **Behavioral CQ: Acting Appropriately**
> Behavioral CQ, which is what it is also called in the original research, measures our ability to *act* appropriately when interacting cross-culturally.[17]

Livermore points out that these four types of CQ together represent an interdependent grouping of aptitudes that must be nurtured for effective STM to occur. While most cross-cultural preparation models do invest some time in training students for understanding and behavior, Livermore argues that the higher level skills of interpreting cultural cues and persevering through conflict are of critical importance on account of the role they play in cross-cultural communication and service. To satisfy our students' need to become culturally mindful, therefore, we as leaders should both employ continuing mission education replete with cultural examples and equip STM participants for the specific beliefs and practices of the recipient culture (see fig. 11.4).[18]

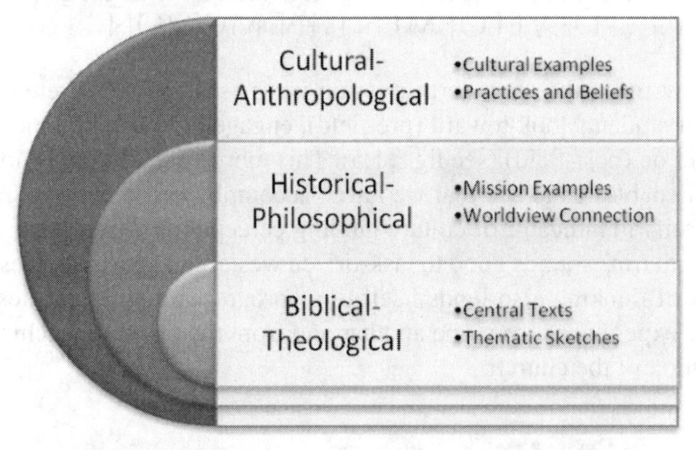

Figure 11.4: The Subcategories of the Curricular Spheres

Transformissional Activities

For discipleship truly to take place, we must reinforce the missional concepts we teach (content) with concrete actions (method).[19] As Chris

[17] D. Livermore, *Serving with Eyes Wide Open* (Grand Rapids: Baker, 2006), 111.

[18] D. Sills, "How Shall They Hear the Gospel?" *Southern Baptist Journal of Theology* 9 (2005): 71. Sills uses the term *culturalities* to depict the distinct "types and dynamics" of each culture, which includes how they conceptualize reality.

[19] M. Clendinning, "Strategies for Mission Education in the Local Church," in *Missiology,* ed. J. M. Terry, E. Smith, and J. Anderson (Nashville: B&H, 1998), 613.

Folmsbee says, "Discipleship is not solely about learning more about God. It's about learning how to live one's life to glorify God."[20] Missional content and action together must be perennial components of what we passionately communicate to students. As Monte Clendinning reminds us, "Continuous, ongoing, missions education is one process whereby every church member can experience consistent obedience to Jesus' commands (Matt. 28:16–29; Acts 1:8) by being involved simultaneously in missions learning, missions action, and missions support in the world."[21] This synchronized involvement between the church as a whole and the student ministry in learning, action, and support is exactly what a seamless transformission approach offers. It engages students in mission education and practice, simultaneously and consistently, to afford them the opportunity to put their faith in motion.

FOLLOWING AND LEARNING: PUTTING DEVELOPMENT IN MOTION

Many times the short-term mission trip is seen as a discrete experience our students look toward (pre-field), engage in (on-field), and return to reflect on (post-field) (see fig. 11.5). This more "linear" way of looking at STM enables us to see that we have "accomplished something."[22] This is, in itself, an indicator of culture guiding perception. "We just finished a short-term trip" sounds good to task-driven westerners like ourselves. This manner of thinking also lends itself to a "progression" that isolates each of these experiences from one another and from the ongoing teaching and application of the church.

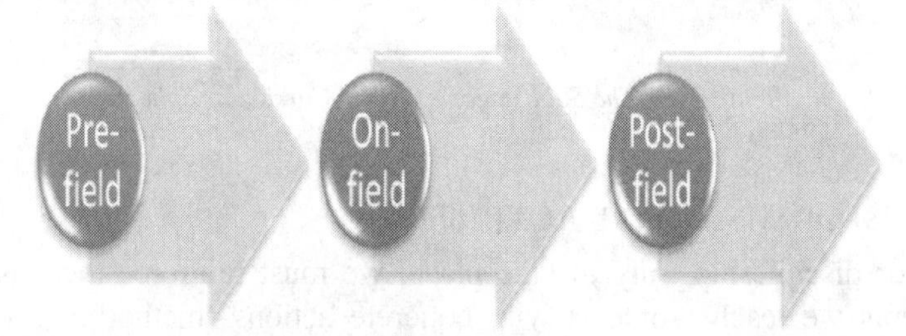

Figure 11.5: Linear Progression of STM Process

---

[20] C. Folmsbee, *A New Kind of Youth Ministry* (Grand Rapids: Zondervan, 2007), 39.

[21] Clendinning, "Strategies for Mission Education in the Local Church," 601.

[22] R. Peterson, G. Aeschliman, and W. Sneed, *Maximum Impact Short-Term Mission* (Minneapolis: STEM, 2003), 128.

A transformational approach, on the other hand, sees in the process an ongoing cycle that serves as an essential means of developing disciples. Thus, this approach mandates that we coach our students to see even the stages of STM preparation, deployment, and reentry into our own culture as *part* of what God is doing to shape us and those to whom we minister cross-culturally, rather than a rare and isolated vacation from the norm. Students would always be either in preparation for their next STM, on the field, or going through the posttrip process, which would lead seamlessly to laying the groundwork for the next STM (see fig. 11.6).

Each of these developmental events in a cyclical STM process occurs concurrently and in tandem with the student's ongoing participation in mission education, service, and living in his community and world.

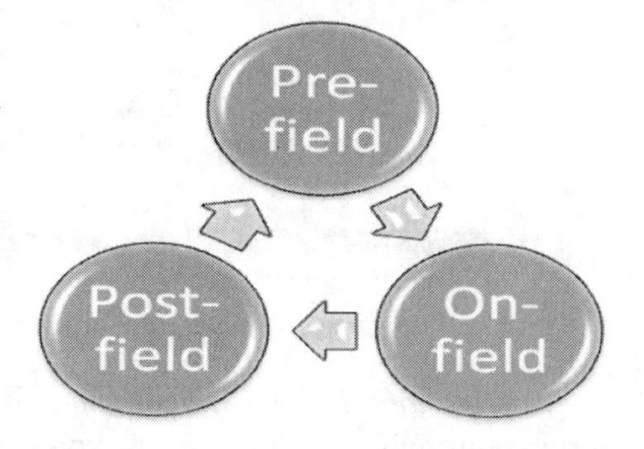

Figure 11.6: TransforMission's Cyclical STM Process

Pre-Field: Training Ground

Preparation for something that matters is always intense. A playoff game means weeks of longer practices and a lot less goofing off. A big exam means less time for fun and many more late nights spent studying. Students are accustomed to tightening the bolts and focusing on something that is valuable. A trip across continents and cultures, for the sake of His name, seems pretty valuable, but we can be guilty of treating it as less important than the "big game" or a test no one is going to remember a month from now. When we make requirements and programming for mission trip preparation light, we subtly do just that—downgrade its importance—because we thereby communicate that the "weight" of the trip is light too. We also hinder the students from seeing the value of mission through pouring out time, energy, and their own money to be a part of what God is doing.

In order to get them to see the value of mission, we should place fairly stringent requirements on all wanting to participate as part of the team. We know what you are thinking, "Not everyone is going to go, if I do this." Good. The point is not to get every student to go on the trip; rather, the goal is to see each student develop. The next developmental step may not be a cross-cultural trip for some students. For them it may be getting involved in local service projects or connecting more directly with their parents. Yet for those who do want to explore going, make sure to orient even your preparation toward challenging discipleship. Some example items might include: (1) application, (2) fund-raising, (3) cultural research, (4) mission book review, (5) team service projects, and (6) mandatory training meetings (see fig. 11.7).

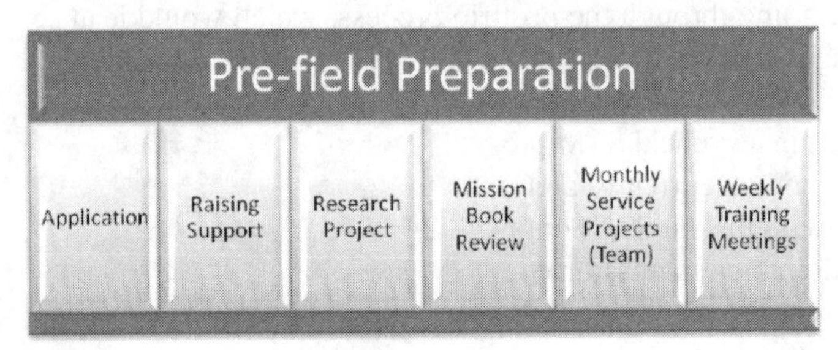

Figure 11.7: Sample Pre-field Preparation Requirements

Application: Forming the Team. If your student ministry team is serving through a sending agency, you will have at hand application materials from that agency's office; however, we would suggest that you require an additional *application* of applicants. In addition to basic information, you might request: (1) a written account of their conversion and spiritual journey, (2) reasons for interest in the trip, (3) any health concerns, and (4) personal references.[23] We can tell you from experience that these items can serve several helpful purposes:

1. They allow you to get an early assessment of the maturity level and rationale of those wanting to join the team.
2. They give you other perspectives (references) on the student or adult.
3. They may alert you to some spiritual or emotional needs of which you were unaware.

Once the deadline for submitting applications has come, you might also want to interview each applicant to discuss their materials.

[23] J. TenElshof, "Selecting and Screening Volunteers for Service," in *The Short-Term Missions Boom: A Guide to International and Domestic Involvement,* ed. M. J. Anthony (Grand Rapids: Baker, 1994), 65–66.

Raising Support: Partnering with Others. Raising support for mission may or may not be necessitated by the state of your student ministry budget. Whether or not the ministry can cover all expenses, however, we recommend instructing students in how to craft a support letter, and requiring them to raise some of the support. If you pay their way, there is a strong likelihood that they will not value the mission, as much as they will value the free international church trip (minimal justification). Raising support is part of the reality of mission for many of those spread out all over the globe. Their agencies, or independent ministry structures, require them to obtain financial backing from donors. Understanding a little bit about this process gives students a fuller picture of missionary realities. Moreover, raising support furnishes an opportunity for people to partner with your students in ministry, through praying and giving.[24]

Cultural Research and Book Review: Learning to Understand. Another responsibility missionaries have is to learn about the people among whom they are living. Assigning each student, or groups of students, to research the history and culture of the people group, area, country, and world region to which you are going is another way to get them involved in preparing for mission. Their findings can then be presented at your training meetings to fill in any gaps in the research.

In addition to research projects, having students complete an integrative review of a mission book can get them to interact with some of the biblical, historical, and cultural issues and figures you have been discussing throughout the curriculum. They can also bear down on some of the ways in which these commands, people, and cultural observations might intersect their lives on mission, specifically as they get ready for the trip. Having them review the book and include several ways in which the content connects with their experience and maturational needs is a great way to challenge them to think critically about mission concepts.

Service Projects: Like the Real Thing. We have to realize that people practice the way they play, and they play the way they have been practicing. Service projects will tell you a lot about your students and their preparedness to cross cultures and serve—if you make sure that the service projects are as close as possible to what you will be doing on the field. Also, if at all possible, the service opportunities need to involve people that are representative of the culture you are entering. These opportunities will also be important for continuity in service placement and type when you return from the field.

---

[24] K. Hicks, *Scaling the Wall* (Waynesboro, GA: Authentic, 2003), 183.

Training Meetings: Mandatory and Motivational. Training meetings should be regularly held, beginning several weeks or months before mobilizing for the short-term mission. Components of pre-field training meetings include some of the aspects above (e.g., presentation of research, tips on raising support), with the addition of logistical information (e.g., passports, travel, immunizations, etc.), and team study and prayer. Since these meetings are your informational and team building hub, make them mandatory. If some cannot make the meetings, they cannot be prepared for the STM, so they do not need to be on the team. This might seem like a rigid stance, but it is a matter of discipleship process and team strength. If you are calling them to commit to the team and the STM process, then do not relax that charge. Your team will maintain great solidarity if you have the same expectations and standards of participation for each of them, and they may more clearly see the significance of the process as well.

Preparation for STM needs to be extensive, but it also needs to be nonstop. Chances are, not all of your students will go on your next mission trip. Some may never go. Even though this is the case, you should always be preparing them for cross-cultural ministry.

ON-FIELD: THE PROVING GROUND

Anyone who has been knows that when you get off the plane in Africa, you know immediately that you are on another continent. That first breath of African air is just different, and that moment can be uneasy. Stepping into any new culture can have that disconcerting effect, no matter how much adrenaline is pumping and how much you have prepared before going. That uneasiness is the beginning of the "crisis" you have worked tirelessly to direct your students toward.

Now your task, as a leader, is to help them navigate these few days or weeks and facilitate their conscious framing of the experience in the proper light. Your charge is to uncover the tension (dissonance) they are experiencing and direct them to resolve it for life change, as the Spirit transforms them. Some activities that might assist you in this are as follows.

Trip Tasks: Relationship First. Make sure the students understand what they are there to do and not to do. The most beneficial "task" is to spend time with the people, live life with them, and learn from them. This will not give you video footage of putting on a new roof or putting in a well, unless that is what the people in the area happen to be doing and your students join them in it. The more important matter is that whatever you are charged to do, make sure your students understand that people connections, and communicating the truth of the gospel through these, are more important than task completion.

Bible Study, Prayer, and Journaling: Disciplines for Change. We connect these two activities because they need to be closely associated on the field. As you select Bible study texts and themes, think through patterns and topics of prayer that you also want to lead the students to engage. Study topics should, again, call students back to a full-orbed critical assessment of what they experience. Here they can begin to assess the new culture and ideas against the biblical material. Informed by this study, they can then pray in keeping with what they have learned. The Word can shape their thoughts, which shapes their prayers.[25]

While we will treat the issue of debriefing at greater length in the next chapter, it is necessary to mention it here. Debriefing will be an invaluable tool for you to guide students, and the team, to assess and manage their experience. Having them keep a daily journal can serve as a tributary of their individual thoughts, feelings, and attitudes about the people and places they are experiencing.[26] These thoughts can then flow into individual, small group, or team debriefing sessions on the field.

Cultural Study: Living to Understand. Even if ongoing cross-cultural exposure and pre-field cultural study are a part of your plan, what you study in the class may not fit what you discover in the lab. Because of the nuances of culture—and even groups and individuals within each culture—your students need to be learners *of* the culture while they are *in* the culture (see fig. 11.8 for an example outline of on-field practices). Sherwood Lingenfelter puts it aptly: "We must love the people to whom we minister so much that we are willing to enter their culture as children, to learn how to speak as they speak, play as they play, eat what they eat, sleep where they sleep, study what they study, and thus earn their respect and admiration."[27] This deferential attitude, tempered with your instruction on the avoidance of cultural practices that might be ethically or morally compromising, is

[25] D. Whitney, *Ten Questions to Diagnose Your Spiritual Health* (Colorado Springs, CO: NavPress, 2001), 34–35.

[26] D. Whitney, *Spiritual Disciplines for the Christian Life* (Colorado Springs, CO: NavPress, 1991), 206–7.

[27] S. Lingenfelter and M. Mayers, *Ministering Cross-Culturally* (Grand Rapids: Baker, 2003), 24–25.

what we must instill in our students in pre-field training and continue to encourage as they serve cross-culturally.

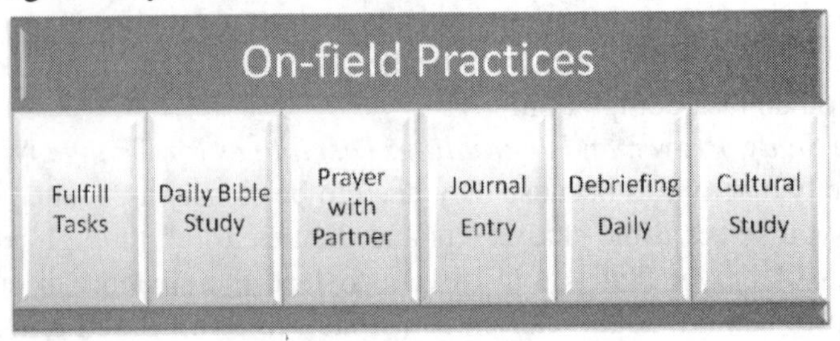

Figure 11.8: Sample On-field Practices

While the on-field portion of the STM cycle is the shortest, it will tend to be the most intense and unsettling. A flexible but well-developed, discipleship plan can enable your students to wrestle with the realities they experience while recognizing the safety line of relational and emotional support that are in place.

POST-FIELD: FERTILE GROUND

Once your students return from crossing time zones, oceans, and even cultural barriers, the work seems finished when in fact it has just begun. The ability to harness and capitalize on the energy and dissonance that the experience will inevitably bring to many of your students will make the difference in long-term impact. Keeping these issues in front of them, while also providing them with the tools needed to continue living on mission, is the challenge for you as a leader. In dissonance terms, you are still focusing on selective exposure through relationships while also providing activities and environments that encourage postdecision reassurance and commitment.

Reentry, Debriefing, and Next Steps: Framing the Experience. While assessment needs to take place consistently within the relationships students have with parents, mentors, and leaders, the reentry period needs to include several specific relational forms:

1. Reentry Meetings: Parents and mentor-coaches meet with each student in order to hear about his experience and to provide some feedback and basic direction.

2. Debriefing Meetings: These include both individual and team meetings in which the team leader, or student minister, leads guided discussions about the experience, moving students toward discovering possible next steps.
3. Follow-Through, Next Steps: Based on student observation, team discussion, and leader insight, a follow-through plan of next steps needs to be established and executed in concert with all of the influence connections (parents, mentor-coaches, team, church).

These post-field steps enable students to continue missional thinking while pointing them toward the next cross-cultural action or behavior.

Communicating to Supporters: Reporting the News. Communicating with those that supported the students—through written correspondence, phone calls, and in corporate reporting services—is another important aspect of the posttrip period. This not only informs those who have prayed and given, but it can also strengthen students' postdecision commitments. The resultant encouragement that they may receive from some supporters can also supply the postdecision reassurance they need to maintain these mission commitments.

Service Projects: Like the Real Thing, Again. Just as they were before going, students need to be involved in similar cross-cultural service at home after they return. Mission principles and practice have to live and breathe as they do—wherever they are and wherever they may go. As was the case in their preparation to go, service projects provide continuity of action for students once they return home. These projects, then, become another step in their pre-field progression to the next overseas effort (see fig. 11.9 for a summary of suggested post-field activities).

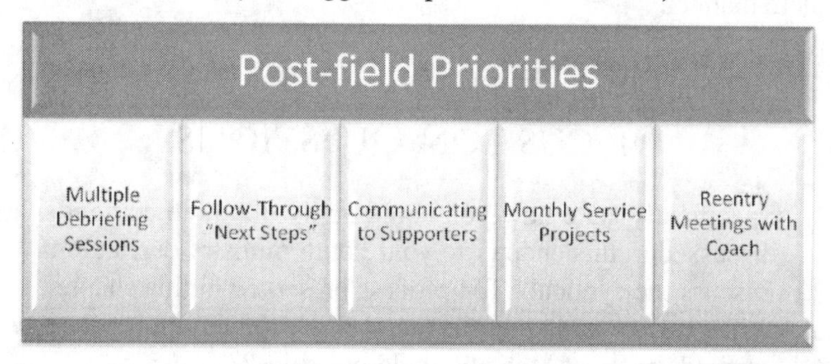

Figure 11.9: Sample Post-field Priorities

Missional discipleship for students involves influences consistently converging on the student's life, the use of the STM cycle as a tool for targeting growth outcomes. The pre-, on-, and post-field movements must be understood in light of, and as subordinate to, this disciple-making transformative work.

WE MAKE DISCIPLES

One of the chief training grounds for the U.S. Armed Forces is the Marine Corps Recruit Depot at Parris Island, South Carolina. When young men and women, facing some of the most intensive weeks of basic military training in the world, first ride in to the training facility, they cannot miss a sign over the road that reads simply, "We Make Marines."

Before they ever hear the first of thousands of screams from their drill instructor, do the first of thousands of push-ups, or run the first of hundreds of miles, they know what they are becoming. They know from the start that they are taking every step to be molded and fashioned into a capable warrior. Those training them also understand, from the beginning, that preparation and testing will be necessary as means to that end. The sign that hangs over our efforts in mobilizing students and adults in STM needs to be:

We Make Disciples.

If we start out with this objective, both for our students and those they reach, we will then be able to develop and engage them in STM in a more complete manner.

DISCUSSION QUESTIONS

1. Specifically state how you could apply the three content spheres discussed in this chapter to your youth ministry curriculum.
2. Discuss the cyclical STM process presented in this chapter.
3. What are the strengths of: the pre-field preparation process? the on-field practices? the post-field priorities?

CHAPTER 12

ENGAGE: MOBILIZE THEM FOR CHALLENGE

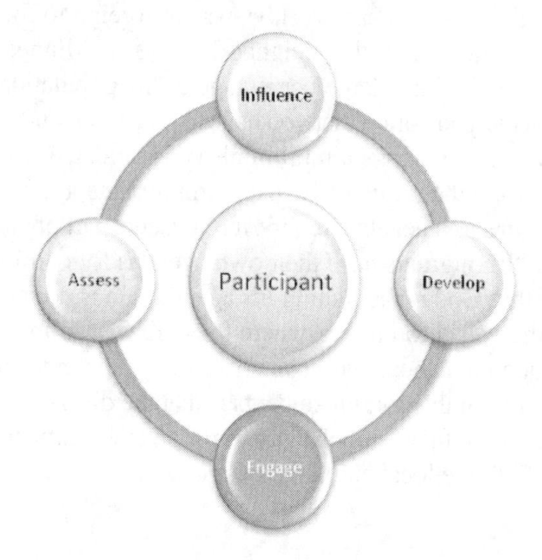

EXECUTING THE PLAN

A discipleship process and curriculum is, in essence, about focusing on life transformation, rather than simply gaining information about our global mission.[1] Bob Roberts argues that "the emphasis in discipleship must shift from information to transformation. . . . Right living doesn't come from more information but from more imitation."[2] This is why the curriculum must emphasize mission engagement.

Students and adults need to be engaged in activities characteristic of how we ultimately want them to live. Their initial involvement prompts dialogue and critical assessment about life and their place in global service. In short, the "imbalance or dissonance" they experience can push them

[1] B. Roberts, *Transformation* (Grand Rapids: Zondervan, 2006), 68–69.
[2] Ibid., 69.

harder to integrate more cross-cultural thinking and acting into their lives.[3] If we want them to be missional, we have to get them acting on mission in directed and specific ways.

GETTING CROSS-CULTURAL: NEXT DOOR

Some of my best friends live in an African neighborhood filled with Somali nationals. The customs and worldviews are foreign to these Americans from Virginia—even though this neighborhood is in Minneapolis, Minnesota. It is "African" in that a large percentage of the population is composed of Somali refugees. The notion that you have to take your students "overseas" to get them engaged in cross-cultural ministry is outdated. Michael Pocock points out that while the influx of Hispanic immigrants, for example, is seen by some Americans as a negative reality, it represents part of God's providential movement: "Immigrants have their own agendas for coming to America, but we believe that God is facilitating *his* agenda! He is doing it by bringing the people of the world to an area where they are free to make choices and are likely to encounter those who can share the gospel and their lives with them."[4] The beauty of this for our students is that the diversity of our national makeup, and many of their schools, allows for an environment in which they can connect to both the local and global community.

GETTING CROSS-CULTURAL: GLOBALLY AND LOCALLY

In an attempt to capture the need to influence all spheres of life simultaneously, several writers have used the term *glocal*. In terms of mission impact, being glocal means intentionally affecting all geographical dimensions simultaneously: "The Great Commission was not sequential steps but dimensions we operate in simultaneously. It's not Jerusalem, then Judea, then Samaria, then the uttermost parts of the world. But Jerusalem, and Judea, and Samaria, and the uttermost parts of the world."[5]

[3] K. Tuttle, "The Effects of Short-Term Mission Experiences on College Students' Spiritual Growth and Maturity," *Christian Education Journal* 4 (2000): 137.

[4] M. Pocock and J. Henriques, *Cultural Change and Your Church* (Grand Rapids: Baker, 2002), 19.

[5] Roberts, *Transformation*, 132.

While Luke outlined these specific geographic areas in Acts 1:8 to detail the historical spread of the gospel, it appears that the ultimate scope of the gospel's reach is all-encompassing, as it has been from the start.[6]

Therefore, as we mobilize students, we want to see the *world* affected by their lives and ministries, not just their neighborhood. We also want to see them emerge as faithful witnesses to His grace in their homes, at work, and in their neighborhood. They need to see service to their "own people" as within the scope of their missional responsibility and influence.[7] As we mobilize cross-culturally, we maximize the potential for both international and local mission to focus their living.

The old adage still rings true: the light that shines farthest shines brightest at home. In other words, the more intentionally involved in international mission our churches and student ministries are, the more that exposure will inform and enflame their passion for local service. In order to harness this potential, however, we need to look at how these spheres of mission relate to one another, and how they are touched by a transforming short-term mission.

In order to do this, we first have to admit the glaring weakness of short-term mission trips: they are, by nature, brief. They happen for a few days or a few weeks, after which time the student's "normal life" can crowd out their effects. This occurs, in part, because a few days of microwaving does not provide the necessary time or life experiences to comprehend and absorb deep, pervasive biblical truths and gritty global realities in a consistent way; slow cooking is needed. In order to see perseverance develop, we all need to live out truth day by day and week by week. In the student mission sphere, this requires continuing involvement in mission, locally and globally.

Ongoing Engagement: Glocally

Consistent, ongoing STM training and engagement can help establish a mission pattern in the lives of your students. Because of school, work, and general life schedules, most of us will only mobilize students for overseas missions once a year.

The natural question then is, How is something that takes place once a year "ongoing"? This is where constant relational influences and discipleship plans undergird the STM process and keep it before the student

[6] A. Köstenberger and P. T. O'Brien, *Salvation to the Ends of the Earth: A Biblical Theology of Mission* (Downers Grove, IL: InterVarsity, 2001), 127–28.

[7] B. Stearns and A. Stearns, *2020 Vision* (Minneapolis: Bethany House, 2005), 219–20.

by facilitating global cross-cultural engagement and consistent involvement in local cross-cultural ministry, which leads to subsequent short-term experiences.

The real crux of the matter is to make sure that what is done overseas is done, on some level, at home. I had a friend in college who served in youth ministry at the Salvation Army in downtown Columbia, South Carolina. To say that he sacrificed his time and energy to serve young people others would rather forget is an understatement. That is why nothing got on his nerves more than classmates who were imbalanced in their hard push toward cross-cultural service. He often said, "I would respect them more, if they did here what they say they are going to do there. If they are not doing it here, I do not see it happening overseas."

If we are cause oriented, and our cause is cross-cultural mission for the sake of His name, then we can advance that cause anywhere we find ourselves. However, if we are occasion oriented, we may justify different behaviors and values at different times and stations. Pushing ourselves toward mission life, no matter where we are, is part of what ongoing engagement can foster.

RELATIONAL TIES: PEOPLE OVER PLACE

The burning question for a lot of us at this point is, Where do I take my students? This question needs a careful and considered answer. While issues of climate, access, safety, and existing language skills are important, these are probably not the preeminent ones they are many times made out to be. The selection of a target people group and place should be prayerfully considered in terms of your church plan to engage long-term in *ongoing relationship building*.

Daniel Rickett's suggestion of a "narrative" approach to short-term excursions involves the primacy of relationship building: "If we are to seize the promise of short-term mission, it must be made subordinate to and in the service of long-term relationships in the work of the gospel."[8] For Rickett, time is the "missing element" and the "fundamental flaw" in poorly conceived STM because the lack of time spent dealing with cross-cultural issues and people of another culture feeds a misunderstanding

[8] D. Rickett, "Narrative, Communion, and Development," in *Mission Maker* (Minneapolis: STEM, 2008), 33–35.

of the issues and strategies. His proposed remedy is to make STM trips "episodes in a narrative—short stories in the long story of transformation among a specific people in a specific place. The answer is accomplished through long-term mission partnerships."[9] Orienting your student short-term efforts around partnerships with the host people will encourage initial relationship building, but it can also encourage lifelong relational ties between those whom you take and those who receive them.

Thomas and Elizabeth Brewster see these ties developing in a purposeful way. They draw a parallel between the birth experience for an infant and the entry of someone into a culture that is new to him. They point out that American hospital births, in many cases, do not allow ample bonding opportunity between parents and baby immediately following the birth. This is principally due to the presence of drugs in the systems of both mother and baby, as well as the removal of the baby to the nursery following labor. The authors point out that a lack of bonding can lead to rejection. They observe:

> There are some important parallels between the infant's entrance into his new culture and an adult's entrance into a new, foreign culture. In this situation the adult's senses, too, are bombarded by a multitude of new sensations, sights, sounds, and smells—but he, too, is able to respond to these new experiences and even enjoy them. Just as the participants in the birth experience, his adrenaline is up and his excitement level is at its peak. Upon arrival, he is in a state of unique readiness, both physiologically and emotionally, to become a belonger *[sic]* to his new environment.[10]

The readiness to enter the new culture can be short-lived if this pivotal bonding takes place with "other foreigners," rather than nationals. The authors point out that, for a long-termer, "the way a new missionary spends his first couple of weeks in his new country is of critical importance if he is to establish a sense of belonging with the local people."[11] This can create a dilemma:

---

[9] Ibid., 34.

[10] T. Brewster and E. Brewster, "Bonding and the Missionary Task: Establishing a Sense of Belonging," in *Perspectives on the World Christian Movement,* ed. R. Winter and S. Hawthorne (Pasadena, CA: William Carey, 1986), 453–54.

[11] Ibid., 454.

> When his sense of belonging is established with the other foreigners, it is then predictable that the missionary will carry out his ministry by the "foray" method—he will live isolated from the local people, as the other foreigners do, but make a few forays out into the community each week, returning always to the security of the missionary community. Without bonding he does not have a sense of feeling at home within the local cultural context. Thus, he does not pursue, as a way of life, significant relationships in the community.[12]

Anticipating the question many would raise, the Brewsters make distinction between their "bicultural" method and what has been traditionally called "going native." They mark the contrast in the following way:

> "Going native" generally implies the rejection of one's first culture—a reaction which is seldom seen and which may not be possible for normal, emotionally stable individuals. Nor is being bi-cultural the same as being schizophrenic. The schizophrenic is a broken, fragmented self. But the bi-cultural person is developing a new self—a new personality.[13]

To put some flesh on this bicultural bonding idea, they educate all who join their projects through "prior preparation of perspectives and expectations." These include four primary conditions:

1. Be willing to live with a local family.
2. Limit personal belongings to 20 kilos (approx. 44 lbs).
3. Use only public transportation.
4. Expect to carry out language learning in the context of relationships that the learner himself is responsible to develop and maintain.[14]

The timing of this bonding is of the utmost importance. The Brewsters designate the first two or three weeks as the window in which bonding will either successfully take place with the nationals or default to deeper relationships with the other expatriates. Since the STM experiences we are suggesting develop completely within this rough time frame, it may be that practices

[12] Ibid.
[13] Ibid., 460.
[14] Ibid., 458.

similar to those suggested for long-term missionaries may prove to concretize both the relationships of the students with the people and with their part in ongoing service to them.

Angie Fann gives several practical steps, specific to STM participants, which translate some of the bonding ideas for use in these brief experiences. We have adapted four of those:

1. Integrate rather than separate.
2. Learn as much as you teach.
3. Get to know their whole lives.
4. Try to speak the language.[15]

Integrating with nationals, rather than remaining separate, allows you to have a more meaningfully engaging impact. It is one thing to live in a culture for a week. Tourists do this all the time. It is a far different, and more challenging, exercise actually to connect your life to the people who call it home, to understand them, and to experience things with them.

If you make a conscious effort to get your students to spend time with nationals, you can then foster in them a desire to *learn with* them through trying to understand their *whole lives*. We do not mean that your students can get a comprehensive grasp of what reality is like for the nationals in a few days, but what they can do is safeguard themselves against thinking that they have everything figured out. When they seek to be students of the culture through visiting the homes and communities of the people, they can begin to see both the complexities of cultural understanding and the simplicity of the central need for Jesus that each person possesses; this takes place through bonding with the people.

Finally, if you prepare your students to know at least some of the *language*, make sure they use it. Talking with people in their own language can be, admittedly, one of the most difficult and embarrassing things one can do, especially when little is known of that language. But it is also one of the most rewarding and exciting activities. It is rewarding because it shows students that language learning is a key piece in being able to communicate, and understanding the language gives them not only that ability but also the respect of the people, who witness the genuine desire to communicate with them in their own language. The joke that makes us cringe every time we hear it goes like this:

---

[15] A. Fann, *How to Get Ready for Short-Term Missions* (Nashville: Thomas Nelson, 2006), 66–67.

> Question: *What do you call someone who can only speak one language?*
> Answer: *An American.*

Do not feed this stereotype through your students. Involve them in the whole cross-cultural experience through helping them bond with nationals by trying to live *and* speak with them.

RELATIONAL INVESTMENT: PEOPLE AND PLACE

Chris Leake is convinced that the building of relational ties to a cross-cultural people is essential to the long-term development of students and adults. So much so, that he advises that we not only mobilize students for bonding but also strategically determine to what type of people group we want them to attach for the long haul:

> Short-term mission involves a similar bonding scenario. It takes people who are willing and eager to follow God's call and serve in missions and throws them into their first experience on the field. This becomes the bonding period. During this critical initial plunge, the bright-eyed participant undergoes a period of extreme receptivity to the leading of God. Perhaps you know people who have made significant decisions, commitments or changes in life direction as a result of STM participation. But with what are they bonding, and what types of commitments will they make as a result? Few will deny the role of STM in mobilizing long-term mission laborers. Ask any full-time, foreign missionary if his or her first time on the mission field was during STM involvement, and chances are the answer will be yes. Is it possible, though, that the way we are doing STM is one of the reasons we are seeing so few long-term laborers going to the most unreached areas of the world? If we do not bring short-termers into contact with the unreached and teach them this need, they will not bond with the unreached.[16]

[16] C. Leake, "Bonding Through Short-Term Mission: A Lifeline to the Unreached," Lausanne World Pulse, n.p. [cited 10 December 2008]. Online:http://www.lausanneworldpulse.com/themedarticles.php/264/03–2006?pg=all.

Leake intends for us to be methodical in our church strategy for engagement so that when we mobilize students and adults we will connect with specific relationships, in a specific cultural group and place, so that these relationships will have long-term impact on the participant and the recipient cultural group.

Connecting with a People and a Place

The Global Adopt-A-People Network assists churches in researching and carefully deciding on a people group of the world to adopt for ministry and mission. They point to this historical shift in mission thinking as the reason for their ministry:

> The Old Mission Model: Focus on Missionaries. For generations, the local church's perceived responsibility to world mission was often summed up in the person of the missionary. As long as the missionary was sent, clothed and fed, his prayer letters read and the requests mentioned, many churches felt that they had done all that was possible in fulfilling the Great Commission mandate.
>
> The New Mission Model: Focus on Peoples. In a growing number of churches, a new mission model is taking hold! This is a vibrant, strategic model that goes right to the heart of the harvest: PEOPLES! This model, Adopt-A-People, has emerged from the very heart of God for all peoples. In the world's 234 geopolitical nations, there exist over 16,000 distinct, ethnic cultures.[17]

Connecting with a people group not only allows your students, and your church, to direct their thoughts, prayers, and energies to a specific people and place; it also enables your STM to have direct correlation to other mission experiences that are taking place through your church ministries.

For example, if your church chooses to focus on reaching the unreached Senufo people of Mali, your overarching strategy to engage them might include: (1) praying for them as a church; (2) sending mid- and long-term missionaries from your church, and supporting others at work among them; (3) funding these missionaries and the indigenous church (as it is established); and (4) sending STM teams to assist in the work and to get to know the people and their culture (see fig. 12.1).

[17] "The Adopt-A-People Movement," Adopt-A-People Clearinghouse, n.p. [cited 5 December 2008]. Online: http://www.adoptapeople.com/whoweare/vision.asp.

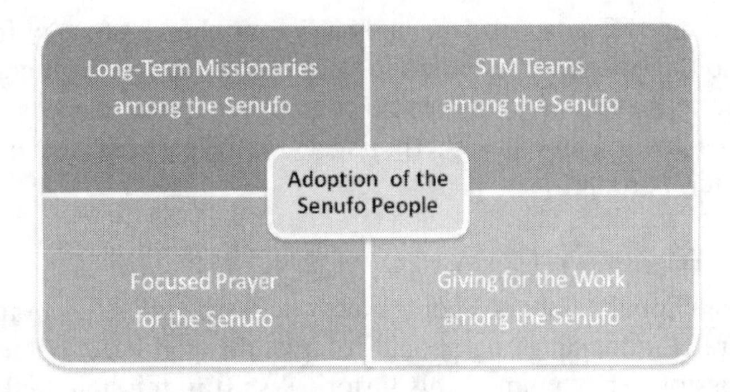

Figure 12.1: An Example Template for People Group Adoption (Senufo of Mali)

Here, the STM experience is *one* piece of who the church and your student ministry is doing to reach people whom students, as a part of your church, know and engage on the field in repeated ways.

While you might pray, send, and support missions and engage students short-term in a more general manner, having your student trip(s) stand alone does not take a long-term view of their time on the field because there is no cohesive vision. This does not preclude sending or giving to other peoples or areas, but it does mean streamlining what you do for long-term impact on the recipients as well as your students.

NETWORKING FOR ENGAGEMENT: AN OVERLOOKED RESOURCE

As teachers in Christian higher education, we recognize the potential importance of Bible colleges, Christian liberal arts, graduate schools, and seminaries in STM. This may seem like an odd place in our discussion to look at this variable, but for churches and student ministries seeking effectively to engage a people in long-term partnership, the resources of a Christian college or seminary may prove pivotal.

In his ministry to Muslims, David Cashin has offered personal invitations to 11 mosque leaders to study the Bible with him. Only one turned down his offer.[18] We mention this because it demonstrates his personal concern for the unreached peoples of the world to be engaged by believers through the church. Having witnessed the common church and aca-

[18] D. Cashin, "Rejoice, the Muslims Are Coming to Jesus!" *Connection* 8 (2008): 16–17.

demic approaches to identifying and adopting a people group, he makes this observation: "I find it interesting that in the 36 articles on adoption of people groups that I have read, none mentions the role of Christian centers of education. The typical topics discussed are, Churches, mission agencies, the process of adoption and even conflicts arising between these two wings of the Christian movement."[19] The "interesting" part for Cashin is that individual congregations, or ministries, often navigate through this adoption process with little or no research or resource base to guide their thinking and acting. Cashin argues that "Christian educational institutions, particularly if their faculty has missions experience, can play an important role in bringing this expertise to the often short-term efforts of churches. The relationship of educational institutions with mission agencies allows for a significant level of cooperation in the preparation of workers."[20] He proposes that there be a partnering of church, sending agency, and institution in the adoption of and ministry among a people group.

Each of these entities brings a substantial piece to the table of deliberation over whom your church is going to work among. Your *church* has both the potential missionaries (personnel) and the prayer, relational, emotional, and financial support (partnership) for those whom they send. The college or seminary possesses a research and expertise base. Many of them also have experience in mobilizing short-term teams with a participant development orientation. Finally, the sending agency has a broad-based strategy and existing pathways of networks to get students to the field (see fig. 12.2).

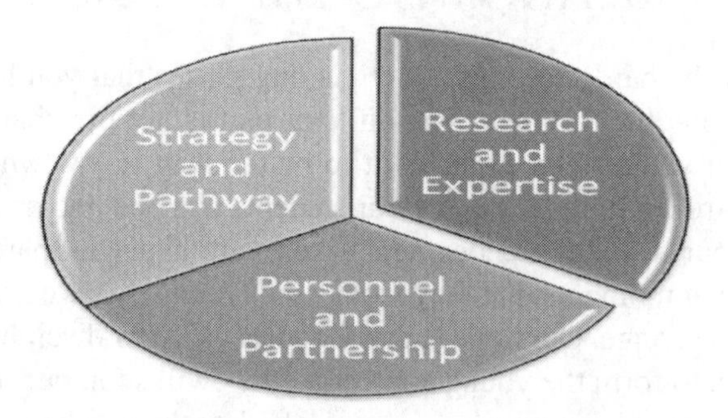

Figure 12.2: Necessary Resources for Effective Mobilization

The coupling of these to each other allows for discovery, training, and mobilization of those called to connect to this team of entities; in other

[19] D. Cashin, "Facilitating a New Student Volunteer Movement," TMs (photocopy), 1.
[20] Ibid.

words, it provides a full complement of resources to the student missionary (see fig. 12.3).

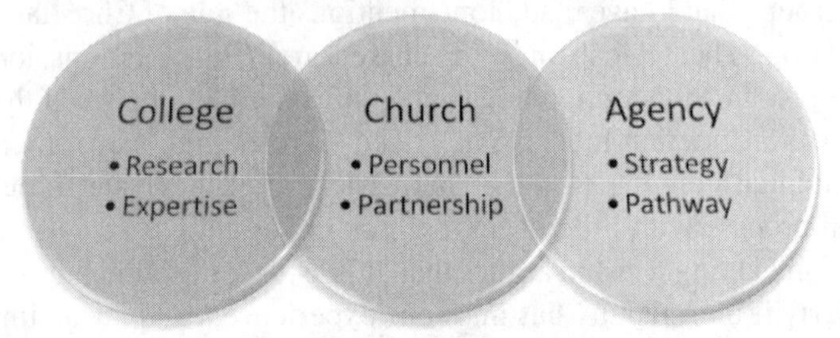

Figure 12.3: Distinct Resources Provided by College, Church, and Sending Agency

While it may not seem readily apparent, there is a direct benefit to youth as well as college ministries in partnering with Christian institutions of higher education. The resourcing of students and churches with the faculty and educational capital of a Christian university or seminary could not only assist in an informed selection of place and people, but it could also lead to a broader partnership between the institution and your church, youth, and college ministry for the purpose of training and future mobilization.

CHALLENGING STUDENTS: SEEING INTO THE FUTURE

One of the hardest things about visiting places that you have not seen in years is that they change. The difficult part is not the change itself but the fact that you always expected it to be the way it was when you were younger—frozen in time. Seeing our students married and having children interrupts our nostalgic tendencies. Like many if not all parents, we privately wish at moments that they would stay young, but we know they will develop and change. Our hope is that God has used our discipling efforts, in some sense, to form the young adults that they will soon become.

What can tend to evoke fear in us is a look at the numbers of post-youth ministry dropouts. If roughly 70 percent of students between the ages 18 and 22 leave the church for a period of time, we begin to wonder if engaging them in STM, or any other activity, is even worth the effort.[21] If their time

[21] "LifeWay Research Uncovers Reasons 18 to 22 Year Olds Drop Out of Church," LifeWay Research, n.p. [cited 13 December 2008]. Online:http://www.lifeway.com/lwc/article_main_page/0,1703,A=165949&M=200906,00.html. See also B. Shields, "An Assessment of Dropout Rates of Former

on the field is an isolated "activity," which is disconnected from church relationships and mission, then the answer is probably yes, it is a wasted effort.

After taking a detailed look at "dechurched young adults," or post-youth ministry dropouts, Thom and Sam Rainer observed: "Why do these students take a break from church? It isn't because the college is drawing them away. It's because the church is unimportant to them. We push them away. Why is it so easy for them to leave? The church is not a meaningful part of their lives. Why is the back door so large and the front door so small? The church is nonessential to them."[22] Insightful for our discussion of discipleship through mission engagement, they found that "the church that teaches and disciples all teens to think outwardly has a much better chance of retaining them inwardly."[23] The three identified areas of "outward focus within the church" were "service, giving, and missions." Students who were involved in these missional activities were more likely to remain connected to the church through the college years.[24]

This is not simply about church growth and retention. It points to the heart of long-term engagement that is the result, in part, of ministry habits built into the handful of years that these individuals are students. It is in these years that engagement in STM, wed to relationships that are part of a larger discipleship process, can influence and develop students into lifelong world Christians.

Discussion Questions

1. What is a "glocal" mission approach? How might this idea influence your international STM efforts?
2. How do these two cross-cultural spheres of ministry work together to encourage student development?
3. What are some of the aspects involved in a church or ministry "adopting" a people group? What are the benefits of adopting a people group for the development of students?

Youth Group Participants in Conservative Southern Baptist Megachurches" (Ph.D. dissertation, The Southern Baptist Theological Seminary, 2008). Shields examines the convoluted origin of the dropout statistic. Also, he found in his study that 88 percent of students actively involved in dynamic youth ministries of select SBC megachurches remained actively involved in local church contexts in young adulthood. See also B. Shields, "Family-Based Ministry: Separated Contexts, Shared Focus," in *Perspectives on Family Ministry: Three Views,* ed. T. P. Jones (Nashville: B&H, 2009), 100–6.

[22] T. Rainer and S. Rainer, *Essential Church* (Nashville: B&H, 2008), 83.

[23] Ibid., 86.

[24] Ibid., 86–87.

CHAPTER 13

ASSESS: EVALUATE THEM FOR CHANGE

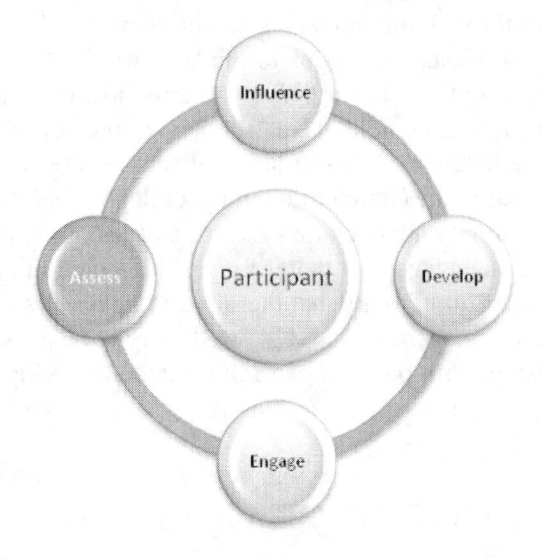

THAT WAS GREAT, NOW WHAT?

We have heard from numerous short-term practitioners and theorists that what happens *after* the STM is the most important ingredient in the entire process. Yes, even more important than the on-field time. Their reasoning for this is that exposure to something does not ensure right thinking and acting, and many short-termers have experienced just enough to be dangerous. It takes a thoughtful and intentional follow-through plan to help students fit the pieces of the experiental puzzle together.

Assessment or evaluation sounds either corporate or academic—or a little of both—but it happens all the time in life. In fact, your students are used to it. They take exams and try out for sports teams, band, and drama presentations, but they also get feedback from friends, enemies, and family members about who they are and how they are acting. People evaluate people, and it is not always an accurate or well-informed assessment.

In our attempts to be accepting, we often buy into the lie that we cannot make evaluations of student learning, attitudes, and perceptions in ministry because we believe that our churches should be places that refuse to levy unfair, judgmental criticisms.[1] The problem is that this tactic undermines the hopes you have for students to grow and change because without evaluation, you have no gauge to determine if transformation is actually happening. Also, the students are left with no mature guide to help reinforce their resolve to be dynamic followers of Jesus, or clarify what and why they are experiencing tension in living out faith on mission.

Assessing where the students are, and where they might be going, can be a key educational and relational part of ensuring long-term commitment to global evangelization. More than that, guiding them to self-assess their thoughts and perspectives is paramount to their ability to derive the maximum educational benefit from the dissonance-creating experience.[2] The need for appraisal is particularly important for a successful return home, as it helps to clarify what occurred and what those events mean for the rest of the students' lives, and to establish long-term commitment to mission.

Reentry to Reassurance: Watch Your Step

Long-term missionaries ending their service and making the move back home face the difficult task of "reentry." Peter Jordan writes:

> Like the astronaut guiding his craft back into the earth's atmosphere, retuning missionaries must negotiate many potential hazards. They too must cover dangerous territory; dangerous in terms of the emotional, spiritual, and relational damage that can occur if the process is not handled correctly. Indeed, if it is not handled correctly, the

[1] J. Estep, M. Anthony, and G. Allison, *A Theology for Christian Education* (Nashville: B&H, 2008), 290–91.

[2] S. Brookfield, *Developing Critical Thinkers* (San Francisco, CA Jossey-Bass, 1987), 26.

> returning missionary may barely escape with his or her emotional well-being and faith intact.[3]

Your students will not face the same degree of testing that a missionary returning from years of service might, but some of the same types of strain and temptation are possible if not probable. Taking time to alert your students in the pre- and on-field phases can help them anticipate such challenges.

Moreover, a comprehensive plan to understand and address these transitional issues post-field is essential. Jordan offers a sampling of these re-entry transition challenges that some long-term missionaries have faced:

- From being primarily concerned with the spiritual to being primarily concerned with practical matters.
- From being daily surrounded with Christian encouragement and fellowship to deriving your fellowship and encouragement from Wednesday evening and Sunday morning services.
- From having a fixed and measurable goal to perhaps having none at all.
- From seeing abject poverty firsthand to perhaps experiencing seemingly overwhelming wealth.
- From a high degree of self-motivation to searching for new motivation.
- From being somebody special in the culture in which you were serving to being nobody special.
- From serving with people who have a world perspective to being with people who, in many cases, do not care much for those outside their own circle.[4]

Not every missionary experiences all of these struggles; however, even short-term student missionaries encounter some mixture of these or associated barriers. Student challenges might look like this:

- From STM experience to daily life experience.
- From full-time cross-cultural mission to part-time.
- From having a group and individual focus for mission to having none.

---

[3] P. Jordan, ed., *Re-entry* (Seattle, WA: YWAM, 1992), 13.
[4] Ibid., 52.

- From seeing poverty to living in relative luxury.
- From having the highest motivations to experiencing lesser ones.
- From being seen as exceptional to being seen as normal again.
- From a global team to an individualized culture.

These obstructions can interfere with the anticipated growth you have been praying for and planning toward. Left unchecked, these transitional hiccups can then tempt students to be overly critical of their own culture, to find fault with the practices and people in the church, or merely to return to life as usual because dealing with these unanticipated obstacles seems like too much to handle.

Helping students see their way through these issues is largely a matter of leveraging methodological and relational capital against these thoughts and attitudes through a process of debriefing aimed at clarifying their experience. This can then lead you to provide an informed outlook for the next mission step planned for them.

Debriefing for Clarification: Getting It Right

In order to provide care and stability for soldiers and units who have been involved in battlefield situations that are potentially traumatic, the Army Behavioral Health professionals debrief them:

> Battlemind Psychological Debriefings (BMPD) are structured group discussions designed to support military personnel in their transition back to duty after a significant incident (in-theatre) or from the combat environment to the home environment at post deployment. Battlemind Psychological Debriefings use a set of specific questions to guide participants through a series of phases in which combat events or deployment experiences are acknowledged among unit members, common reactions are discussed, and actions that can be taken to facilitate the transition are reviewed.[5]

[5] "Traumatic Event Management," U.S. Army Behavioral Health, n.p. [cited 6 December 2008]. Online: http://www.behavioralhealth.army.mil/provider/traumatic.html.

While the trauma suffered by combat troops has no business being compared to the tension students face on short-term mission, their experiences have been challenging.

In the military system, "structured group discussions" focus on "specific questions" that are asked of the "participants" and the group so that they can "discuss" their "common reactions" about their "deployment" and allow the leader to "guide" them and "facilitate their transition."[6] These are the same terms and to a degree the same activities that are used when debriefing students who have been on STM. Meetings that are set before, during, and especially after the trip can allow the group and the individual students to *recognize* both the highlights and the negative elements of the experience.

Debriefing also allows the student to *reflect* on the experience, with the help of leaders, mentors, and other short-term team members, and to evaluate the impact of the trip on their present and future.[7] From a leader's standpoint, debriefing helps ensure that "the actions previously taken do not drift along unquestioned, unrealized, unintegrated, or unorganized," and this goal connects to making sure the students get the postdecision reassurance they will be seeking.[8]

DEBRIEFING: TEAM AND INDIVIDUAL

Whether you have them on-field or during the post-field follow-through period, both individual and group debriefing sessions need to take place. Having both types of sessions allows you to tailor next steps for each individual while also gleaning group understanding and suggestions for future actions. It is important to have a group debriefing process that encourages both individual and collective reflection.[9] Building from individual to corporate reflection can encourage and extend the clarifying process.

Through the debriefing process the leader should guide each student to: (1) reflect on his own experience so that he can identify goals, anticipate obstacles, and begin to develop an action plan to achieve those objectives; (2) reflect with a team small group, which can provide feedback and prayer support for the student; and (3) engage in team reflection, which al-

[6] Ibid.

[7] L. Joplin, "On Defining Experiential Education," in *The Theory of Experiential Education,* ed. K. Warren, M. Sakofs, and J. Hunt (Dubuque, IA: Kendall/Hunt, 1995), 19.

[8] Ibid.

[9] Jordan, *Re-entry*, 141–42.

allows each participant to interact with the group reflectively and the group to dialogue collectively (see fig. 13.1).[10]

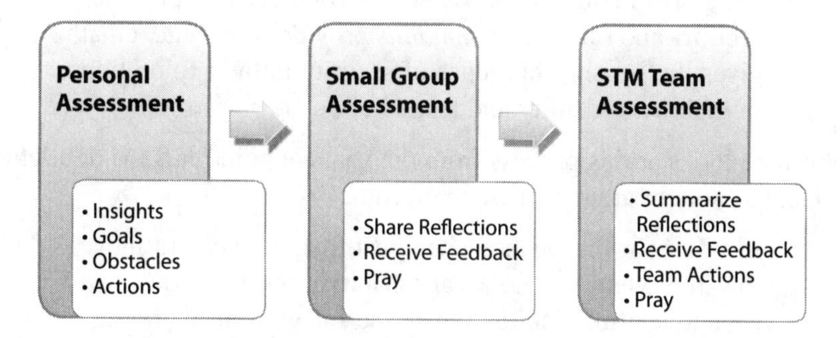

Figure 13.1: Debriefing Process Stages and Activities[11]

The tension (dissonance) students are experiencing can and should show itself in this debriefing process. This tension and struggle are not the transformational goal but simply a vehicle to reach it. As leaders and disciplers, we do not want students to remain in a constant state of tension at its peak, but we also understand that dissonance is a tool to be used in pursuit of life change.

Debriefing: From Realization to Integration

Jim Mannoia's approach to "critical commitment" is helpful in clarifying the nature of dissonance as it relates to life transformation. David Johnstone summarizes Mannoia's view:

> Dissonance by itself does not bring the student to a level of understanding or wisdom. The purpose of dissonance is to encourage the student to identify and integrate the implications of their reflections into a way of life that exhibits more integrity. These applications are translated into *habits,* patterns, and "ways of living" which reflect a thoughtful and critical response to these situations which provoke questions. However, living examples that demonstrate and provide options for responding to these issues

[10] Ibid.

[11] Some structural elements are adapted from the debriefing process outlined in Jordan, *Re-entry,* 141–42.

> must be present. These *models* are individuals that provide students with multiple responses are paradigms for responding to situations or living their life. Besides modeling, a student also needs an environment that provides security and safety. A *community* provides the context that gives the student this sense of security in the exploration of their own identity and learning.[12]

Johnstone looks at this process from the vantage point of STM debriefing and makes note of an important connection:

> In order for dissonance or angst of experiences to move towards what Mannoia calls habituation a person must be purposeful. Habituation is the integration of the lessons a student has learned into their thinking and actions. One helpful tool for assisting a student in this direction is found in the biblical book of Proverbs. Throughout the book there is the recurring theme of gaining "knowledge, understanding and wisdom" [Prov 2:6; 19–20; 17:27; etc.]. This is a progressive approach which begins with observing what is happening [*knowledge*], grasping the context [*understanding*], and applying the implications [*wisdom*]. It is a simple biblical paradigm which enables the student, team leader, and others to assist someone in processing an experience.[13]

The reflection on an intense (dissonance-inducing) experience can be guided by models (influences), in a supportive community (team, student ministry, church), which can lead to altering attitudes, actions, and beliefs (adopting a more missional lifestyle). Using this *knowledge*, *understanding*, *wisdom* paradigm allows you to walk students through their self-assessment, and your own evaluation of them. Figure 13.2 lists the guiding question behind each level and includes a sampling of questions that might be asked after a dinner in the home of a national host family.

[12] D. Johnstone, "Closing the Loop: Debriefing and the Short-Term College Mission Team," *Missiology* 34 (2006): 525.

[13] Ibid., 526.

Level of Reflection and Perception	Foundational Question	Example Questions After Dinner in a Host Culture
Knowledge	*What is happening?*	*What did I hear?* *What did I see?* *What did I feel?* *What did I eat?*
Understanding	*Why is it happening?*	*Why were our hosts hospitable?*
Wisdom	*What do I need to do because it is happening?*	*Am I as generous and hospitable to my guests?*

Figure 13.2: Debriefing Levels of Reflection and Perception (Johnstone)[14]

In each level the student must answer questions that relate to the stage of evaluation. The level of wrestling with the issues and motivations that underlie what the students observe increases as one moves from knowledge to wisdom. Along with this struggle the potential for the student to integrate further cultural awareness and greater biblical consistency into his thinking, attitudes, and actions (transformation) should increase.

Debriefing sessions must also be spread out over the weeks, and even months, that follow the STM, in order to have extended impact. On-field and minimal post-field debriefing does not tend to provide the long-term context to facilitate lasting change.[15] As Johnstone indicates, the knowledge, understanding, wisdom paradigm can take place before, during, and after the on-field experience, offering continuity for follow-through steps.

Following Through for Commitment: Making It Count

Post-field follow-up can involve returning students in any number of assessment and instruction activities.[16] Brian Heerwagen argues that following *through* rather than following *up* is much more than a matter of semantic preference: "Follow-up implies one event or action. Follow-through communicates the idea of continuing—something that is not bound by time

[14] Ibid.

[15] T. Linhart, "Planting Seeds: The Curricular Hope of Short-Term Mission Experiences in Youth Ministry," *Christian Education Journal* 2 (2005): 268.

[16] R. Peterson, G. Aeschliman, and W. Sneed, *Maximum Impact Short-Term Mission* (Minneapolis: STEM, 2003), 144–45.

or event. You start with the end in mind."[17] Starting with long-term mission living in mind, Heerwagen has developed what he calls, "The Triage Concept for the Next Mile," which provides a long-term follow-through approach for STM. He points out that just as doctors must sort patients based on their specific level of need, leaders of short-term teams must use post-field assessment tools to discover what the next step is for each of the team members.[18]

The prospect of following up with each student seems overwhelming even if you have a structured transformational process in place. On the other hand, if you are going to follow up with one, you have to follow up with all to an *equal degree*, right? Let us ease your mind by saying, definitively, no. Not all students, or adults, want or need the same measure of follow-through after a short-term experience. They are at different points in their development. Therefore, the ways you offer to help them grow need to be diverse.

Heerwagen's own data give us a concrete example of how this might work. If one were to take 10 participants on STM this summer, three distinct groups, he notes, would return. First, six participants will not have a high level of interest in going on a short-term mission trip again.

These are labeled "Level One" team members. The next group, "Level Two," would be the estimated three team members likely to go on another STM. Finally, out of the 10 participants, there would be one "Level Three" student. The statistical breakdown looks like this:

- Level One Team Members: Those who are not likely to participate in another STM—six (60 percent)
- Level Two Team Members: Those who are likely to participate in another STM—three (30 percent)
- Level Three Team Members: Those who are likely to move on to mid-term or long-term service—one (10 percent)

The next action item for you, as a leader, is to develop and implement individual follow-through plans for each of these team members. *The Next Mile* curriculum offers several example action steps to solidify the level of commitment for each participant, as indicated in figure 13.3 on the next page.

[17] B. Heerwagen, *The Next Mile: Leader Guide* (Waynesboro, GA: Authentic, 2005), 2.

[18] Ibid., 48. Although these statistics may not generalize to all STM experiences, the example is provided to focus the reader's attention on the fact that he will need to discern with which students to invest additional time and resources.

Next Steps	Level One	Level Two	Level Three
1. Attend three follow-through team meetings. 2. Participate in the Reporting Home service. 3. Receive a field update from the team leader two months after the STM.	X	X	X
4. Lead an aspect of next year's STM. 5. Join the church missions committee. 6. Challenge them to organize items from the 20 Mile Markers.		X	X
7. Encourage them to attend (or you take them to) missions conferences. 8. Arrange appointments with sending organizations. 9. Recommend books, videos, organizations, Web sites, and magazines related to missions.			X

Figure 13.3: Next Steps for Follow-Through as Indicated in The Next Mile[19]

Here, the first grouping of three steps is for every student participant, while steps 4–6 are for Level 2 and 3 students. Finally, suggestions 7–9 are for those Level 3 participants who are looking beyond STM to longer terms of ministry service. The paradigm establishes follow-through for each team member while also providing tiered commitment steps and relationships to those desiring them.

Setting Goals for Lasting Commitment

The importance of working with students to set these goals cannot be overstated. Ver Beek states that "many of our everyday experiences and lots of research, including my own, have shown that two *factors* are key in helping people bring about lasting positive change in their lives. I will call

[19] Ibid.

these two factors accountability and encouragement."[20] Working from the goal-setting theory of Edwin Locke and Gary Latham, he argues:

> Individuals are more motivated and will work harder to achieve their goals if: a) their goals are made public b) if the goals are specific (not just do your best) c) if the goals are more demanding as long as it is within the individuals [sic] capability (most people have little motivation to achieve simple goals). In addition, it matters little if the individual sets their own goal or if the goal is set for them, as long as they accept and commit to the logic and importance of the goal. In summary, goal-setting theory would argue, that short-term missions participants are much more likely to successfully experience lasting positive change in their lives if they set specific, public, demanding goals and then are regularly held accountable for their progress.[21]

In Ver Beek's estimation, if we actually expect students to make permanent changes in their way of thinking and behaving, we must develop an ethos of accountability that includes goal setting and feedback.

Locke and Latham's theory gives us insight into how we can facilitate the greatest amount of transformation among the participants. They tell us that it is necessary that a person must make his goals *public*, *specific*, and *demanding*—yet *attainable*. They also note that it does not matter who sets the goals—the student or the adult—as long as the student accepts the goals and acknowledges the underlying logic and importance of them.

Ver Beek argues that "in seeking to make lasting change in the participants, the key ingredient is the creation of a structure which will provide accountability and encouragement to the participants before and especially after their experience."[22] The encouragement component, he suggests, relates to the appropriate relationships that are involved in the accountability (influences) process, as well as to social support networks in general. These provide the needed encouragement, understanding, and

[20] K. A. Ver Beek, "Lessons from the Sapling," in *Effective Engagement in Short-Term Missions*, ed. Robert Priest (Pasadena, CA: William Carey, 2008), 492.

[21] Ibid. The original goal-setting theory may be found in E. Locke and G. Latham, "Building a Practically Useful Theory of Goal Setting and Task Motivation," *American Psychologist* 57 (1990): 705–17.

[22] Ibid.

friendships.[23] Accountability and encouragement can help cement one's "good intentions from the field" into a way of living.[24]

Assessment Shows You the Way to Transformission

At the end of any youth ministry event, the biggest and most difficult job is figuring out what the next step is for all the students in attendance, whether 20 or 200. When students return from their STM, the same difficulty faces you. They have come back challenged and energized for mission, and they expect you to have an idea of what all of that means for them.

The ability to assess them, through debriefing and reentry exercises, allows you to tailor these action steps to their level of commitment, without getting overwhelmed. This is a strong weapon against the tendency for students to return home and resume life, unchanged. If their postdecision commitment is going to stick, they need the glue of further investment and greater challenge in mission. Comprehensive follow-through provides an environment for commitment to mission to be established and animated for long-term devotion.

Discussion Questions

1. What is debriefing? Should debriefing be done in groups or individually? Give reasons for your answer.
2. What is the difference between a philosophy of posttrip "follow-through" and "follow-up"?
3. What is Heerwagen's "triage" concept for follow-through? Do you agree with this philosophy? Give reasons for your answer.

[23] Ibid.
[24] Ibid.

Conclusion

Challenging Them to Death: The Gravity of Mission and the Weight of Student Ministry

It is no diminutive thing to challenge students to invest their lives in reaching the nations. In fact, the gravity of the mission pulls mission-oriented student ministry into the orbit of global revolution. This is a much bigger enterprise than making youth and college students "better" by getting them to stop doing some things and to start doing others; than pushing them to speak about Jesus to their friends, or to invite them to an event you have planned; than getting fraternity and sorority members to join your campus ministry, so you can influence those parts of the university. While these goals are certainly positive, missional student ministry involves something greater, namely, seeing students commit their lives, in biblical devotion and holy adoration, to the Lord and His global mission. This challenge will transform the world *and* their lives.

Challenged by Headhunters: A Personal Journey to Mission

Having experienced it firsthand, we know what transformation to a mission perspective for life and ministry looks like. For me (Shane), it was just another day that I was required to be in chapel. As soon as I walked through the door, some guy handed me a brochure. I looked at it and immediately realized that we were going to hear a choir. At that point the temptation level to leave and take an absence was extremely high, since just about the only thing I like to sit through less than a choir program is a Broadway-style musical production. My take is: just say the lines instead of singing them, and we can be done with the play in half the time. I know, I have a real heart issue, as my wife often reminds me. But I also had plenty going on—serving as a full-time student pastor and a full-time college student (no, the math on that does not compute). I am sure I had students whom I could meet for lunch, upcoming events to plan, or even Greek exegesis that was calling my name. Compared to what I could be doing, sitting there seemed like a complete waste of valuable time.

In the end, however, I stayed. Slipping into my usual seat in the back right corner, I started reading for class. Like an unsuspecting driver heading toward a jarring collision, I had no idea what God was about to use to get my attention; but it was coming, ready or not. As it turns out, the choir was filled with children, Indian children. What they presented was not simply an arrangement of standard songs but a story. In fact, it was their story, and it was gripping.

The account chronicled their ancestry, as members of the Hmar tribe of northeast India. From the beginning of their tribal history until their grandparents' generation, the Hmar were known for one thing—being vicious headhunters. But one day that collective reputation and the course of their eternal lives changed forever. As the story is told:

> In 1910, a missionary, Watkin Roberts, sent the Gospel of John to a Hmar chief. The chief invited Roberts to come and explain the Scriptures. He went, despite a travel ban by the British Colonial rulers, and five young tribesmen chose to follow the Lord Jesus. The converts grew in faith and became leaders of a new and growing church. Within two generations, the entire tribe was evangelized.[1]

That tribe is now known for their mission efforts among neighboring tribes and other regions in their homeland.

The recounting of that history was wrenching enough, but at the conclusion of the program, they did something that, I am sure, seemed sappy to many. Normally, I would have been the first one to say just that; however, that day was anything but normal. While they were finishing their final song, the children left the stage and embraced some of those in the audience who happened to be seated at the end of the rows. As I am an "end-sitter" by habit, one of the boys eventually made his way back to where I was sitting.

[1] India Children's Choir, *From the Hills of Manipur* (Colorado Springs, Colo.: Bibles for the World, 1997), 1.

He approached me and gave me a hug. It was only for a few seconds, but in that brief moment, I came to the stark realization that if God had not sent Watkin Roberts—at the expense of his safety, comfort, and, potentially, his life—to take the revolutionary gospel of Jesus to an Indian tribe of ferocious murderers, this boy in all likelihood would have grown to be just another in a long line of headhunters. Instead, I was meeting him as a brother, and we will one day bow down around the throne of the Lamb with others such as him, purchased "from every tribe and tongue and people and nation" (Rev 5:9).

I had no idea that a simple hug from a child, whose name I still do not know, would play a part in my coming to terms with the latent dissonance in my own life. I had a malformed view of the Great Commission of our triune God. He gave this charge to His church so that He might be worshipped among *all* the peoples of the world, but I was the guy who frequently complained about repeated calls to go overseas and had no interest in getting caught up in taking the gospel where it had never been. I had typically felt that we have enough to do here without worrying about going overseas. That moment, along with many subsequent ones, radically changed my perspective. In fact, since that day I do not remember having thought or said anything close to that.

That experience was not the only one God orchestrated to rattle me. Add to that encounter the fact that I was taking classes on mission theology, surrounded by classmates that were going to the field, and being informally mentored by a professor who repeatedly went to India. I was surrounded by relationships that were influencing and reinforcing my burgeoning decision to become a world Christian.

Over the next few years, I began reading missionary biographies, integrating mission understanding into my study and teaching, and going on multiple short-term trips to Africa, Asia, and Central America. I also began to do research on student ministry and short-term mission. My steady development and engagement in mission is the by-product of the Holy Spirit's orchestration for the purpose of stimulating me to worship God through mission awareness and activity, and each form of engagement has occurred concurrently with my involvement in ministry to, and with, students. I have grown in Jesus through the simultaneous influences and practices of mission and student ministry.

Mission and Student Lives: The Glorious and Severe Truth

Therefore, the passion that Michael and I share for both student ministry and mission engagement is not dichotomous because we see these two streams of ministry as organically linked. We have realized that for students to become true disciples, they must themselves become concerned and active disciplers of the nations. If this generation will be influenced and developed toward, engaged in, and assessed for growth unto a global vision and life, God will raise them up to change the lives of whole tribes, communities, and nations. Who knows who will be sitting in the audience that day when those they impact are singing their story, and who knows how their lives might, in turn, impact others for the sake of His great name?

As thrilling as this prospect of our students changing the world may be, there is a sobering caution for us here. What we are challenging them to is nothing short of death. If it seems like you can suddenly hear the shrill screeching of tires and like the reading experience just derailed into a ditch, gather yourself and hang on to the book for one more moment. We are talking about the sanctifying death to self-dependence and isolation—as we have discussed here—but we are also talking about real physical death, if that is what it costs to see His mission accomplished.

This is not quite as radical as it appears. To connect loving Jesus and the absolute willingness to pay with the understanding that it might cost me as much as my life should comprise a baseline understanding of our life with Christ. Dietrich Bonhoeffer seemed to recognize this, as he famously observed that "when Christ calls a man, he bids him come and die."[2] Jesus certainly communicated our relationship to Him in these terms:

> Then Jesus told his disciples, "If anyone would come after me, let him deny himself and take up his cross and follow me. For whoever would save his life will lose it, but whoever loses his life for my sake will find it." (Matt 16:24–25 ESV)
>
> Remember the word that I said to you: "A servant is not greater than his master." If they persecuted me, they will

[2] D. Bonhoeffer, *The Cost of Discipleship* (New York: Macmillan, 1963), 99.

> also persecute you. If they kept my word, they will also keep yours. (John 15:20 ESV)

When we call students to follow Jesus in eastern Kentucky, southern California, North Africa, Southeast Asia, or Central Europe—or wherever they may go—we are challenging them to a discipleship of death. But, as Jesus indicates, it is also the way they find real life in Him (Matt 16:25).

When I speak to students who are preparing to serve as businessmen, teachers, media specialists, pastors, and student ministers overseas, I think about their parents, because I think about my care and concern for my own children. Most nights, before my kids go to bed, we read a book that mentions each one of our family and friends, reminding them how much we love them all. But the last page simply says, "Most of all, Jesus loves you."[3] Some children's books are worthless, even though they cost eight dollars for just a few pages. This one is pregnant with a truth I need to hear each night. The truth is that as much as I would joyfully forfeit everything I have for friends and family, including my life, I will never demonstrate the divine, perfect, sovereign love that Jesus Himself has shown for them.

Unlike me, Jesus always knows what is paramount to both His receiving glory and to the real happiness of my children. If this means that God uses my influence toward cross-cultural understanding and involvement, lived in front of them, to direct them to hostile places, even among a Christ-despising people, then Jesus is demonstrating His perfect love for them through that calling, not in spite of it, and should thus do what pleases Him with their lives. I am amazed at how easy this is to write, but I do not think it will be as painless to live.

It will be much more difficult to experience because I have seen what happens to some young men and women who answer this call. Probably no more than 100 feet from where I was sitting that day in chapel is a men's dormitory named Memorial Hall.The reason for the name is simple. When you enter and exit the dorm, as students do multiple times each day, there are bronze plaques on the wall that include the names of former students, their years of graduation, and the dates of their *martyrdom*. Each of these men died on mission, and the call to both remember and emulate their commitment is always in front of the students that call the building home.

Those plaques represent people who had a passion for His honor among the nations and understood the temporal yet severe cost. The cost

[3] N. Piper and D. Anderson, *Most of All, Jesus Loves You* (Wheaton, IL: Crossway, 2004).

of calling the students of today and tomorrow, which includes my young children, to this Great Commission carries the same price tag. In the case of these martyrs, God granted them the grace to follow the course and to make the final decision of their earthly lives—to no longer struggle with tension over obedience and mission but to resolve to endure the rounds of bullets, the stabs of the knife blade, the blows of the club, the eventual snuffing out of their lives on earth. They chose this course so that others might see what it means to be a disciple who has been transformed by the God of all mercy and grace. They chose it because they had real life in Him.

Our word of warning to each among us who serves students and their families is not to stop calling them to this great privilege of being men and women of extreme love for Jesus. Our admonition is that you demonstrate an attentiveness to the gravity of discipling students through STM and cross-cultural awareness by partnering with parents and other wise models in the church to challenge them. We must recognize the vital importance of this call for their lives and their families so that we can systematically engage and encourage students, while pleading with God that He might develop and change them to be more consistent followers of Jesus, among the nations, to the praise of His glorious grace.

Name Index

Scripture Index